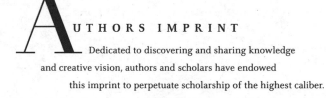

UTHORS IMPRINT

Dedicated to discovering and sharing knowledge
and creative vision, authors and scholars have endowed
this imprint to perpetuate scholarship of the highest caliber.

Scholarship is to be created...by awakening a pure interest in knowledge.

—Ralph Waldo Emerson

The Stickup Kids

The Stickup Kids

RACE, DRUGS, VIOLENCE,
AND THE AMERICAN DREAM

Randol Contreras

UNIVERSITY OF CALIFORNIA PRESS

BERKELEY   LOS ANGELES   LONDON

University of California Press, one of the most distinguished university presses in the United States, enriches lives around the world by advancing scholarship in the humanities, social sciences, and natural sciences. Its activities are supported by the UC Press Foundation and by philanthropic contributions from individuals and institutions. For more information, visit www.ucpress.edu.

University of California Press
Berkeley and Los Angeles, California

University of California Press, Ltd.
London, England

Library of Congress Cataloging-in-Publication Data

Contreras, Randol, 1971–
    The stickup kids : race, drugs, violence, and the American dream / Randol Contreras.
        p.   cm.
    Includes bibliographical references and index.
    ISBN 978-0-520-27337-5 (cloth : alk. paper) — ISBN 978-0-520-27338-2 (pbk. : alk. paper)
    1. Youth—Drug use—New York (State)—New York.   2. Drug dealers—New York (State)—New York.   3. Cocaine abuse—New York (State)—New York.   4. Cities and towns—New York (State)—New York.   I. Title.
    HV5824.Y68C673 2013
    363.4509747'275—dc23
                                                                        2012022291

Manufactured in the United States of America
20 19 18 17 16 15 14 13 12 11
10 9 8 7 6 5 4 3 2 1

In keeping with a commitment to support environmentally responsible and sustainable printing practices, UC Press has printed this book on Rolland Enviro100, a 100% post-consumer fiber paper that is FSC certified, deinked, processed chlorine-free, and manufactured with renewable biogas energy. It is acid-free and EcoLogo certified.

I dedicate this book to the South Bronx men, women, and children who were swept up in the drug trade during the crack era and who still struggle to recuperate from its destructive impact on their lives.

CONTENTS

ILLUSTRATIONS (AFTER PAGE 114)

ACKNOWLEDGMENTS

I would like to thank the people who supported me and made this book possible.

Karina Bautista: Thank you for convincing me to return to school and attend a community college in upstate New York. Thank you for introducing me to a world where ideas and justice mattered, which started me on the path toward a sociological understanding of life.

Felix Collado: Thank you for providing guidance as I made my transition back to school. Thank you for being my *compadre* for life, who always comes through when I have much to lose.

Mehdi Bozorghmehr and Lily Hoffman: Thank you for your support during my undergraduate years at the City College of the City University of New York, for introducing me to the rigors of the field of sociology and taking a gamble on me with letters of support. I hope you both feel that it has paid off.

Keith Thompson: Thank you for the many hours you spent encouraging my graduate school aspirations and answering the countless questions I had of this unknown milieu. Thank you for treating me like a colleague though I was an undergraduate and for introducing me to the world of teaching.

Gail Smith: Thank you for your magnificent lead as head of the CUNY Pipe Line Program, a wonderful program that supports undergraduate inner-city minorities pursuing careers in research and teaching. You are truly an inspiration, always knowing what to say to get us over the barriers and obstacles that were our lives. In the end, all your efforts were truly worth it.

Rebecca Tiger and Salvidor Vidal-Ortiz: Thank you for being gracious with your time, putting off your own graduate work, just to provide me with feedback as I started writing up my project. It was great to be in the company of brilliant minds and I hope to return the favor one day.

Philip Kasinitz: Thank you for being a patient dissertation advisor, who made sure that I got through the program. And thank you for being a patient colleague, who takes the time to listen, but makes sure to interject when I get off track.

Dana Collins: Thank you for being a gracious colleague and for the illuminating discussions on our train trips from our Cal State Fullerton campus to Los Angeles. Those talks, where you listened so patiently, are the basis of my methodological insights.

Anonymous Reviewers: Thank you for taking the time to read the manuscript draft and pointing out its gaps, inconsistencies, and ambiguities. The final product is certainly better for your comments and suggestions.

Ramona Perez: Thank you for acting on my behalf in New York City when I had to tie up all those maddening little loose ends from over two thousand miles away. You are the greatest big sister in *el mundo,* who showed me that she would try her best to assure that her little brother made it through.

Naomi Schneider: Thank you for being a wonderful editor, who saw promise in my work and understood its intricate goals. Thank you for having faith in me as a writer and scholar to weave together the social, racial, economic, and gendered complexities of this South Bronx world.

Scott Brooks: Thank you for providing a nuanced critique on a late manuscript draft, which made my place in the research a lot clearer for readers. More important, thank you for extending your friendship and being someone that I can count on and call at anytime. *You're my bro.*

Randall Collins: Thank you for your open mind and love of ideas—for taking the time to read an earlier form of this manuscript despite not knowing me. Thank you for having my research contributions as the basis of your continued support of my work and career.

Loic Wacquant: Thank you for sharing your magnificent insights on this manuscript, and especially for sharing your love and enthusiasm for ethnography. Thank you for letting the world know that I exist, for creating the opportunities and "stages" so that my work can be known. This is something no one has ever done.

Philippe Bourgois: Thank you for being a strong advocate of my work, for wanting to open up new career possibilities despite me not being your student. Thank you for making me feel that my research is important, that it is a valuable contribution to the study of human suffering and despair. *Te debo, mi hermano.*

Lauren McDonald: Thank you for being a wonderful partner, who has always tried to facilitate my scholarship and love of writing. You have always put my passions ahead of us; you have always been so generous with your love, care, and time. It is the most wonderful thing to have a partner that could intellectually topple giants if she wished, yet is modest and humble. You have stimulated my thinking more than you know; with this book, I hope to have made you proud.

Scott Ochs: Thank you, thank you, for giving me a hope, a dream. When I was a South Bronx kid attending Tompkins-Cortland Community College, you told me that my work was worthy of great expectations, that I should pursue a career in "academia." Your words would open a new world of possibilities, which I have yet to let go. Thank you for caring about the most marginalized, misplaced, dream-deferred students of our nation—the hardest ones to reach, the hardest ones to teach.

This book has mostly resulted because of you.

PREFACE

During the late eighties, Dominican drug dealers were a highly visible lot. I could not miss them. They drove expensive cars, with shiny rims, with the sunroof open, or with the convertible top down, for all to see (everyone had to see the driver, the King of the Avenue). They wore extravagant clothes, custom made—a stylish suit for the day: baggy slacks, Italian button-down shirts, "Miami Vice" style. They wore summer dress shoes with no socks, even during winter, the time to show off fancy leather coats. And their hair (inspired by Michael Jackson) was done up to hide the rough texture, the kinkiness—*el pelo malo*—through a "Jerry curl" style, all oiled up, coiled up, dripping wet, with a tissue in hand to wipe the drops running down the face and ears. The jewelry was large, exaggerated, overblown, making one wonder how these skinny men weren't anchored to night club floors or were able to lift their heads for greetings *("Que pasa, mi pana?")*.

The New York City–born drug dealers (second- and third-generation Dominicans and Puerto Ricans) wore the finest urban gear: Adidas, Puma, and Fila sweat suits; Nike sneakers, Gucci shoes, and Bally slip-ons. The jewelry was flashy—Cuban and Gucci links and rope chains, with large gold crucifixes, Madonnas, anchors, nicknames, and initials. Some with kinky hair—*moreno* hair—did away with the "Jerry Curl"; they shaved their heads close, Caesar style, or sported flattops, towering high above their foreheads. Those with *pelo lacio,* or *pelo bueno,* had fades with a fluff of hair on top, either spiked or wet down to get the wavy look. Facial hair was Arabic style, or fifties Bohemian, to look like *malos:* goatees, thin and thick, sometimes with helmet-strap strips running from ear to chin, making people look "hard"; and if worn with a baldy or a barely visible Caesar, dudes looked like they just came out the "pen."

And their women *(las palomitas de los jodedores)*—they were "fine": all hues and colors, voluptuous, *con carne;* all done up, in tight jeans or slacks, big bamboo earrings or hoops, gold chains, gold bracelets, gold rings; all displaying themselves, to an adoring crowd, attracting attention—lots of attention. They were at their finest in the passenger seat of the luxury car, with gold rims, shaded windows (rolled down, of course) and a *jodedor* driving (her King for the Night)—she knew she was on display.

These men (young and old) oozed a sense of security, of confidence—the neighborhood knew that they were building luxury estates "back home," in "D.R.," the Dominican Republic, supporting entire families, on both shores, in different neighborhoods, off their drug profits—and for a time (a two- or three-year span that felt like eternity) it appeared as though they would never get caught, it would just continue, the money would never slip away.

. . .

As a teenager, I wanted so badly to be like these magnificent drug dealers. Despite coming from poverty, they had found a way to become rich. But poverty was something my parents could never avoid. They had come from the Dominican Republic during the late 1960s and settled in the South Bronx. Since neither of them ever finished middle school, they could only secure low-wage jobs: my mother, a dressmaker at a local sweatshop; my father, a clothes presser at dry cleaner. Shortly after my two siblings and I were born, my parents divorced, leaving my mother as the sole breadwinner. Sometimes my siblings and I accompanied her to the grim, filthy, and windowless factory to help her earn more money by putting belts and tags on hundreds of garments. However, her efforts to secure higher pay and better places to live would be futile. The crumbling South Bronx would remain our home.

Despite this, I had gained admission to Brooklyn Technical High School, one of the city's three specialized public high schools. To most New Yorkers, it might have seemed like a great opportunity. But I was fourteen: the classes were boring, and I hated the commute—over an hour each way. So after a year, I transferred to my neighborhood's locally zoned high school, William Howard Taft.

Now Taft—or *Training Animals For Tomorrow*, as the students called it—warehoused the area's most unprepared students. Here, I cut my way through some classes and clowned my way through others. Sometimes I just napped, like in one English class where we were told, *Define and write sen-*

tences for these ten words. A few dedicated teachers made their courses fun and challenging, which motivated me to do well in creative writing and math. Mostly, though, teachers just checked out, leaving students lost.

After graduation, I attended CUNY's Hunter College. Since I possessed little structure or cultural capital (not really knowing what to say or do), I failed most of my classes during my first year. Looking ahead, I imagined a mediocre future at best—no *riquezas* in sight. Then that dangerous question began pelting me, striking me harder and harder every day: *Go to school for what?*

So one day, as I headed to a final exam in sociology, I stopped in my tracks. *Fuck it.* No more school. I was going to strike it rich in the crack market. Later that day, I established a business partnership with a neighborhood friend, and we pooled money from our legal earnings—we worked in fast-food joints and grocery stores—to buy an ounce of cocaine. We also found what seemed like the perfect selling spot: a run-down building whose superintendent was a "crackhead." Under the watchful eye of my best drug-dealing friend, Pablo, we cooked the cocaine into crack, producing a huge mound of the substance. Then, with razor blades, we sliced off tiny pieces to insert into small perfume vials.

Any other time, this would be a boring, mindless task. But right then, we were exhilarated, with me repeatedly yelling out, *Yo, we gonna get paid! We gonna make crazy dollars, bro! Ha-ha!* At the time, it was one the greatest moments in my life. I had never felt so sure, so confident of success. I was going to be rich.

Be somebody.

Little did I know that the big time would never come for me. I was too late: it was the early nineties, and the crack era was almost over. According to urban anthropologist Ansley Hamid, the crack epidemic featured six stages: onset, incubation, widespread diffusion, and *peak;* then decline and stabilization.[1] In New York City, the peak stage occurred between 1987 and 1989. So the riches my peers and I saw were from the peak stage, when freelance and corporate-style groups sold crack in our buildings and alleys, on our stoops, sidewalks, and corners. By the time I entered the crack game, dealers had begun to struggle, and crack use had declined.[2] And I would suffer, indeed.

For instance, after setting up our crack spot, my partner and I gave local crack users free samples to appraise our product. Anxious, we waited for the good news. Yet one by one they returned, saying that our crack was "garbage," or "wack." *Shit. Fuck.* If we continued selling our product, our brand would get a bad reputation. But we had no more money; we *had* to sell our "garbage" drugs for new start-up cash.

Eventually, we convinced a neighborhood crack user to sell our drugs. At first, he was reluctant, agreeing only after we promised him not the typical one dollar for every five-dollar sale, but two dollars instead (we were pathetic capitalists). Nevertheless, sales were slow. We only sold about six or seven crack vials a day and got serious customer complaints. Worse, our worker started showing up late—only after his other money-making opportunities ran out. So we spent hours waiting with the crack in hand, sometimes doing risky hand-to-hand sales. This was not the plan.

After an excruciating three or four weeks, we made enough money to buy more drugs. This time we purchased wholesale crack through a neighborhood friend, Manolo, who had connections to a reputable dealer in Washington Heights. Yet as we sliced and packaged the crack into vials, I was cautious in my predictions. This time, I simply hoped over and over again: *Please, please, let it turn out right.*

It didn't.

Slow sales. Days, and sometimes weeks, went by with no action. Often, we sat around for hours, just watching, waiting, desperately trying to convince crack users to buy our product. We even tried to sell crack in two other South Bronx locations: in a small park near the Cross Bronx Expressway and in a run-down block in University Heights. But no matter how many times we put the key into the ignition, our crack operations wouldn't start. Slowly and painfully, my dream was evaporating into New York City's hot, humid air . . .

Yet I was determined. With an eager new business partner (his girlfriend had just dumped him for a successful crack dealer), I raised some more capital to sell angel dust (or PCP). But selling "dust" was just as hard. The best locations had drug-dealing landlords that demanded a "rent" for sidewalk space. But we could not afford a "rent." Eventually we gave up, frustrated and broke.

As a repeat drug market failure, I was forced out of the drug game. Fortunately, a concerned neighborhood friend filled out an application for me to attend a rural community college near her state school. Later, she introduced me to politically engaged students who challenged global inequalities. I *dug* them and *got* what they were saying. With some strong encouragement from a community college professor, I decided to pursue sociology. Drug dealing—*no mas.*

My neighborhood friends—the focus of this book—continued as drug dealers. They avoided crack's downturn by dealing in other states. Almost overnight, they would become superstars, living the ultimate high life, spending money on cars, clothes, jewelry, liquor, drugs, and women, with no end in sight. But then their drug-dealing success ended, abruptly. They turned to brutal drug robberies as way to recapture their glory years. Now their lives would be filled with misery, violence, and pain.

So this book brings me back to my South Bronx drug market roots. But this time I am equipped with theoretical and analytical tools for exploring the hidden social forces that influence and shape South Bronx lives. Without these sociological tools, even I—a South Bronx product—could get lost in the gore that makes up a good portion of this book. For the violent scenes and episodes can stir up our worst fears and nightmares, prompting us to define people as inherently evil. As monsters.

Yet I must tell this story. We must understand how despair can drive the marginal into greed, betrayal, cruelty, and self-destruction. An ethnographic approach allows me to document and analyze those key social, historical, and personal moments on which lives pivot, turning already marginal lives into nightmarish suffering. But even with a sociological eye, studying my childhood drug market friends has been a heart-wrenching task. Because in doing so, I would suffer along with them too.

November 2011

Introduction

BY THE EARLY 1990S, the South Bronx had changed. On my visits home from an upstate community college, I noticed that more and more neighborhoods had dried up. The "crackheads" and "crack whores" were gone, along with the drug peddlers who had barked: *Red Top! Gold Top! I got Blue!* Someone had cleaned the streets, dusting the drug dealers and drug users off the planet, leaving the South Bronx a ghost town. *Coño, que pasó?*

Eventually, my sociological interests landed me at the Graduate Center of the City University of New York. Since I still lived in the South Bronx, it was easy to stay in touch with neighborhood friends. So I often visited their homes, went out for drinks, and hung out on street corners. Mostly, we reminisced about the good ol' days, going on and on about the old adventures and loves. Sometimes, though, they would ask me to go with them to see "this kid" or "this dude" about something. On the way, they would explain the meeting's purpose: to set up a drug deal or organize a drug robbery.

Once the "meeting" started, I stayed away from it, leaning on cars or brick walls several feet away. I wanted no blame if they were busted by police. *I didn't hear nothin', so I don't know nothin', papa.* I still got the lowdown afterward. My friends just wanted my opinion and support—my: *You're right, bro.* Yet I kept seeing how their new crack and cocaine ventures always failed. Their only success was in drug robberies and they began calling themselves "stickup kids," or *joloperos.* Soon I heard stories of them beating, burning, and mutilating dealers for drugs and cash.

Then the irony struck me. For the last several years, criminologists and politicians had been debating the big crime drop of the 1990s. In cities across the United States, crimes such as murder, robbery, rape, car theft, and assault had dropped dramatically. New York City, in particular, had experienced

crime lows not recorded in thirty years.[1] Public officials cited tougher policing and more incarceration. Criminologists cited several factors: a shrinking
crack market, a change in youth attitudes toward crack, a natural drug cycle,
community initiatives, improved policing, and a reduction of people in the
crime-prone years.[2]

At the same time, I was witnessing an alarming phenomenon in the
South Bronx, a phenomenon that was not revealed by crime statistics: an
increase in unreported drug violence. Unable to sell drugs within a shrinking crack market, some former dealers had become violent drug robbers.
And since these offenses occurred within a crime market, the victims never
reported them to police. I saw a double irony. First, at a time when reported
violent crime was dropping, unreported violence within the drug world
seemed to be rising. Second, violence had increased among men who were in
their late twenties—beyond the "crime-prone" years. This observation countered the statistical picture as well as common criminological wisdom.

I told Pablo of my research interests, and he suggested that I hang out
several blocks away, where Gus, another old friend, was staying. There, I met
other drug market participants—Neno, Topi, and David—who mostly relied on stickups to earn money. Drug market insiders recruited them to rob
drug dealers storing large amounts of cocaine, marijuana, heroin, or cash.
Little did I know that I would be embarking on a tumultuous journey. I
would learn about violent drug robberies, but I would also witness the self-
destruction of these Dominican men.

Over the next several years, I observed them ride a violent roller coaster
that ended in a horrific crash. As crack dealers, they had never been so brutal. But in the drug robberies, beating, burning, and maiming became routine. Worse, their economic uncertainties made them anxious, depressed,
and suicidal—made them Fallen Stars.

Que pasó? How would I explain their rising violence and their self-
destructive turn?

Sociologically, I started framing them within a declining manufacturing
sector, a worn-down community, and a shrinking crack market. For more
insights, I turned to the latest qualitative, interview-based robbery research.
Its researchers, though, sped the other way, framing their work within emotions and street culture. I became concerned with their rare mention of social inequalities, shifting drug markets, or a punitive state.

To clarify this unease, I must do a theoretical rewind to one of the most
pivotal years in criminological thought: 1988. In a thrilling tour de force,

sociologist Jack Katz argued that economic swings, racial discrimination, and social position mattered little in understanding crime.[3] Instead, the emotional allure of evil mattered most. Regardless of social class, he argued, criminals were sensually attracted to deviance, to acts that, like brilliant fireworks splashing against a midnight sky, exhilarated them.

To make his case, Katz argued that since robberies provide only sporadic income—and if the robber is caught, a lot of prison time—then robbers must be seeking more than just money. For instance, why would some robbers do grocery shopping while holding up a supermarket? Or why would some of them sexually assault a waitress while holding up a bar? In short, why would some robbers increase their risks during a robbery? It was, Katz argued, because risk-taking behavior itself is thrilling.

But there was more. For Katz, robberies were just one piece of a larger life of illicit action: a life of heavy gambling, heavy drug use, heavy drinking, heavy spending, and heavy sex. At the extreme, these behaviors led to money woes, which then led to robberies as the logical—read: chaotic and thrilling—solution.

Almost overnight, enthralled researchers followed Katz' lead, leaping over the root causes of crime. By 1992, criminologists Neal Shover and David Honaker had devised the concept of "life as a party" to explain crime among property offenders.[4] By the mid-1990s, other criminologists—Richard T. Wright, Scott Decker, and Bruce A. Jacobs—were following this path in their interview-based studies of St. Louis street criminals. Crime, they concluded, resulted from the allure of both street culture and emotional thrills.

Their assumption that "street culture" was distinct—or disconnected from mainstream culture—disturbed me.[5] In particular, I was disturbed when I read statements like the following about the criminal world (I'm paraphrasing):

1. Nothing is done for free, for no money.
2. Flashing material success is a goal.
3. Drinking and drug use are serious recreations.
4. Men pursue sex with many women.

It seemed as though they had never hung out on a college campus or in a local bar. It seemed as though they had never paid attention to the Wall Street or Orange County crowds. It seemed as though they had no idea of the individualistic and materialistic foundation of the United States. Worse, it seemed as though they had gone back in time, to the days when cultural reasons alone were believed to explain why the poor remained poor and engaged in crime. Thus, rather than situating Katz' ideas within structural factors such as poverty, social class, and the economy, some researchers would *strictly* ride down the emotional and cultural landscape of crime.[6]

Not that I, too, wasn't taken by Katz' work. His writing was electric and metaphoric. His emphasis on emotional thrills was novel, inspiring. And as later chapters show, I use his ideas to understand drug robberies. Also, I use the insightful ideas of the aforementioned robbery researchers. In terms of in-the-moment robbery dynamics, they did magnificent work.

Still, their goal was to mine deeper into street culture, and even deeper into the emotional fulfillment of doing evil. By the expedition's end, however, the analytical canary was dead. They could not answer how a given offender's biography was tied to the criminal underworld. They could not explain how that criminal underworld had emerged. Everything was just there, always existing—the evil, the streets, the drugs, the violence.

The emotional-cultural box, I came to realize, had to be opened to let in the dazzling lights of historical, social, economic, and drug market forces. Otherwise, readers would have to believe in magic: criminals had just popped up out of thin air. Because at the turn of the twentieth century, when White ethnics were *the* inner-city crime problem, street culture and evil surely existed.[7] Yet as the century progressed, White street crime would decrease dramatically.

Wait. If evil emotions and criminal cultures are as powerful and entrenched as some criminologists claim, how did Whites exorcize those crooked-faced demons? Answer: Historical moments and structural shifts. World wars. Unions. Booming industries. Ignoring such factors is not the sociological promise as I see it. Instead, it is almost a criminological sleight of hand.

I take a cue from C. Wright Mills, situating the Dominican drug robbers I observed within a salient historical moment.[8] This is not only my sociological promise, but also my promise to the study participants. Because when I ask them about their rising violence and depression, of their sense of being "trapped," their answers are limited to what Mills referred to as their "private orbits." Like most people, they fail to grasp the "big picture" and rely on day-to-day experiences to understand their lives. But larger structural transformations—such as a shifting drug market—had influenced and shaped them too. Because:

When a drug market rises, a struggling college student becomes a drug dealer; a tough kid, an enforcer; a poor building superintendent, a lookout; and a dishwasher, a drug kingpin. When a drug market expands, a mother mourns her dead dealer son; a dad laments his drug-using daughter; a child visits a parent imprisoned by the state. When a drug market peaks, an ill-affected sibling becomes a social worker; a storefront preacher, a community organizer; a stay-at-home mom, an after-school volunteer. When a drug market fades, an ex-con is perpetually unemployed; a recovering female addict, forever humiliated; a New York City mayor, despite doing nothing special, applauded and praised.

And during the crack era, some of my Dominican study participants became crack dealers. Like typical Americans, they badly wanted money, power, and material status symbols, everything the U.S. ideology claims as real success. And through crack, they succeeded. Cash, cars, women, and clothes—they got them. Status, masculinity, and respect—they got those too. These men were Kings.

But by the mid-1990s, their reign had ended; the crack era, without warning, was gone. And that salient moment would remain within them, becoming the eternal barometer of their marginal lives. They then became drug robbers. They then became more violent rather than aging out of crime. True, in their everyday orbits, they sounded and appeared as some criminologists would have it. But the crack era—and its demise—framed their emotions, their violence, and their crime.[9]

Following C. Wright Mills' call to examine the big picture, I use Robert Merton and Cloward and Ohlin's "strain" theories to make sense of the study participants. In his classic statement, Merton argued that when people lack access to the approved ways of achieving society's sacred values and goals, they may feel a strain, or pressure, to break the rules.[10] As a result, a frustrated few become *innovators*, creating criminal paths to success. Cloward and Ohlin added that the *existence* of innovative opportunities mattered too.[11] So along with factors such as race and gender, the absence or presence of criminal opportunities shaped *if* and *how* a frustrated person innovated to do crime.

Under strain theory, I could integrate these South Bronx Dominicans within the historical context of the crack era. Crack's rise during the 1980s had swiftly changed the city's criminal opportunity structure. Now, as long as they had the start-up capital, thousands of marginal residents could turn to the drug market for American-style success.[12] And these Dominican men took advantage of this new opportunity and, in time, lived a material life that most South Bronx residents could only dream.[13] Drug dealing became their best bet at overcoming the great American contradiction: the strong cultural emphasis on achieving the American Dream, yet the reality that little legal opportunity existed for its achievement. However, during the 1990s, the crack market shrank and reduced their drug-dealing opportunities. They then responded to this new "strain" through an *extraordinary innovation*: becoming stickup kids who earned money through brutality and violence. In all, strain theory helped me place Jack Katz' emphasis on crime's emotional allure within a larger frame

In this book, I describe and analyze the drug robbery violence of South Bronx Dominicans. Politically, this leads to *un tremendo problema*. Some readers may feel that I reinforce popular negative imagery of Dominicans. Their questions will be: Why study stickup kids, a group that is hardly representative of the South Bronx Dominican community? Why not study legal Dominican workers, like cab drivers, sales clerks, or *bodega* owners?

Given the conservative backlash against inner-city minorities, I understand those concerns. I can only respond by saying that I grew up with these Dominican drug market participants, so I care about them personally as much as I do sociologically. Also, I understand the great challenges in studying a vulnerable population, especially the danger of falling into psychological or sociopathic frameworks. This is why I go beyond pure interpretive ethnography and show how brutal drug robberies do not happen within a cultural vacuum.

Moreover, throughout the book, I present the study participants as complete human beings. Like most people, they juggle multiple statuses and roles: they are fathers to children, brothers to siblings, and sons to mothers and fathers. They experience economic hardship and romantic problems. They laugh, they cry, they have legal hopes and dreams. They show many mental and physical symptoms related to social distress.

They also engage in violence, which I cannot omit.

I am studying *drug market participants* who came of age during the crack era.[14] Specifically, I examine the crack market's varied negative consequences on one of its populations. Because the rise and fall of crack affected different parts of the drug market population in different ways: for some it led to committed crack use; for some, it led to crack-related sex work; for some it led to being the victims of beatings, stabbings, and shootings; and for others, it led to long-term incarceration. For the study participants, it led to becoming drug robbers, the worst perpetrators of violence in the drug world.

Thus this book is about a particular group of people, but it also speaks to the generational cohort of Black and Latino/a men and women across the country who lived through the crack era. It speaks to the individuals who invested their young adulthood in the crack game and now cannot find legal spaces to apply their drug-specific cultural capital. It speaks to the economic issues facing the prisoners of the harsh, politically charged drug laws, who, on returning home, find that incarceration prepared them poorly for capable citizenship.[15] It speaks to those who have, in both a real and a symbolic sense, experienced "social death."[16]

. . .

The book is divided into three parts. In part 1, I contextualize the drug dealing and drug robberies I observed, discussing the South Bronx decline and the rise of crack, the study participants' trajectory into the crack market, their brutal jail and prison experiences, and their drug robberies as a response to a shrinking crack market. In part 2, I analyze drug robbery dynamics—its stages, accomplishment, and violence (the place where most robbery studies start and stop). Thus, I explain gender roles, torture, and status within drug robberies, and drug robbery lifestyles on the street. In part 3, I explore the final outcome of study participants' drug market involvement. Specifically, I show how these men became fallen stars—how they became suicidal and self-destructive as they made sense of their diminished drug market status.

But first: the South Bronx, the participants—and a methodological note that I avoided until I no longer could.

THE STICKUP KIDS AND ME

Between April and September, and lately in October, the number 4 train carries tens of thousands of city residents to its most celebrated stop, "161st Street, Yankee Stadium." Mostly White fans from all over the city come to watch the magnificent Yankees play baseball. Clad in Yankee caps, T-shirts, and jerseys, they engorge the local area, forming a dizzying sea of blue and white and pinstripe. They visit fast-food joints, cafes, pubs, and Yankee retail shops.

Then they attend the game.

Surely, these visitors never get beyond one block of Yankee Stadium. Not that they should. The west side of Yankee stadium borders a highway, and to its south stands a filthy marketplace where vegetable and fruit merchants sell produce to wholesale customers.[17] By the afternoon hours, the market is empty except for the occasional emaciated prostitute trying to score a John. To its north, the retail and food shops end abruptly, not daring to step into local neighborhoods.

Only the stadium itself crosses local borders. At night, its bright lights illuminate the local sky, a cherubic glow seen for several miles. And if the Yankees score a run, strike a batter out—or do anything spectacular—the unison cheers of fans are electrifying, momentarily muting the sounds of the streets, the cars, the radios, and the chatter of people. For an instant, local residents pause to think about the cause for such jubilation. Then they carry on.

Other than stadium sights and sounds, local people routinely encounter the rumble of the number 4 train. On a quivering platform, this silver metallic fleet of cars shoots through the entire Jerome Avenue. On the platform's east side, past the first uphill block, is the borough's administrative center. It holds the county courthouse and the offices of the borough president, district attorney, and county clerk. Farther up, across the Grand Concourse—past the historic Concourse Plaza Hotel—are the family and criminal courts.

Now on the west side of the elevated train platform, and immediately north of the stadium, is John Mullay Park. The three-block public park offers a worn outdoor running track, a Little League baseball diamond, and an undersized pool. Running parallel to the park's west side is a lonesome area the city books call "High Bridge." The neighborhood seems to have it all: elegant art deco buildings, a scenic view of the city park, and a daytime atmosphere resembling the Bronx's northern, upscale sections. Still, the decorative mosaic that adorns the structures is covered in soot, and the sidewalks are worn and uneven, a checkerboard of grays.

But in between two buildings stands a public good: a steep, four-flight cement stairwell. The stairs act as a shortcut for residents living on the perched city blocks behind the street. Otherwise, they would have to circle about three long, uphill blocks to reach those neighborhoods. In all, other than traffic heading toward the highway and a bridge, the neighborhood is peaceful, with little pedestrian activity.

And that is most of it. Unless I include a local *bodega,* or grocery store, that operates out of an art deco building next to the public stairwell. By day, the *bodega* caters to working poor Mexicans, Central Americans, Dominicans, and Puerto Ricans. By night, though, the *bodega* attracts a certain Dominican male clientele. These mostly young Dominicans gather outside its entrance and on the public stairwell to listen to its blasting *merengue* music, drink liquor and bottled beer, argue about sports, gamble with dice, or play cards. Sometimes they sell marijuana, heroin, or cocaine. But that business is slow—so slow that drug transactions are not obvious. Their only obvious crime is smoking *hierba,* or marijuana.

Their main work takes them far from the neighborhood, deep into other boroughs, onto other streets, inside other apartments, where they beat, choke, and burn people. Simply put, they rob drug dealers holding large amounts of drugs and cash. And if you ask them in Spanish, they describe themselves as *joloperos.* In English: stickup kids.

Researching Violence: A Night in the Life

Nightfall. The neighborhood air was hot, thick, and sticky, New York City style. It was so muggy that people perspired after walking just a few feet. The aroma of the damp street was also strong, a mixture of car fumes, moisture, and sidewalk. But a light breeze came in from the park that brought us momentary relief.

Block residents left stuffy apartments and were scattered everywhere. In front of the first building, several mothers sat on parked cars and talked while watching their children play street games. Kids just learning to walk (the ones that fall easily) played with bottle tops, empty wrappers, and empty soda cans. They threw them as far as they could, at parked cars, or at each other. Other kids hopped from one sidewalk square to another, trying to skip over the dividing lines. Sometimes they bumped into each other, sometimes they fell.

Older kids rode bikes in zigzags or raced. Their recklessness almost caused collisions with people standing around. *That little nigga better watch that shit,* warned a young male. *Yo, shorty, watch that bike!* Others played tag, running in circles, dodging each other, hiding behind pedestrians, trying to avoid being "it." *You're it!* Sometimes, the older ones cheated by going into the street. Running through a maze of cars, they made drivers honk horns and laughed at how the others could not follow. *Stop cheatin'! I'm not playin' any more,* the sidewalk kids pleaded. Yet they all kept playing.

Neighborhood teens, mostly males, separated into groups that sat or leaned on old cars without alarms. Their owners never fussed about scratches or dents. A smaller group smoked weed and drank beer on the block's far side to avoid neighborhood gossip. But most just talked, joked, and listened to rap music from a parked car nearby. The car's radio played Big Punisher's rap album throughout the night.

> From San Juan to Bayamón,
> I'm the Don Juan beside the Don,
> Live long,
> Get your party on,
>
> Don't let the liquor fool you,
>
> 'Cause I'll stick you,
> Something sharp to the heart,
> Or somethin' big to move you.[18]

Some young Dominican guys played cards on car hoods and gambled dice against the storefront. They always played for money, for those wrinkled, crunched-up dollar bills they sometimes threw to the ground. The winner, who usually grinned ferociously, turned solemn-faced as he counted and straightened the bills. Then another round of dice started. When a player tried to leave early, especially after winning, others urged him to stay. They wanted to win their money back. *Where you goin'? Don't leave yet. Come on, let's play again.*

Now and then, a player trotted backward toward the sidewalk's edge, glancing left and right to detect police cars.

Nearby, Pablo, Tukee, Dee, and I prepared mixed drinks. The liquor for tonight was "99 Banana" rum and Tropico, mixed with orange juice. We drank, joked, and listened to music blasting from the *bodega*. The grocery store played classic *merengues* from the 1980s, popularized by Dominican singers like Fernandito Villalona:

♪

> *Vamos pronto darno un trago*
> *Que esta noche es la mas buena . . .* [19]

♪

Showing off, a young Dominican guy sometimes danced alone, smiling as he improvised steps. All grin, he chopped his steps, from side to side, jabbing each fist sideways, giving us no clue to his next move. Suddenly, he lunged forward, then stepped back twice in staccato. We were all happy faces. Pablo slapped him a five. *"Coño, tu ere' el mae'tro,"* Pablo said. *"Diablo 'mano— vi'te eso?"*

It was the perfect summer night to hang out—people were chatting, people were laughing, people were smoking, people were gambling, people were drinking. And some, I should add, were preparing for a drug hit.

While some of us drank on the public stairwell, Gus, David, and Neno stood across the street, by the park, going over the details of a *tumbe* (drug robbery). With them was Jonah, a drug robber everyone said was *loco.* He was using a tall Jeep—the getaway car—to hide his cocaine snorts. Shortly, Melissa appeared, and as they had earlier in the park, her body proportions caught everyone's attention—she was petite from the waist up, and voluptuous from the waist down, with protruding buttocks. Within a half-hour of her arrival, she was driven off to set up the drug dealer.

Throughout that emotionally charged night, Gus repeatedly updated us on Melissa's progress, informing us on how far the dealer had fallen into her trap. For instance, at one point, Gus told us, "Yo, this nigga [the driver] just called, ha-ha."

"He called?"

"Yeah."

"What he said?"

"He said that she was makin' out with that nigga [the dealer], ha-ha. They sittin' at a table and they makin' out and shit. Yo, that nigga's fuckin' drunk already, ha-ha-ha. He been buyin' all these drinks for her and shit, ha-ha, and they been drinkin' all this time. He's all over her, all drunk and shit, ha-ha-ha-ha. Yo, that nigga's an old man and he thinks he gonna get some young ass tonight! That nigga's gonna get a big surprise, bro! What you think, Randy?"

"He's goin' d-o-o-o-w-w-n," I answered, inebriated.

After a few hours of such updates, the driver appeared and drove Gus, Jonah, and David to the apartment where they would later sequester and brutally torture the dealer.

By three o'clock in the morning, Pablo, Dee, Topi, Tukee, and I were the only ones hanging out on the block. We had just finished the liquor and waited for the crew to return. I asked Pablo if he thought they would find anything or get any information out of the dealer.

"Yo Ran," a drunken Pablo answered, "all they gotta do to that mother-fucka is put a hot iron on his fuckin' ass, bro! Nah, in fact, they just gotta put a hot fuckin' hanger in his ear, bro. You know what a hot hanger would do to you, bro? Yo, like we did to one motherfucka one time, bro. Yo, that nigga didn't want to talk so we said, 'A'ight, you don't want to fuckin' talk, bro? A'ight.' Yo, we fuckin' heated a fuckin' hanger on the stove and then put that shit [the uncoiled wire] in his ear, bro. That nigga started talkin' fast! Ha, ha. He was like, 'Okay, okay, okay!' Ha, ha, ha. You shoulda seen that nigga, bro."

"Listen, man," Tukee added, in his cool style, "all you gotta do is tie that nigga up with some duct tape, boom, wrap that shit up all around his arms, his legs, and be like, 'Just tell me where everything's at, B[ro]. We know what you got, B. If you don't tell us where everything's at, we gonna have to do some th-i-i-n-n-g-s-s to you, B. You know what I'm sayin'? So, just tell us where everything's at and everything's gonna be alri-i-i-g-h-t.' Ha-ha-ha. And if that nigga don't say shit, just smack that nigga up a little bit, B, ha-ha. And if he still don't talk, B, 'Gonna have to turn the iron on,' and be like, 'Now I'm gonna have to make you tell me, B.' Just put that shit on his back and everything's gonna be alr-r-i-i-i-ght. 'Oh, now you know what I'm talkin' about, B? I thought you didn't know, B.' Ha-ha."

By sunrise, only Pablo, Dee, and I remained on the block. We still talked about everything young drunk guys talk about when they break night wait-ing to see what has come out of a drug hit their boys were in. Women. Cars. Sports. Torture. Drugs. At 8:00 A.M., though, I told the guys that I was leav-ing. *They still haven't come back and I'm tired, bro,* I explained.

Nigga, you just pussy-whipped, psshh-pshhh, Pablo joked, imitating a whip-ping sound.

Nah, man, I'm tired.

Yeah, nigga. Just admit it bro, you whipped, ha-ha. Nigga, I'm only playin', ha-ha. I'm ready to break the fuck out too. I'm goin' to Neida's [his girlfriend's apartment].

Pablo gave Dee and me fisted handshakes and quickly walked away. Still walking, Pablo turned halfway and yelled, *Yo, Ran, I'll let you know what happens tomorrow, a'ight? Call me. Don't forget, call me, nigga.*

I walked home, six blocks away.

· · ·

I already knew some of the stickup kids in this scene. During the 1980s, I lived in a nearby South Bronx neighborhood with Pablo, Gus, and Tukee. In fact, Pablo and I spent lots of time together during summers and after school. Since Gus was three years younger (a huge span in teen years), we had a closer relationship with his older brother, Sylvio, who eventually became a big-time drug dealer. But after Gus proved his daring (he shot some people), we hung out with him too. Tukee also lived in our neighborhood, but then moved a few blocks to the High Bridge area, where most of the research is based. But since he visited often, we kept our friendship tight.

I met David, Topi, and Neno through Gus on a winter night in 1999. Gus introduced them to me outside a local pool hall as they got set to do a drug robbery. They were young and Dominican, only spoke Spanish, and wore the latest urban, baggy clothes. Meeting them like this, on the eve of a drug robbery, gave me a head start on some key robbery aspects. For instance, here I first learned of the role of "the girl" as I spoke with Pablo, who had accompanied me. This critical robbery role was sometimes played by Melissa, whom I would meet a few months later.

Initially, I recorded my observations through extensive field notes. However, after about three months, I began using a medium-sized tape recorder, which just fit into my jacket or pants pocket. The tape recorder improved my recollection of events since I often got back home in the early morning, usually intoxicated from heavy drinking. Nevertheless, I wrote up extensive outlines before going to bed (which sometimes took over two hours) and then wrote elaborate field notes the next day. These notes supplemented and guided the tape recordings, especially since street sounds sometimes interfered with the sound quality, and sometimes weeks passed before I found time for transcription. I followed this pattern intensely (about three or four days a week) between 1999 and 2002; then again for the autumn of 2003 and winter of 2004; and then intermittently from the summer of 2004 to the present.

The tape recorder also took on a critical social role during the research, especially with Pablo and Gus. After getting used to it, they often eagerly asked if I was carrying it with me and searched for the tell-tale bulge in my jacket or pants pocket. During conversations or interviews, they often spoke to the tape recorder—or to the world "out there"—rather than to me. Sometimes, the tape recorder was therapeutic, letting the study participants voice their hopes, dreams, sadness, and anger in ways they never had. They even cried.

As to participant dialogue, I only put tape-recorded conversations in quotation marks.[20] All italicized dialogue is based on field notes. This lets the reader know whether a conversation is precise (or close to it) or relied on memory alone. In both instances, I edited or removed long or confusing dialogue, like the run-on sentences with no clear beginning, middle, or end. Also, I sometimes removed extra slang or colloquialisms like, "You know what I'm sayin'?" and "You feel me?" and "bro" and "yo." Although not distracting (to me) in real conversation, too many of them on paper may distract readers from a dialogue's meaning.

Also, some study participants only spoke Spanish. In such cases, I translated their accounts into English; they are so identified in the text. However, the translations stripped those accounts of their richness. To avoid a total loss, I sometimes kept in Spanish slang, phrases, and words. Moreover, I retained ungrammatical speech and mispronunciations, especially their tendency to skip the letter "s" at the middle or end of words. In the latter case, I placed apostrophes to indicate the absence of letters and purposely spelled some words according to their sound. Although purists may complain, I must maintain the lyrical and verbal integrity of the marginal, who do not speak Castilian Spanish and use language as play.

As to field data, I provide many accounts that include me. Sometimes, though, I provide ones where study participants recollected previous events. On their face, they may appear purely autobiographical or not validated. However, since I grew up with most of the guys, I was "there" for many of those events: I observed them from their teenage years, to their drug-dealing years, to their brutal years as drug robbers. I provide their words so that readers can hear their voices and grasp their meanings.

That said, sometimes I was not "there." For instance, when they took drug-dealing trips to other states, I did not accompany them, but only heard their stories upon return. However, I always validated those accounts through speaking with others that witnessed the same events.

I ordered the material chronologically, though I am purposely vague about exact dates and years. Disclosing time-related information could be dangerous to the study participants. And I promised them that the research would not lead to their arrests or to drug dealer retaliation.

In all, I interviewed, spoke with, or observed twenty-seven people in and around the South Bronx neighborhood. I have used pseudonyms to protect them all. I disclose the field site and give some character descriptions. That, I hope, is enough.

As to robberies, I was mostly unaware of a robbery's exact day and time. There were just too many in the works. I would often learn of them when unfamiliar guys came to the block and pulled study participants aside. Sometimes, they returned from these sidewalk meetings and continued robbery preparations in my presence. Mostly, I stood silent, never asking about their plans. I commented only when someone asked for my opinion. Like a sounding board, my responses were in the form of, *Yeah, you're right, bro,* no matter what was asked.

For instance, one afternoon, Gus, Neno, and I were hanging out on the public stairwell as they smoked weed. While we were standing there, two middle-aged Dominican men pulled up in a car, got out, and walked to a sidewalk space about ten yards away. Gus and Neno met them with partial hugs. Neno then offered one of the men a hit of the weed. Smiling, the guy accepted and inhaled deeply. For about the next five minutes, they spoke furtively. I heard nothing, only observing nodding heads, moving lips, and puffs of smoke. After the men left, Gus and Neno returned to our spot and discussed an upcoming robbery.

"It's like I told them," Gus said, in Spanish, "if we use the girl, she can get us in the apartment without a problem. Without a problem. How many times did we use her? Tell me, how many times did we get inside the apartments?"

"No, I know," Neno responded.

"Then he's [the man he just spoke with] saying that it's not going to work," Gus continued, "that if we send the girl to knock on the door, it's not going to work. That guy was just talking shit. He doesn't know what he's talking about. He doesn't know shit."

Neno was silent. Gus then addressed me in English. "Yo, tell me, if we send Melissa to the apartment, aren't those niggas gonna open that door?"

"Yeah, they probably will," I answered.

"'Cause these niggas were like, 'Nah, nah, that's not gonna work. They never open their door.' I'm tryin' to tell those niggas that we used Melissa before and that that shit always works, man. We don't got to pull out no guns and shit on those niggas in a [building] hallway. Bro, that shit's just gonna attract mad attention. Tell me, bro, that shit's just gonna make a lot of noise, right?"

"Yeah, that shit's gonna make a lot of noise," I agreed. "You right."

"That's what I'm tryin' to tell them. But those niggas just don't want to listen, man. Like I said, yo, the niggas we goin' after been doin' this shit for years, bro. For years. Tell me, if they carryin' eight kilos of coke, they been doin' this like for a real long time, right?"

"If they movin' that much, yeah," I responded. "That shit just don't happen overnight."

"You know what I'm sayin'?" Gus continued. "Those niggas are gonna be lookin' to get robbed, right? They gonna be prepared for that shit. Man, the way they want us to do it, man, that shit ain't gonna work, bro. I know it, man. But those niggas just don't want to listen." He pulled out a lighter and relit the weed blunt that had gone out. He and Neno then resumed smoking.

Such moments represented the scope of my participation. I never asked about a robbery being planned. In fact, I told Pablo and Gus not to inform me of upcoming stickups. I only wanted accounts of ones that were done. *Just give me after-the-fact information, bro.* True, I had received a Federal Certificate of Confidentiality from the National Institutes of Health. This protected me from law enforcement wanting to subpoena my field data. But I was unsure if the federal protection extended to me having "heard something" about future crimes.

Yet, one day, I did think aloud about how *that shit would be dope, kid, to see how a stickup started from beginning to end.* I would understand it better, right? Gus, who believed that "experience is the best teacher," tried hard not to disappoint. So he sometimes informed me of upcoming drug hits, and even invited me to tag along. Only through observations, he insisted, would I learn what robberies were all about. As always, I declined, citing moral and ethical obligations.

Nevertheless, Gus would persist. And after several months, I figured out why: I was his opportunity. Not only could his exploits garner possible media attention, but they also might accord him a higher street status. This was why he introduced me to everyone as his "cousin," the journalist. Never as the sociologist. The guys perhaps understood the work of reporters, who sometimes glamorized criminals in news articles and trade books. By calling me one, he was announcing to the world that his brutal acts were worthy—he even had a journalist, or personal biographer, following him around.[21]

In fact, Gus fell in love with earlier drafts of the robbery chapters, sometimes asking me to carry them when he hung out with girlfriends. Since he had given a lot to the research, I complied. Often, he would have his girlfriends read the chapters and get off on their wide-eyed reactions. *That's you? You're crazy!* Other times, he would get lost in his own rereading of the accounts, ignoring his girlfriends and leaving me to make conversation. Yes, Gus wanted a superstardom that transcended these streets. He wanted to be famous, to have everyone know him, worldwide.

That said, I must address some other methodological matters, critical ones that I can no longer hide from, no longer duck and dodge. In truth, I have grown weary of running from what I have perceived from the start to be a politically charged methodological note. This is ironic because while I sometimes feared for my life during my South Bronx research, I feared even more that disclosing my insider view would harm me professionally.

Insider Research: Standpoint Crisis

Most inner-city ethnographies have been done by upper-middle-class and elite-educated researchers. For them, fieldwork is often their first sustained contact both with poor people of color and with exciting and unfamiliar social phenomena—the streets, the sounds, the language, the black and brown bodies. They admit their race and class privileges and discuss how these might have influenced their observations.[22] Then they provide wonderful ethnographic insight, mostly for upper-middle-class readers who are just like them but who would never travel to those exotic worlds.

Now me: I came from a poor South Bronx neighborhood. I attended bad public schools. I used a plastic shopping bag as my school backpack. I wore torn, "holy" sneakers as my only shoes. I starved on many dreary afternoons, often having only soda crackers and government cheese to eat. I shivered in freezing *cold* apartments that landlords refused to heat. Struggling Black and Brown people—those were my neighbors and best friends. For me, the exotic "others" were the professional Whites in Manhattan subways and the middle-class Whites teaching in public schools. Later they were the middle-class Whites, Blacks, and Latino/as that I met as a graduate student. I was not privileged in race, place, or class. And as I started writing this ethnography, an uncomfortable feeling welled up inside me. In fact, it made me freeze.

Fear.

I was afraid of the repercussions of this unprivileged position: I was afraid of how critics would say that my insider knowledge of these South Bronx drug robbers had produced a less objective, less insightful ethnography. I was afraid that, unlike privileged ethnographers, who were praised for studying dangerous urban worlds, I would be vilified for revealing violence in marginal communities. I was afraid that the Black and Latino/a scholarly communities, who wanted no more negative images, would become angry at me for studying violent Dominican men.

Most of all, I was afraid of taking on the dominant White-male, scientific voice, which, for me, is neither neutral nor authentic. I was afraid that I could not be me, that I could not write from my social space, one that cut across social statuses and time: educated, street, Dominican, 1980s to 2000s, criminalized, marginal, and male.

Sandra Harding and Dorothy Smith's call for researchers to use their unique standpoints, or gendered social positions, was useful here.[23] Patricia Hill Collins complicated this idea by showing how standpoints are based on intersections of race, class, and gender.[24] As an unprivileged researcher of color, I could appreciate these methodological breakthroughs. Yet my unprivileged position, with its unique epistemology, or ways of knowing what I know, made me feel uneasy. Would I be as entitled as privileged ethnographers to reveal my standpoint? Would I get the same sympathetic nods as privileged ethnographers did when they revealed their positionality within the research?

Given my experiences within the privileged world, I thought not. Reinforcing this gut feeling was the reaction of colleagues when I talked about the focus of my work. *It could ruin your career,* I was told, behind closed doors. *But if I die tomorrow, what I leave behind won't reveal the true workings of a Dominican drug market insider,* I responded, dramatically but sincerely. *Don't do it,* I was told again. *The academic community will judge you. Just knowing that you grew up with these violent men will have them thinking twice about you.*

Afraid, I would listen to these privileged insiders.[25] *They're probably right.* I grew silent. I hardly discussed how my background shaped the research; I endlessly sought distractions to avoid writing it up.

Yet no matter which way I ran, I was always dragged right back to this issue. When I discussed my work in public forums, audiences wanted more on my insider status. *This is a fascinating topic,* they would say, *but I want you to discuss more about how your position as an insider affected your research. I also want you to address why you're so different from them, or how it is that you had such a different trajectory.* I would then answer strategically, not revealing entirely how I had felt during the fieldwork. Even the original version of this book manuscript had limited insider discussions. Reviewers criticized this silence—vehemently—and demanded to know more.

So now it has come to the moment I call *standpoint crisis,* where I have to decide whether to fully disclose my background. As a person of color, I have faced many levels of oppression in my everyday world. The risk of adding one more in the academic world—a place where the dominant paradigm is positivistic—makes me hesitate.[26] Yet for the sake of being open about the methodology, I will reveal the truth: that my South Bronx experiences during the crack era *did* significantly shape my feelings and interpretations during fieldwork. They also shaped the way I sometimes wrote this ethnography as to language, tone, and style. Here goes.

Desensitization

I grew up in drug-ridden neighborhoods, witnessed violence, and heard lots of talk about violence, so I was partially desensitized toward many violent acts. When study participants recounted torture stories, I simply nodded, chuckled, or smiled. Occasionally, I added a *Damn, that shit is crazy, bro.* Sometimes, I even slapped fives while laughing aloud. For instance, one night, Gus and Neno recounted a torture incident to Pablo, Tukee, and me as we drank liquor on the public stairwell.

We kept fuckin' him up real bad, bro, Gus explained, *and the nigga didn't want to talk, yo. Like we was doin' all type of shit to him, bro. I was punchin' that nigga and shit. These dudes was chokin' him, pistol-whippin'... all that shit, bro. Fuckin' him up real bad. Real bad. Then this nigga got the iron and forget it, bro, ha-ha-ha!* [To Neno in Spanish] *Tell them what you did.*

I took out the iron and heated it, Neno explained, in Spanish, *and told him, 'I'm gonna burn your ass, ball-sucker! Tell me where it's [the drugs] at! I'm gonna stain your ass if you don't tell me!' Forget it, when the guy saw the iron, and that it was hot, all of sudden he remembered everything.*

Now the motherfucka remembered he was a fuckin' drug kingpin, B! Tukee added, laughing. *The shit just came to him, B.*

Yeah, I added, *now he's like, 'Oh shit, that's right, I'm a dealer movin' pounds of coke. I just ain't recall that shit a minute ago. Ha-ha!*

Sorry for puttin' you through all that trouble, continued Pablo, acting like the dealer. *You can put the iron away now—ha-ha!—that shit won't be necessary.*

And as Gus finished the story, we continued joking and laughing—including me. During these moments, I was more enthralled than bothered by their brutality. Rarely did I think about the victim, who had been brutally beaten, maimed, and burned. In fact, I saw those atrocities as coming with the drug-dealing turf. Drug dealers knew that this was a business hazard, I reasoned; everybody knew that at some point they would have their day. It was all part of the "game."

Afterward, I would go home and write up the stories or transcribe the tape-recorded interviews. I would then read the accounts on paper, line by line, word for word . . .

Shocked. Disturbed. Those were the words that described my reaction to their drug robbery violence. On the streets, the magnitude of their violence was hardly apparent to me. Also, I had justified their violence by blaming the dealing victim. I was embarrassed, disappointed. I would never have blamed the victim of race and gender persecution—even within the drug market. In fact, the stories that disturbed me most dealt with gender and racial injustices and stereotypes. This was why they hardly mentioned such accounts around me. If they did, it was because they thought that their comments were "safe." Overall, they understood that any sexist or racist remarks would have me logically tear them apart. But in the realm of drug robberies, I was just like them. I blamed the dealer.

Then it hit me: after hanging out with these men so much, I momentarily went back to my old status and role as "wannabe" drug dealer. On the streets, the cold capitalist rationalizations had returned, those justifications for making money no matter the human costs. Beating, burnings, mutilation— *Man, you gotta do what you gotta do to get that loot.* Sometimes, I even felt that certain magic moment again, that time during late 1980s when I believed that the drug market was my only way to financial success. This was when I saw the world as my study participants did, when I felt their lofty desires and emotional pain. I was damn tired of being penniless, broke. I was desperate to earn tons of money and prestige. Drug robberies were the only way out of poverty, out of misery, out of the damn South Bronx . . . Drugs, guns, and violence—*Fuck it.* Just put me down. I'm ready to go.

I was "one of them" again.

On the streets, I romanticized them—I saw them as street heroes jumping over social hurdles and obstacles. But when I read their isolated accounts afterward, alone, the stories *leaped* at me from the page. Then, I interpreted them from the other extreme: stone cold sociopaths. This is when I thought that there was something mentally wrong with them, when I thought that they were hopeless and irredeemable. Without a social context, their words and actions made it hard to see them any other way. *These people are my friends?* I often asked myself, in disbelief.

But then I would remember the time when I would have done anything to make "crazy" money. So I put myself in their shoes: *If I were in their social position today, and had invested my prime years in the drug market, and had a criminal record, and had no legal options for economic success, would I join them on robberies? Would I be capable of the violence that they do? Which one would it be: would I be utterly shocked and disgusted at the brutality, or would I understand it as instrumental to getting the drugs and cash?*

A long pause . . .

The long pause in my reply, though, would disturb me, making me answer a definitive *No!* But that long pause occurred for a reason. I knew that I currently answered from a different social space. In the past, I was like them: I was poorly educated, a child of Dominican immigrants, and spent my childhood and teenage years in burning South Bronx neighborhoods. I had also seen little prospect in schooling and legal work, which had led me into drug dealing. But now I was close to getting a doctorate in sociology. Now I saw my life chances differently.

What had led to this difference, though, was ironic: unlike them, I had failed miserably in the illegal drug market. Had I experienced drug market success and then gone to prison (every drug dealer I have ever known, except for one, has been jailed or imprisoned), there was a good chance that I would have joined them on drug robberies. Most neighborhood drug market participants with criminal records had done robberies, or desperately wanted to do one. Why would I have been so different?

It was those thoughts and questions that would get my sociological thinking to kick in. I would then search for meanings and patterns on the current page, then for their links to the pages from days, weeks, and months before. Throughout this process, I turned to the sociological and criminological literature. I wanted to find links between my observations and other scholarly theories and empirical findings. Soon, I saw that there was logic and reason to these men's violence. At the micro-level, I saw how their in-the-moment violence was shaped by the emotional processes associated with drug robbery. At higher levels, I saw how their violent robberies grew out of larger cultural and material goals, deteriorating economic and community conditions, and especially—especially—the shrinking of the crack market. The challenge was weaving these different levels of analysis into one consistent descriptive and analytical pattern. With this book, I hope to have met that challenge.

There was more, however, to being an insider than past experiences. My in-the-moment appearance, words, and behavior counted too. Let me explain. When I started attending graduate school, I found the academic environment new and strange, and its people equally new and strange. My new classmates had different world experiences and most came from privileged spaces. So I often gravitated back to the familiar—to my South Bronx neighborhood and its people.

And the neighborhood guys still saw me as one of them. They never forgot how I had walked the same streets, joked and talked on the same corners, and experienced their high-fiving joy or *fuckin' heated* anger. In other words, they still expected the same ol' Ran, the same dude who had lived and felt just like them, who felt at ease in the company of drug dealers, who knew what to say and do: the grin, the fisted handshake, the *What-up?* the *Chillin'?* the *A'ight.* So despite being a graduate student who was busy learning both the sociological way and the way through an upper-middle-class milieu, I was expected to continue the neighborhood groove.

For instance, one afternoon as I walked with Pablo down a street, I stumbled over a sidewalk crack. Quickly, I recuperated my balance, showing, I thought, serious athleticism and cool. *Yo, you losin' it, Ran,* Pablo still joked, shaking his head. Another time, I arrived to the block clean-shaven and wearing blue jeans, running sneakers, and a baseball jersey, Yankee blue. *Yo, you look like a fuckin' cop,* Pablo remarked, laughing. *Yeah,* Tukee agreed, *you look like one those Hispanic DTs [detectives], those motherfuckas.* Though I laughed along in both cases, the comments stung. In a grander sense, they were sanctions: I was not supposed to stumble, in words, acts, or dress. I was an insider, one of them.

Even Gus hinted at his expectations of my insider status. One summer afternoon, I played dominoes with some guys in the public park. After several games, I asked a guy to take my place, offering my milk-crate seat. As I drank a Corona, Gus—who was always watching—walked over to me. *Yo, don't give your seat up to him,* he said, annoyed. *He's a fuckin' cokehead, man.* I was stung again. True, this was a pedagogical moment, one where he described the neighborhood pecking order. But his tone was sharp. I had done a serious wrong.

On these streets, then, my slip-ups were unacceptable. In other words, I could not act naïve. For other researchers, outsider naiveté is often a wonderful ethnographic tool.[27] Whether real or contrived, it often forces participants to teach researchers the do's and don'ts of the field site. However, the prevailing attitude toward me was: *Don't act like you don't know.* So I received no sympathy, no empathy—just a researcher-participant relationship full of no's. No hand-holding. No learning the ropes. No protection from sponsors. No acting like a dope.

Nonetheless, to gather rich data, I would pretend that I "didn't know" and ask a multitude of questions—sometimes to the point where they appeared annoyed. *It's that I need this information in your own words*, I explained when I saw their exasperation. *This research is more about how you make sense of everything, not just about how I make sense of what's goin' on.* Eventually, they became accustomed to my avalanche of questions and enjoyed being the "experts" in the research.

Being an insider also meant that I had some protection. Gus, the most violent robber, vouched for me as his "cousin," and Pablo and Tukee called me their "cousin" too. So guys like Topi, Neno, and David, whom I had just met, would never rob or pull a gun on me. But I also knew that with acceptance came adherence to group norms. The guys always enjoyed a good fistfight and believed that men should physically establish their social status, or manhood. My protection, then, was limited to them stopping anyone from potentially killing me. That's it. Anything beneath that point, I was on my own.

For instance, one autumn afternoon, I discussed with Gus and Pablo an interesting but troubling observation. I had noticed that whenever David, Neno, or Topi accompanied me to the *bodega* to buy beer, they stared at my money as I pulled it out of my pocket . . . stared at it as I silently counted it . . . stared at it as I handed it to the grocer . . . and stared at it as I put it away as change. Every time.

"Don't worry about those niggas, bro," Gus said, laughing. "They ain't gonna do nothin' to you. I already told them you was my cousin. Those niggas won't dare do shit to you, bro. Trust me on that, ha-ha."

"Those are some funny niggas, ha-ha," Pablo added. "They be staring at your money and shit. Just fuck those niggas up, bro. They try some shit, just fuck them up. They ain't shit, man. Psst. Those niggas is ass, man."

"I mean, I ain't worried about them," I said, showing bravado. "It's just that it always happens, bro. Every time they in the store with me, they always starin' at my money. Like I take it out of my pocket and I go like this [I circled my hand with imaginary money], they be goin' like this [I circled my head as though it was following the circling money hand]."

"Those niggas are like dogs and shit, ha-ha-ha," Gus said, bursting into laughter. "You ever had some food in your hand, bro, and you start goin' like this to a dog [circling his hand], they start movin' their heads like . . . they start followin' your hand and shit, ha-ha-ha! Those niggas is funny. . . . Like I said, man, they ain't shit. Those niggas is real pussy, bro. You could handle them niggas, bro."

"Just fuck' em up, Ran," Pablo repeated. "They're bullshit, bro. They ain't shit."

"I'm not worried about them, bro," I said again. "It's just something I noticed, bro, that they always lookin' at my money. I know they not gonna do nothin' to me, like personally, bro. I know they won't do that. But they could send somebody to rob me, bro. They don't have to do it [themselves]. They could send somebody to do it, you understand? They lookin' at my money too much, man. They look like they want it re-e-a-a-l bad, ha-ha."

"Nah, man, don't worry about it, man," Gus said, reassuring me. "Yo, on the strength that I told them that you was my cousin, they won't try that shit, bro. They won't. Trust me, man, they ain't gonna send nobody to rob you. They crazy if they do that shit. They know how I am, bro."

Like Gus said, everyone knew he had my back. In fact, I sometimes sensed that Topi, Neno, and David deferred to me because of him. They never raised their voice at me. Never put me down. They always smiled and said, "*Y que?*" whenever I came around. Initially, I thought it was because I always played it *cool*. When I drank liquor with them, I never dominated conversations; I just listened, nodded, and took slow sips. In fact, we mostly got into in-depth conversations when we were alone. Even then, I was intent on getting their story, their side. Now, though, I see how Gus' violence probably loomed large in the backdrop—a mighty force field of protection that shielded me from a fight.

Insider Biography

I admit that I had preconceived ideas when I first started the research. Given my previous drug-dealing experiences, I was inclined to a Mertonian analysis of drug robbers. As a youth, I had grown up desperately wanting what society said I should want: lots of money. Big houses. Luxury cars. Designer clothes. Respect and status through showing off material goods. I was not alone. Most of the neighborhood youth who later became drug dealers had wanted the same. On the street corner, conversations that revolved around *if I had the money* had taken much of our time.[28]

And as a teenager, I was rather pragmatic about how I could reach these material goals. The neighborhood reality was that most adults had legal jobs, yet struggled to make ends meet. Even those who left after purchasing homes lived in unexceptional houses and suburbs. Their new neighborhoods had blight and their homes were cramped and small (their previous South Bronx apartments were actually bigger). They were also overwhelmed with mortgage payments and unforeseen household bills. To me, they had not "made it"; economically, they were still close to their former South Bronx home.[29]

Also, at an early age, I was an indoctrinated American, infused with the capitalist spirit. Thus, I wanted to join the ranks of the financially successful. I thought nothing of improving the social conditions of the poor. Instead, I searched for that catapult to fling me over the social fortresses surrounding the rich. In the vernacular of the time, I wanted to dress fly, make crazy money, and drive fresh cars. But I also dreamed of achieving that other lifestyle, where, like the people shown in the Nautica ads plastered on building facades and subway walls, I sailed yachts and wore preppy clothes. I wanted badly to be Captain Elite.

But, again, from what I had observed, school was not the move for folks like me. The only people that I had seen rise from the South Bronx ashes were a handful of Dominican and Puerto Rican drug dealers. They were young men of color who eventually made more money than their social conditions should have allowed. With intelligence, drive, ambition, and luck (crack cocaine emerged just on time), they had paved a new economic path. Since they earned more money than the neighborhood adults working legal jobs, they won my admiration, hands down.

Another admission: I had also seen a few of my extended family members strike it rich in the drug market. It was an amazing observation. Only a few years before, I had visited these poor cousins in the Dominican Republic. On the island, they lived in decayed housing that lined dirt streets, had no running hot water, and hardly had electricity. Worse, as older teenagers and young adults, they begged me for money and clothes—me, their little twelve-year-old New York City cousin, who started every Spanish utterance with the English street slang prefix, "Yo."

But later, in the U.S., the tables were turned: they had the designer shirts, pants, and shoes; they wore the big gold chains, bracelets, and rings; and they carried rubber-banded wads of cash. Sometimes, they would pull out a knot of money, unroll several twenties, and hand them to me: *Here, so you can take some girls out.* I was impressed. Clearly, most of my extended family worked legally and never committed crime. But it was these men that stood out. Although unschooled, they had created a different way to booming economic success.

So this was what I had seen: the drug market—an innovative and alternative path—was the way to go. Merton 101. Since this was how I had roughly framed my drug-dealing experiences, it was the preconceived idea that I had brought to the field. To be clear, I was not deliberately testing or advancing Merton's or his successors' theories of anomie. My experiences had just made this theme familiar, even before I had seen its academic form. So whether I wanted to or not, I was thinking in those terms when I started my South Bronx fieldwork. And when I flipped the research switch and asked why these Dominican men had become drug robbers, Merton's anomie was the first lighted bulb.

But as I did fieldwork and read literature, I saw that squeezing my data into this preconceived frame was lopping off crucial parts of the theoretical picture. It was like placing the *Mona Lisa* in a small frame, revealing her hair, her eyes, her nose, but not that important part: her smile. I would, I realized, need a larger frame, and I found it in Philippe Bourgois' drug market spin on resistance theory; Jack Katz' emphasis on crime's emotional allure; and later, Randall Collins' micro theory of violence. These theoretical contributions were just as relevant and strong.[30]

The Triple Representational Dilemma

I must admit to one other reason for being absent in an earlier manuscript draft. Clearly, I believed in *reflexivity,* where a field researcher explains how his or her social position affected the research.[31] Weaving themselves into the analysis, they show how they saw what they saw and how they dealt with their race, class, and gender position.[32] Still, I balked at putting myself alongside South Bronx drug robbers. I wanted no one—*no one*—calling me a cowboy ethnographer.

The cowboy ethnographer. I use this term to describe ethnographers who are *perceived* to exploit research for their own professional or narcissistic end. In other words, researchers who are thought to glorify themselves at the expense of the study participants.[33] Surely, no one knows whether this is true of any ethnographer. But behind closed academic doors, the word is that this happens, and the cowboy is ridiculed and scorned. So the perception, not the reality (as the Thomas theorem states), makes the cowboy real.

Mainly, the charge is aimed at researchers studying dangerous or hidden populations. For most laypeople (and academics), these exotic others are distant, only seen roaming the streets or as images on the nightly news. Through ethnographies, though, middle-class readers can live vicariously through a researcher, one with a background similar to their own. Now they get a sense of how they would feel among the homeless or among the urban poor. Now they get a sense of how they would react around violent men, women, or outlaws on the down low. Now they were *there*.

The word is that some ethnographers capitalize on those middle-class curiosities. They project themselves as bravely risking life and limb, as tight-roping dangerous race and class lines—and making it back to tell the tale. Whether such cowboy ethnographers truly exist, I do not know. Neither do I care. As long as ethnographers advance knowledge within certain moral and methodological limits, they can do as they wish.

That said, I wanted no part of that label.

As a result, I retreated further, limiting my reflexivity until it was almost gone. If I did include my thoughts and feelings, it was when I was touched by suffering study participants. Those moments were not prone to sensationalism; their pain would remain front and center. Still, in discussing or depicting violence, I not only risked glamorizing the study participants, but myself too. This was the start of the *triple-representational dilemma*.

The first representational dilemma: if I discussed drug robbery torture in depth, then I could be accused of glorifying the study participants' violence. Yet if I played down drug robbery violence, then I could be accused of sanitizing violent study participants.

The second representational dilemma: if I failed to place myself within the text, I could be accused of not showing how my social position affected my research. Yet if I regularly placed myself within the text, especially during violent moments, I could be accused of cowboy ethnography.

In both cases, I was *damned if I do, damned if I don't*.

But there was one more representational dilemma. As alluded to earlier, I was risking being a called out as a minority scholar who willingly reinforced racist imagery for professional gain. In a sense, it was like being called, as Mark Fleisher would say, a pimp, but this time with all of its racial connotations.[34] Thus:

The *third representational dilemma:* if I discussed violence among minorities, I could be called an exploiting Uncle Tom. Yet if I failed to discuss violence, which was central to my study, then I would not only fail my intellectual promise, but also my study participants, who, like me, wanted to know what was going on in their lives.

In all, as a minority scholar, I faced this *triple-representational dilemma.*

This is what I did: As to the cowboy label, I could only go through my manuscript and look for spots where the action seemed centered on me. I needed to be reflexive, just like the ethnographers who have taught me most. But I also needed to try to remove myself from the center of analysis—unless my emotions clued me in to what was going on. Most important, I did not want to sanitize the world of these South Bronx drug market participants. The violence, the rage, the despair—all was depicted in relation to larger shifts in the social structure. Last, I did the research with intellectual integrity, which meant, to me, no omissions. I would deal directly with violence among marginal minorities.

In the end, I could not let others dictate my research. I would never politicize the research of others, especially on topics that are deviant, taboo, controversial, or that challenge the sociological mainstream. Also, I was not a cowboy who had ventured into the "unknown." The world of these South Bronx Dominican men was familiar—their neighborhood was my neighborhood, their past was my past. And I wanted to learn about what had gone on with *our* community, the factors that had shaped *our* lives. As an academic, especially one with close ties to the research, this was my freedom, my right. And if these men had not existed, then there would be no need to research them. But they did. This alone merited their study. As humans, they needed understanding too.

Danger, Writing, and Representation

Throughout the research, I was grateful to the Dominican men (and one woman) who let me observe them, tape-record conversations, and write their stories despite the great risks. For this, I wanted to repay them. It was only fair. But I had no money or big payday in sight. For instance, I had yet to secure a book deal, so I could not promise royalties.[35] Even if I did have one, I was almost sure of two scenarios. First, it would be a laughable pittance to men accustomed to earning big money. In fact, given the small earnings of an academic book, they might think that I was secretly pocketing profits.

Coño. This unsettled me. From the capitalist streets, I had learned that *money does funny things to people.* Money could even trump close bonds.

For instance, one winter evening I sat in Pablo's home, listening to him complain about Geraldo, a drug dealer and restaurant owner. According to Pablo, he had allowed Geraldo to register a car under his name. Geraldo then accumulated twelve hundred dollars in traffic violations. Pablo, who did not want jail time, demanded payback. Geraldo, however, refused to pay. As retribution, Pablo set up Geraldo for a robbery. These men, I should add, are biological brothers. Pablo did not care.

"Yo, Ran," Pablo said, angrily. "He told me, 'I don't give a fuck about you, that's your problem.' I mean, he didn't say that, but that's the way I take it since he doesn't pay me. That's why I already talked to some people to have him bagged [robbed]. He's lucky, yo. I sent people already to have him bagged, but he's never alone, bro. Like in the mornin' when he opens the restaurant, he's with his wife. I don't want her to be involved, you know what I'm sayin'? Or his kids either, bro. I don't want them to go through that trauma. I want him to go through the trauma. But he's gonna get bagged, yo. Watch, I'm just waitin'."

A couple of months later, Pablo was still angry at Geraldo.

"Can you believe that shit, Ran?" Pablo asked. "That nigga still hasn't paid me one dime, bro. Not one fuckin' penny. Yo, and that shit's been goin' on for a over year, bro. Over a fuckin' year."

"You think he has the money to pay it, bro?" I asked.

"Yo, he *had* the money. Even if he don't have it now, the point is that he had it, yo. He could'a gave me my shit, man. I'm tellin' you, man, nigga's shysty, man. Especially that nigga, man. You don't know, I just want to fuckin' [Pablo paused, took a deep breath, and exhaled slowly] . . . I can't wait for that nigga to start makin' money. To tell you the truth, somebody's gonna be knockin' on that nigga's door. That's to the point that I'm in. I'm waitin' to hear that he's doin' good, bro."

"Why don't you tell him every week to, or every month to—"

"Yeah, I tell him, man!" Pablo said angrily. "Yo, he's with some bullshit! Always with some bullshit. I'm just dyin' for that nigga to start makin' money. Even if I hear that he's makin' money in the streets, Randy, I swear on [my] moms, yo, I'ma send niggas [robbers] to his house. For real, man."

Again, this was his brother from the same mother. What would he do to me if he thought that I had shortchanged him from book profits? This and other stories had me easily imagine disgruntled research participants gagging and binding me and then threatening me with a steaming hot iron, all for earnings I never had. So whenever we discussed the book, I played down the royalties:

Yo, the thing with academic books, I often told them, *is that they don't sell a lot. I mean, I hope this one does. I'm writin' it to give it a chance to sell a lot. But from what I seen, none of them don't.*

The second scenario was less threatening, but just as real: I would need that royalty pittance more than they did. I was a poor graduate student and, given starting salaries for sociology professors, I saw myself struggling financially for awhile. Most sociologists, I was learning, did the work not for the money, but for a passion to unravel the social world. No doubt that these intelligent folks could have earned much more as accountants, attorneys, entrepreneurs, medical doctors, and corporate managers. They simply loved the sociological game.

Since I loved the game too, I was not going to be filthy rich anytime soon, if ever. The study participants were always shocked when I reminded them of this aspect of my brilliant career. Their usual response was: *Damn, that's it? You ain't gonna make shit. Then what the fuck you goin' to school for, all those years?* But the point, I hope, was made: they knew that, money-wise, I could offer little.

There was one thing, though, that I could give them. Within certain bounds, I could grant them authority over their representation. And I did. Individually, I talked to them about this authority and then asked them about what they would like from the book. Their response? They wanted me to portray them as slick criminals who outsmarted drug dealers as they took dangerous risks. Wait. They also wanted to be on the big screen, wanting the book to become a film script. *Professional Drug Hits: The Movie.*

At first, I laughed at their cinematic dreams. *Man, you all some funny dudes!* But over time I realized that they took their potential fame seriously. This was their chance to be "somebody," more than vacant faces on languid street corners, or black and brown bodies doing push-ups in scorching prison yards. This was their chance to rise above their criminal obscurity and become stars. *Stars, yo.*

Since they had risked a lot for my research, I wanted to honor that wish. But I had to represent them sociologically as well. It was more important to reveal the social processes that shaped and influenced them than to provide sensational stories of their brutal acts. Also, danger loomed in such representations. Conservative critics could use them to further vilify poor, minority communities. General readers might never, ever, see the humanity behind the gruesome acts. In all, I risked reinforcing negative stereotypes rather than providing an accurate sociological account. It was a decisional tug-of-war: I wanted to give them a potential movie. But I wanted to realize my sociological goals too.

First, I wrote a narrative that I felt would be appreciated by both study participants and a general audience. Within that story, I cut in occasionally for sociological analysis. I used my natural writing voice, which embodied our background and past. *Ya tu sabe'*: it had the cadence that we had inherited from our Dominican culture; it had the words and sounds that we had picked up on the South Bronx streets. It had, in all, a voice that I still sometimes thought in, spoke in.

Still, this voice was not *the academic voice*. Like an iron mask, the academic voice was hard, rigid; it sounded neutral and scientific. I could write in that voice, which graduate school had taught me well. But it was not me. I shared little with its history and practitioners. Using it would also concede that the best expression could never come from people like me. This is simply untrue and unfair. Still, I could get in trouble for avoiding The Voice. Academics could charge that I was unprofessional and flippant toward established sociological practices. Worst-case scenario: I would be exiled to sociology's fringes, where I would never be heard from again. *Ay, mi madre.* Using my authentic voice was full of *peligros*.

Que se joda. I took the chance. My study participants had to appreciate and understand the ethnography. So I wrote in my voice, their voice, our voice, a legitimate voice. More important, I kept my word. Despite my academic goals, I wrote a manuscript that could potentially attract many general readers, one of whom could be a screenwriter or movie producer. *Win-win,* I thought, as I submitted some chapters to one university press, and an entire manuscript to both another university press and a trade press. Excited, I waited for the response. Then: bad news. The trade press felt that it had too much analysis. The university presses, the reverse: the story and style overwhelmed its sociological significance.

I was dejected.

I had tried to write an ethnography with both popular appeal and academic breadth. But I had failed. My eager study participants—I did not know what to tell them. Since I had really wanted to publish with a university press, I would now have to cut their stories, change the voice, and use a traditional academic format. Ultimately, I was a scholar, with a responsibility to theoretically and analytically understand their worlds. I then realized that my study participants never had representational authority. I could overrule them, anytime. I also realized that, no matter my explanation, they could call me a liar, *un embustero*. A phone conversation with Gus made me feel even worse. After catching up, we talked about the book's progress. Then he said: *It feels real good to know that people will be readin' my life story, bro. Like they'll see how it all started, like from the beginning to end . . . That shit'll make a good movie, bro. I know it. That's why I can't wait to read that shit. I'm gonna read all of it, all of it. It's gonna make a good movie, bro. Just watch.*

After a pause, I repeated to Gus that I had to make some manuscript changes before getting it published. But I could not bring myself to tell him that I would also delete most of the story. As of this writing, I have yet to tell them. I can only say: *Sorry Gus, Pablo, and Tukee. I tried my best. I really tried.*

The study participants, to be sure, will not like this final version. For sociological reasons, I had to cut their robbery stories and expand the sociological analysis. Left alone, the disturbing and brutal tales overpowered the academic analysis. I know this from the anonymous reviewers, who gave up their precious time to read the earlier version. So this time I wrote it (as much as possible) in reverse: I weaved the stories around the sociological analysis. I truly hope this works.

That said, I have tried to keep some of the original voice, one that both the study participants and general readers can appreciate. In doing so, I hope to make this ethnography accessible to both audiences. I want these South Bronx Dominicans to understand what a sociologist is saying about them. I want a general audience to understand how a sociologist can uncover hidden social processes in marginal people's lives. This is only fair to the South Bronx men and women willing to share their lives with me. To them, I say:

Gracias, for letting me write it all down.

PART ONE

Becoming Stickup Kids

*The facts of contemporary history are also facts about the success
and the failure of individual men and women. When a society is
industrialized, a peasant becomes a worker; a feudal lord is liqui-
dated or becomes a businessman. When classes rise or fall, a man is
employed or unemployed; when the rate of investment goes up or
down, a man takes new heart or goes broke. When wars happen,
an insurance salesman becomes a rocket launcher; a store clerk, a
radar man; a wife lives alone; a child grows up without a father.
Neither the life of an individual nor the history of a society can be
understood without understanding both.*

C. WRIGHT MILLS
Sociological Imagination

ONE

The Rise of the South Bronx and Crack

THE BRONX IS A LAND OF STEEP HILLS, green parks, and elegant architecture. The borough is slightly smaller in square mileage than Boston, but with over 1.3 million residents, it has almost two and half times its population. Still, it is only New York City's fourth most populated borough, coming ahead of just Staten Island.[1] The Bronx is also the only borough attached to the mainland; Manhattan, Brooklyn, Queens, Staten Island— water separates them all. The land borders Long Island Sound to the east, the East River to the southeast, the Harlem River to the west, and the county of Westchester, a wealthy neighbor, to the north.

The natural landscape is beautiful, with parkland covering nearly a quarter of the borough.[2] These parks offer shady trees, green grass, athletic fields, and colorful playgrounds, all for pleasant mornings, evenings, and afternoons. On streets outside the parks stand butter-colored art deco buildings, a signature of curves and arches that soften the Bronx sky. These elegant buildings have housed residents from all over the world; in their early years, from Europe, and later, from Africa, the Caribbean, and Latin America.[3]

But a close inspection reveals severity. Sidewalks wrinkle with cracks, roads crater with potholes. Building facades crumble, litter adorns the street. Every bright color is dimmed by soot, a thick coat of gray. Though reviving, the Bronx is still the Bronx. Next to most New York City boroughs, it is crime ridden, poverty ridden, and uneducated.[4]

It is here that the lives of the Dominican drug robbers have unfolded. Not so long ago, the South Bronx was an urban inferno, with thieves, drug pushers, and vandals roaming its abandoned streets. This was not always so. The Bronx was once a glorious city. But some political, economic, and social woes reversed the borough's forward momentum. Then it was the Hopeless

Bronx. The Shameful Bronx. The City on Fire. Under Siege. These Dominican men came of age then, during the time when the South Bronx was falling apart.

More important to their lives was the crack era. This period coincided with the South Bronx demise and influenced them first to become crack dealers, then drug robbers. Thus, they evolved within a social context in which political, global, and social forces transformed the drug market, forces that would later affect other urban areas too.

And I must describe those historical factors in some detail. My own readings of ethnographies suggest that a superficial "background" section—one or two pages—is like a speck of dust, large enough to notice, but small enough to forget after flicking off. This then leads to a limited analysis that dismisses historical and structural factors. For example, in explaining why Black men are overrepresented as robbers, Katz argues that poverty is irrelevant since other poor ethnic groups do fewer robberies. He then links this crime statistic to Black culture, claiming that it glorifies the criminal "hardman."[5]

I am unsure how Katz discovered this Black cultural trait from just looking at arrest data, police files, or robber autobiographies. Also, "hardmen" can be found in other ethnic cultures, like the *bandido* in Mexican culture or the mafia heist man in the Italian American community. In the end, I wish Katz had considered how history—its social forces and criminal opportunities—matters just as much. Because perhaps African American robbers have less access to crimes controlled by certain ethnic groups. Perhaps the actions of public, business, and political leaders, and a fleeing White (and Black) middle class, drain the community's economic pond, which in turn creates a concentration of poor African Americans, which in turn increases their risks of doing street crime.[6]

Perhaps it is a combination of all.[7]

I pay attention to these historical and structural matters. Though these Dominican men did not create the South Bronx, it set the stage for their lives. In the South Bronx, their criminal opportunities rose and fell, and the effects of the crack era lingered long after the demand for crack had peaked and declined. The South Bronx was where they first became dealers, then drug robbers, then self-destructive human beings. Thus, these Dominican men were situated in a historical and social context.[8] Race, class, history, community, and drug market swings all shaped the motion picture of their lives.[9]

For real, bro? Nah, that's bullshit, man. I don't remember the
Bronx being like that. This shit was always fucked up, at least far
as I could remember. Shit was on fire back then. Fuck, shit's still
on fire now, ha-ha. Nah, I can't believe that, bro. You must got
your facts wrong or somethin'.

PABLO

Like Pablo, I could not believe that our South Bronx was once called the
"Wonder Borough."[10] Yet during the nineteenth century, the area was an
Eden, a tranquil, hilly, and leafy wilderness parceled into large estates. It would
attract prosperous Manhattan residents who were sold on the idea of country
and morality, who wanted to escape the mostly German and Irish slum neighborhoods that were filled with street gangs, drunkards, disease, and crime.

And by the early 1900s, the Bronx had gone from an idyllic country escape
to a posh city, full of style. To make a mark, Bronx boosters built impressive,
large apartment houses. These apartments, which the study participants and
I now called "home," were designed according to the period's French art deco
movement.[11] Resembling French flats, they had all the modern amenities—hot
water, separate living and sleeping quarters, electric lights, telephones, steam
heat, separate kitchens, and private bathrooms. The grand buildings also featured elevators, large hallways, and marbled lobbies, and sometimes had entrance courtyards with water fountains, statuary, and shrub-filled gardens.

Bronx boosters also lavished funds on one grand public amenity: parks.
They wanted a remarkable but tranquil experience in wide-open areas with
grass and trees, where people could forget, if for a day, urban life. Like Manhattan's Central Park, Bronx parks would stimulate modern residential construction, raise property values, and ultimately increase tax revenues. Potentially, the Bronx could rival the grandest cities in the world: London, Paris,
Rome. Indeed, the construction of Crotona Park, Claremont Park, Van Cor-
tland Park, and Pelham Bay Park made the borough's reputation sparkle.[12]

True to plan, by the 1920s, the Bronx was a smash, with modern buildings, large parks, and spectacular public works:[13]

It had the Grand Boulevard and Concourse, a broad, four-mile curving
boulevard that was modeled on the Champs-Élysées of Paris and that show-
cased three roadways, one for pedestrians and horse-drawn carriages, and
two for automobiles.

It had Yankee Stadium, which was made famous after "Babe" Ruth, one of the greatest hitters of all time, awed baseball fans with spectacular home runs and led the Yankees to a string of World Championships.

It had the Bronx Zoo and the Bronx Botanical Gardens, which featured exotic animals and plant life, and attracted visitors from all over the world.

It had respectable institutions of higher education, housing the campuses of Fordham and New York Universities, two intellectual sites that attracted the city's brightest.

It had the Concourse Plaza Hotel, a luxury establishment that catered to a high-end clientele, hosted extravagant events, and was home to athletic superstars.

And it had a powerful Democratic presence—led by "You're in like Flynn" Boss Flynn—which played a crucial role in Franklin Delano Roosevelt's presidential victory.

The Bronx had it all.

The successful borough also attracted a middle class wanting modern living and a working class wanting upgraded housing. In addition, it drew in a mix of immigrants, mostly Americanized German Jews and Irish wanting to escape Manhattan's congestion. Later, oppressed Russian and Eastern European Jews, as well as Italian peasants, would make the Bronx their home. The Bronx became a symbol of accomplishment, a move up on the status ladder.[14]

The Bronx Slides Downhill

Then, like a mudslide during a torrential rainfall, the Bronx went downhill after the Second World War. Many White, middle-class residents fled from newly arrived poor Puerto Ricans (who themselves had fled from a sad island economy)[15] and from newly arrived poor Blacks (who themselves had fled from a tyrannical Jim Crow South). Through the G.I. Bill, which sponsored low-interest loans, they settled in suburban homes.

Poverty in the Bronx would also expand because of a one-man social force, Robert Moses.[16] As a public official, he purposely designed bridges and parkways as cages to contain minorities; and he demolished 113 streets, dispersing tens of thousands of Jewish residents in East Tremont, all for a seven-mile stretch of highway to ease travel for outsiders—the Cross Bronx Expressway.[17] He also cleared Manhattan slum neighborhoods for public housing, which uprooted poor Blacks and Puerto Ricans to South Bronx neighborhoods. The influx of poor residents would allow some Bronx landlords to lower building maintenance, which lowered their expenses while increasing their profit.[18]

The Bronx slid further because of the demise of New York City's manufacturing economy. For generations, manufacturing had provided unionized security for European immigrants and their children.[19] However, between 1947 and 1976, New York City lost about five hundred thousand factory jobs, many to non-unionized regions of the country.[20]

In an intriguing account, sociologist Robert Fitch argues that New York City could have saved hundreds of thousands of those manufacturing jobs.[21] However, city officials sided with the real estate elites, who wanted to develop more office buildings for higher profits and land values. Specifically, the elite persuaded the city to give Title I status to much of the land where the remaining manufacturing sat. Thus, the plants and factories where hundreds of thousands of people had worked were knocked down for the promise of "urban renewal."

Worse, the city whole-heartedly subsidized office building construction by offering developers serious tax abatements and relief. Banks also granted them mortgages in staggering amounts. But after the towering office buildings went up, the projected white-collar economy never took off. And for the next several decades, vast amounts of office space went unused. The city continued to subsidize the empty spaces despite losing the tax revenue. The banks also lost millions of dollars in unpaid mortgages. The winners were the elite; they played with city and bank money, not their own.

Those who lost the most were blue-collar and low-wage New Yorkers. Hundreds of thousands of them lost traditionally secure jobs, all because their presence was a profit blocker to the powerful.[22] And they knew very little about how the city and real estate world had ruined their lives. Instead, they blamed the minority poor, echoing the distortions created by public officials. As a spokesman for New York City's municipal association argued decades later, "It's the fucking blacks and Puerto Ricans. They use too many city services and they don't pay any taxes. New York's in trouble because it's got too many fucking blacks and Puerto Ricans."[23]

For Bronx residents, then, the mighty manufacturing industries were no longer the first-generational step toward the realization of the American Dream. And the borough's postwar newcomers, who were mostly minority, uneducated, and unskilled, would need a higher education to succeed—one that, like the new office buildings, was skyscraper high.

Beware of the Bronx: Las Gangas y los Tecatos

The 1960s was the decade when the South Bronx gained a sinister reputation. The borough's new inhabitants were thought to embrace drugs, welfare, and crime.[24] True, Blacks and Puerto Ricans committed most of the borough's violence and experienced most of its poverty. Critics, though, generally blamed their supposed wayward cultures. The loss of manufacturing jobs, the language barriers, the need for education and training, all were lost in the public's explanation of the Bronx decline.

Worse, during this period Bronx residents witnessed the rise of *los tecatos*.[25] Filthy and worn out, *los tecatos* were well known to us as they roamed the streets day and night chasing *manteca,* or a heroin blast. After copping some *manteca, los tecatos* sought sanctuary in dark alleys, stairwells, abandoned buildings, or lonely rooftops. They wanted privacy to experience heroin's sudden euphoric flush, which, for some, was more pleasurable than passionate sex, more nourishing than a plateful of *mami*'s home-cooked food. *Pura tranquilidad.*

The tranquility, however, was short-lived. Often, the more users used, the more tolerance they gained—and the more *manteca* they needed for the same high. If not, they got "sick," or experienced withdrawal. To support frequent use, *los tecatos* would soon swell the ranks of *joloperos* and *ladrones,* who robbed, burglarized, and mugged residents for that quick dope cash.

Then the gangs began to make their mark on the South Bronx scene. Wearing denim jeans and jackets, thick belts and big boots, all adorned with war regalia and violent emblems, these youths paraded as the new aristocracy of the streets. Like feudal lords, they commanded neighborhoods, setting the rules and meting out the punishments. They claimed to do the good that the police wouldn't do: they beat up *tecatos,* ran drug pushers off the streets, and put up signs that warned, *No Junkies Allowed.* The gangs declared that they were about street justice, about cleaning up the community, about doing what the city had yet to do.[26]

However, gangs like the Savage Nomads, whom I often saw milling about, fought bloody turf wars with rivals. Worse, many gangs terrified neighborhoods rather than protecting them: they mugged, robbed, and burglarized people, while doing heavy drugs too.

South Bronx residents were in trouble. Now they feared both the *tecatos* and the *gangas* lurking in the shadows, eyeing the scene for that *pendejo* walking down a lonely street. *Cuídate . . . que valla con Dios,* said fearful Bronx residents as they bid a safe farewell in the most literal way.

A cold, misty underworld took over the streets. In 1960, there were close to a thousand reported assaults; in 1969, over four thousand. In the same period, burglaries increased from just under two thousand to over twenty-nine thousand.[27] To outsiders, the mere mention of the South Bronx brought the shakes and the shivers, the body moves that showed how it was best not to go there. *Go to the Bronx? You must be crazy.*

Fuego *in the Bronx*

> Yeah, I remember that shit. People just used to put shit on fire back then, B. Fuckin' landlords be like, "Don't wanna pay no more taxes, B." Ha-ha. "Twenty families still in there? Fuck it, they gonna [burn] too, B." Ha-ha. "Time to put you out your misery. Go get Fulano, the fuckin' pyromaniac motherfucka. He's gonna get shit started now." Ha-ha.
>
> TUKEE

Then it got hot. Real hot. The South Bronx was on fire. With the start of rent control laws, many landlords lost money as building maintenance costs rose. Historian Evelyn Gonzalez notes that landlords also lost money because many South Bronx apartments lay empty.[28] Residents that could secure enough resources moved to better neighborhoods, but often had no one replacing them. Landlords lost profits fast.

To keep profits up, landlords simply stopped maintaining their properties. Then buildings crumbled. Then tenants complained: no heat, no hot water, garbage and rats everywhere. *Slumlords.* Hearing the cries of poor tenants and community activists, lawmakers tried to strong-arm landlords: they passed legislation that penalized neglectful owners; they empowered tenants to withhold rents in buildings with code violations.

Landlords fumed, disinvesting in their properties altogether. Buildings then broke down faster. Residents and neighborhood merchants packed up and left. Eventually entire city blocks of crumbling buildings were uninhabited. Only imaginative kids and desperate junkies used the empty space. They created playgrounds and clubhouses, drug dens and homes.

Yet landlords were left with the idle structures, which lost value and cash flow—a capitalist no-no. Then it hit them. They realized that their properties were "worth more dead than alive."[29] It was better to burn them, claim them, and collect money from them than to keep them profitless.

Insurance brokers were also in on the scam. In a complicated scheme, they insured buildings up to twenty times their real values and then resold the insurance on the market. Property owners then hired "torches," who set the buildings ablaze. Afterward, owners collected on insurance claims, with brokers getting a nice cut too.

This fraud was so smooth and so slick that buyers began purchasing abandoned and run-down properties to burn for profit. Derelict buildings bought for a couple of thousand dollars could sometimes be insured for a couple of hundred grand. The South Bronx buildings flamed in a hurry.

It wasn't a victimless crime, however:

Fuego! Fuego! cried South Bronx tenants as they fled buildings just set on fire.

Llamen lo' bombero'! cried their neighbors as they called for firefighters to put out the blaze.

In awe and horror, South Bronx residents crowded on sidewalks to witness the fiery spectacle: blaring fire trucks racing to the scene; firefighters hurriedly attaching the cobra of a water hose to the fire hydrant; the *bomberos,* with a thick lash of water, trying to tame the feral red and orange flames; the burned-out residents staring quietly at their smoldering homes, hoping that something was left among the ashes. *Bendito.*

But some residents joined in on the arson. To slide up the new public housing waiting list, desperate tenants set fire to their apartments.[30] Sometimes they warned other residents in advance and called the fire department as soon as they were safely on the sidewalk. Still, the fire sometimes spread and burned out other tenants too. The South Bronx had gone up in smoke on every end.

Throughout the 1970s, South Bronx residents would experience blazing scenes about twelve thousand times a year.[31] After awhile, the sound of sirens, the smell of smoke, the sight of smoldering buildings—the whole bombed-out scene—were familiar to the community. (When I was a child, my own family was almost burned out of two apartments; the smoky odor, brown and red rubble, and stretches of grayish, abandoned buildings became ordinary to me. So, till this day, whenever I breathe in the fumes of burning wood or visit decrepit, deserted inner cities, nostalgia stirs up fond childhood memories of "home.")

The nation at large, however, got its first glimpse of the burned-out Bronx during the Yankee-Dodger 1977 World Series. During Game Two, a night game, an ABC camera helicopter hovering above Yankee Stadium captured the image of an abandoned elementary school in flames. "There it is, ladies and gentlemen," commented sports broadcaster Howard Cosell, "the Bronx is burning."[32] President Carter had visited a week earlier to observe the ruins. By now the South Bronx looked like it had been bombed out in a wartime air raid. Within a week, the South Bronx became known as the most awful place on earth.

It helped the Bronx little that New York City collapsed during the 1970s.[33] For over a decade, the city had spent more money than it had coming in. This equation produced a growing budget deficit, with no letup in sight. Worried investors pulled their money, fearing a city bankruptcy. The city, which relied heavily on bond sales and banks, was in a trouble.[34] Gotham would act swiftly. The little people, though, paid the price: thirty-eight thousand city workers laid off. Free tuition at public colleges, no longer free.

Turmoil ensued. Police officers picketed City Hall, stopping traffic on the Brooklyn Bridge and cussing out nonprotesting brothers-in-blue. Sanitation workers went on strike, allowing rotting garbage to pile up and litter the streets. Desperate residents took over fire houses, forcing the city to keep them open, to help douse the insurance-fraud flames. The city was angry, out of control.

Like the crumbling, graffiti-scribbled walls that marked the city, Gotham was a mess—it was fear, crime, frustration, abandonment, fire, poverty, chaos, financial loss . . . and the South Bronx would continue to suffer.

Resilience in the Bronx

Not that all was doom and gloom in the South Bronx. It had its own cultural innovation: hip-hop.[35] As in disco, hip-hop DJs used two turntables to eliminate pauses between records, which kept the schoolyard and block party crowds dancing. However, they purposely scratched and mixed records to create new rhythms and beats. Also, they now spoke over the music, shouting out short, rhyming phrases that moved the crowd: *Put your hands up in the air, and wave them like you just don't care . . . Somebody scr-e-e-e-a-a-m!*

Over time, DJs and then rap groups rhymed in longer sequences, in self-congratulatory oratories or in vivid accounts of ghetto life.

Electric boogie and break dancing also made the South Bronx scene. Popular among the younger generation, these movements were performed to underground dance and hip-hop music. On crude cardboard slats, or even straight concrete and wood floors, break dancers creatively spun and twisted their bodies in a whiz of motions. The boogiers pretended to run electricity through their bodies, either in snaky waves or choppy staccato. Sometimes they seemed to move as if by magic; they seemed to glide and float on air.

The older generation of South Bronx residents, mainly Puerto Ricans, stuck to older cultural forms, like salsa. Amateur musicians set up in parks or on sidewalks and played conga drums, tambourines, cowbells, and *guidas*. Crowds gathered to listen and dance to the music, retaining a cultural tradition from a warm Caribbean island far away. For a balmy afternoon or a dazzling sunset, the congas beat out the rhythm of the South Bronx Latino soul:

♪

Poom, Poom, Poom . . . Pum-Poom
Poom, Poom, Poom . . . Pum-Poom

♪

Que viva Boriquen!

The South Bronx was alive.[36]

On the political side, South Bronx neighborhoods started to organize.[37] Led by several church coalitions (mostly Catholic), residents learned to mobilize and force public officials into action. Often, they used the famed Alinsky method from Chicago. First, they agitated about easy, winnable issues, like putting up a stop sign or demolishing an abandoned building. Then, with rising momentum, they tackled more imposing ones, like demanding city-subsidized housing or cracking down on landlord insurance fraud.

It started to work.[38] In small steps, Bronx neighborhood organizations picketed business institutions and government agencies. They took on the banks, protesting about how despite receiving the bulk of their money from neighborhood depositors, they rarely lent to them. They took on insurance companies, decrying how they refused to provide affordable insurance to South Bronx property owners, who would rather abandon properties than pay high premiums. They took on city agencies, which had monies to immediately rehabilitate buildings, yet took their sweet time. Often, South Bronx organizations won these tough battles. Sometimes they even formed working relationships with the targeted institution. The South Bronx was finally unclasping its hands and starting to applaud.

However, as the Bronx entered the 1980s, it would struggle. The once powerful Bronx Democratic machine had become weak and corrupt. The Reagan administration drastically cut social services. Worker unions crumbled. Traditional manufacturing work continued its slide. If the South Bronx was dealt a deadly blow now, it could only absorb it, drop to its knees, and gasp.

Along came crack, the new contender for the heavyweight championship of the drug world.

THE RISE OF CRACK

While poor South Bronx residents were weathering arson and abandonment, better off New Yorkers were snorting cocaine. The powder was all the rage at extravagant seventies parties; nightclub lavatories (a popular snorting spot) became as crowded as dance floors. For users, cocaine provided a powerful combination of stamina and euphoria, the catalysts for unending parties and unfettered sex. It was the caviar of drugs, the drug of choice for the well-to-do, for the doctors, lawyers, and other professionals with the capacity and audacity to snort it through thinly rolled hundred-dollar bills.

This decadent period would, in part, turn out to be the background for the drug-related crimes later committed by the Dominican men I write about. Cocaine would birth the drug dubbed "crack," which would first launch them into superstardom and then drop them as fallen stars. But like all social phenomena, crack and cocaine did not appear or vanish by magic. Social forces birthed and nurtured them, then dug their graves.

We must go global—deep into the jungles of South America, right into the belly of Colombia's economic and political beast. Then to the United States' raging upper-middle-class drug culture and its "tough," politically conservative men. Then a return to an emboldened Colombia; then a stop in the balmy Caribbean; and then back to regressive drug policies in the U.S. Back and forth we must go to understand what shaped the South Bronx drug market and eventually these Dominican men.[39]

Colombia's Cocaine Economy

In the late nineteenth century, cocaine appeared in the United States as a tonic for health and personality troubles. Doctors, quacks, and entrepreneurs—including Sigmund Freud—hailed the stimulant, claiming that it granted strength to the weak, voice to the timid, and vitality to the sick.[40] Soon, popular drinks and medicines featured the drug; it promised to enhance spirits and cure ills.

In the early 1900s, though, the fear of rampant addiction and of the mythical "cocaine-crazed" Black man led to the criminalization of cocaine use outside of medical prescriptions.[41] Even among show biz entertainers, jazz musicians, beatniks, and street hipsters and hustlers, heroin and marijuana would become the drugs of choice.[42]

In the 1960s, cocaine was back. According to drug researcher James Inciardi, its return occurred for two reasons.[43] First, the U.S. government cut the legal production of amphetamines and sedatives, which had gained underground popularity. As a result, many drug consumers turned to cocaine, which had been making silent backstage rounds among rock musicians.[44] Second, the U.S.-supported Pan American Highway provided the means for transporting cocaine. The Washington-based World Bank financed the mega-highway, which benefited corporations wanting better roads for business. From its southern end, the highway started in Buenos Aires, Argentina, then shot straight west into Chile, where it turned north along the western coast and then cut through the tough terrain of Peru, Ecuador, and Colombia, all the way into Mexico.[45]

For cocaine, the crucial part was in Peru. Before the highway, Peru (and Bolivia, its eastern neighbor) produced coca leaf locally as a stimulant. Its chewers and tea drinkers got a healthy burst of energy and stamina while curbing their appetite too. However, producers faced obstacles in selling to outside markets. Mules were the best transportation through the rugged and dangerous Andes. But with the Pan American Highway, coca sellers began moving huge amounts on newly paved roads. Chile, a long and narrow strip of a country, would be the first major destination.[46]

First, Peruvian and Bolivian farmers cultivated the coca leaves. Second, traffickers processed them into a coca paste, or *pasta*. Third, the traffickers transported the *pasta* to Chile via the Pan American Highway. Fourth, Chilean refiners turned the *pasta* into a coca base, and then into its powder form, cocaine. Finally, small-time Chilean traffickers shipped the cocaine to the United States.[47] Simple, smooth, and manageable.

Short-lived. In 1973, General Augusto Pinochet, backed by the CIA, overthrew the existing Chilean government. He detained mom-and-pop drug traffickers, crushing the tiny cocaine industry.[48] Frightened Chilean traffickers fled north, settling in Colombia, which was suffering from its own woes. Politically, it was coming off decades of civil war, which had normalized violence. Economically, it was undergoing postindustrial pains, with a declining manufacturing industry that had citizens teetering on an economic ledge.

Then it happened. Some enterprising Colombians—the seeds of the infamous cocaine cartels that would later run a hugely lucrative cocaine industry— learned the art of making cocaine from the Chilean outlaws. For impoverished Colombians, it was an economic godsend. According to journalist William Adler, cocaine soon surpassed coffee as the country's leading export. Its vibrant market also provided hundreds of thousands of jobs for "private armies to guard coca plants and the jungle processing laboratories, bankers to facilitate money laundering, lawyers, couriers, builders, accountants, bodyguards, assassins, smugglers, real estate agents, pilots, retailers, even zookeepers: one of the cartel founders maintained some two hundred exotic animals at his seven-thousand-acre ranch."[49]

Yet it was violent work. The next couple of decades would witness the tragic deaths of countless innocent civilians and the shocking murders of politicians, police officers, and judges.[50] And many of the slain were, in a cruel joke, artistically mutilated. A relic from the bloody civil war, the "Colombian necktie" became cocaine's symbol of terror: the pulling of a victim's tongue through a slit throat so that it flopped down like a tie, or *corbata*.[51]

But still, it was the first time in years that money widely circulated among Colombians. And by the late 1970s, the Western world's rising cocaine demand had revved up the country's economic engine, producing a multibillion-dollar cocaine industry.

The Irony of U.S. Anti-Marijuana Scares

Meanwhile, back in the United States, cocaine use was getting a lift from misguided U.S. anti-drug strategies. In the 1970s, the country's drug enforcers zoomed in on marijuana, a drug that scientific studies showed to be relatively harmless in moderation. According to journalist Michael Massing, the new focus was a political charade, meant to appease a rising conservative parent movement.[52] With no scientific evidence, these organized parents asserted that marijuana was morally corrupting the nation's youth. Predictably, politicians caved in, fearing the parents' uncanny ability to instantly rally en masse. Marijuana—new drug enemy No. 1.

Through a crop-eradication strategy, the U.S. sprayed Mexican marijuana fields with paraquat, a highly toxic weed killer. The technique scared many U.S. marijuana users, who, as a health precaution, stopped smoking the plant's Mexican strain.[53] Still, the government had targeted the wrong drug. It was U.S. cocaine use that was on the rise, not marijuana. Displaced marijuana dealers, though, would observe the new trend. With smuggling networks and distributors already in place, cocaine became their new line of business. Now, the planes that once flew bales of marijuana to the U.S. would transport tons of cocaine over the Mexican border into California and over the Caribbean Sea into Florida. Now, the U.S. dealers who once distributed pounds of marijuana would move kilos upon kilos of cocaine.[54]

Sociologist Patricia Adler observed how, in Southern California, "get tough" government interventions pushed upper-level marijuana smugglers into the world of cocaine. As a result, drug profits skyrocketed, and the smugglers' already lavish standard of living rose to even more dizzying heights.[55] In Brooklyn, too, anthropologist Ansley Hamid observed how U.S. drug enforcement reduced marijuana distribution. But with smuggling networks in place, dealers immediately switched to selling cocaine, a more powerful—and more lucrative—drug.[56]

In all, U.S. anti-marijuana strategies helped to flood the country with cocaine. Cocaine consumption would climb higher and higher, and drug dealers would prosper more than ever.

The Glamour of Cocaine

In U.S. high society, cocaine became a symbol of glamour, like a sparkling ring or exotic fur coat. Costing about a thousand dollars an ounce, it was enjoyed only by the rich, who basked in its euphoria and thought of it as a fine liqueur. (A 1974 *New York Times Magazine* article touted cocaine as the "champagne of drugs."[57]) Another article reported that an "after-sniff of the fine white powder—either from a bejeweled coke spoon held to the nostril or through a tightly rolled banknote, the higher the denomination the better—is as common as a snifter of brandy."[58]

Its glow would spur a cocaine surge among affluent U.S. consumers. During the 1970s, cocaine use rose by about 300 percent. To keep up with the ravenous appetite, its overseas producers increased supply by 400 percent. As a result of high demand and high availability, purity would increase by close to 30 percent, and its kilo price would drop by about 60 percent.[59] Yet it was still too expensive for poor drug consumers. Their turn would come later, through a chemical variation known as "crack."

The Cocaine Era: Dead

The early 1980s witnessed a sharp reversal in attitudes toward cocaine. Health-care providers started receiving thousands of help calls from addicted cocaine users. Shockingly, most callers were White—upper-middle-class Wall Street executives, doctors, lawyers, and other well-paid professionals, who, of all people, were thought to have their lives under control.[60] Newspapers featured article titles such as "The Shackles of Cocaine" and "Cocaine: Pleasure Fades Fast, Problems Linger."[61]

The most shocking headlines announced the cocaine-related deaths of University of Maryland basketball star Len Bias and *Saturday Night Live* comedian John Belushi. These deaths made the message clear. Cocaine was not a harmless party drug or a marker of high status. Instead, it was anxiety and depression, financial pain and ruin—it was death.

According to Michael Massing, the decline of cocaine would create a two-tier system in drug treatment.[62] Easily costing three hundred and fifty dollars a day, treatment centers offered affluent users long-term rehabilitation, often in facilities with lush gardens and health spa amenities. Lower income users, however, could not pay for such privilege. Instead, they relied on government-based treatment, which featured short stays and outdated facilities—that is, if applicants could ever reach the top of its long waiting lists.

Widening the treatment gap was the Reagan administration's clear break from a public health model. Christian Parenti documents how, in a show of conservative "toughness," the new White House administration dramatically reduced funds for federal drug treatment while pouring more money into repression: high-tech law enforcement, corrections, drug task forces, and drug user arrests.[63] Carlton Turner, Reagan's drug advisor, best captured the White House mood: "If people can afford to go out and buy cocaine, why should the government pay for their treatment? The government is not responsible for their treatment—*they* are responsible. This country has a problem accepting the fact that there are really bad people in society. We've got the belief that nobody's bad—that we can rehabilitate everybody."[64]

Ultimately, the zero-tolerance approach paved the way for a major drug epidemic. For Michael Massing, the conservative turn against drug treatment "effectively destroyed the nation's first line of defense against a new drug outbreak. . . . Then, when the crisis finally hit, the administration— paralyzed by its zero tolerance philosophy—refused to take even the most basic countermeasures. The result was the worst drug epidemic in American history."[65] Crack.

The impending crack-cocaine epidemic would harm poor users the most. The government and public were against treating them, only for incarcerating them, even if it meant destroying individuals, families, neighborhoods, and communities. As Michael Tonry notes, the effect was an explosion in the number of convictions of minority individuals for nonviolent drug offenses.[66] The prevailing conservative attitude—based on racist rhetoric and fear mongering[67]—was reshaping already impoverished urban lives.

Crack

Smoking cocaine—not new. During the 1970s, smoking *basuco,* coca paste in cigarettes laced with marijuana or tobacco, was common in South America. And the instant, powerful high outdid the euphoria that came from snorting cocaine. *Basuco* contained harmful chemicals like kerosene and sulfuric acid, which were used to process the coca leaf into paste form. But it was also cheap.[68] At about fifty cents a cigarette, *basuco* became popular among poor users, especially street youth. In fact, an official Colombian count in 1983 revealed the existence of over six hundred thousand *basuco* users under the age of eighteen—a national crisis.[69]

Even in the United States, some 1970s cocaine aficionados smoked cocaine, or "freebased."[70] An ingenious user (whose identity remains unknown) figured out how to *free* the hydrochloric acid from the powder cocaine, purifying it to its *base* form. Hence: *freebase.* Freebasing, though, involved flammable ether, a glass pipe, and a butane torch as lighter. Like comedian Richard Pryor in 1980, a user could go up in flames while performing the act. However, freebase contained no toxic chemicals and provided an instant rush. The downside: the fleeting rush caused smokers to binge for several days. For instance, in her observations of wealthy White dealers, Patricia Adler notes that "many individuals, once introduced to freebasing, found it increasingly difficult to moderate their drug use. . . . Some heavy users freebased for as long as seven or eight days straight without sleep. One person I knew went through $20,000 worth of cocaine in a week this way, while another used $60,000 worth in a month."[71] The binging, then, made freebasing expensive and a practice found mostly among the well-to-do. And by the late seventies, of the estimated four million users of cocaine, about 10 percent freebased only.[72]

Crack emerged in the Caribbean during the early 1980s. Contributing to its rise was a dual effort by the U.S. Drug Enforcement Agency (DEA) and the Policía Nacional de Colombia (Colombian National Police—CNP) to reduce cocaine trafficking. The DEA learned two vital pieces of information. One: 98 percent of Colombia's importation of the chemical ether was used to produce cocaine. Two: 90 percent of those importations were coming from Germany and the United States.[73] Since ether was used to process coca paste into its powder form, no ether meant no cocaine.

Game on. The DEA and CNP restricted Colombia's importation of ether. Countering, the Colombian traffickers transported their coca paste to Caribbean islands and to the United States, where ether was available. In the midst of this duel, someone on a West Indian island discovered how to smoke coca paste by adding baking soda, water, and rum. This formulation was called "base rock" or "Roxanne."[74] Later, the rum was left out, and the drug became known as "crack," named for the crackling sound it made when it was smoked.

To make crack, cocaine was heated with baking soda and water until its base was freed from the powder, in a large mound. Users then chipped off tiny pieces of the residue and smoked them, mostly through a glass pipe. As with freebasing, the high was intense and instant, and it left users in an unusually low mood. This after-effect produced binging that lasted for hours or days at a time.[75] The binging led to increased demand, and crack use spread quickly throughout the Caribbean, its profits soon surpassing those for cocaine.

Another factor in the rise of crack was the decline of the cocaine market. During the 1970s, the high demand for cocaine led to its overproduction in Latin America.[76] When users later reduced their intake, a cocaine surplus saturated the market. Caribbean dealers would feel the cocaine glut, the price drop, and the profit loss. Their savior was crack, a drug that, after preparation, yielded greater quantities than powder cocaine and invited binging.[77] Earnings could explode.

And they did. In fact, the powerful drug soon made its way through the Caribbean and then into the United States. Almost in chorus, it rose among the Haitians in Miami, the African Americans in Los Angeles, and the Dominicans in New York. Later it spread to other cities, like Baltimore, Chicago, and Detroit.[78] The crack era was born.

In the coming years, the Drug Abuse Warning Network (DAWN) documented crack's rise. DAWN monitored the country's drug-related emergencies and deaths in hospitals and treatment centers. In 1986, it counted close to 52,000 emergency room visits that "mentioned" cocaine. By 1989, the number had grown to about 110,000.[79] The demand for crack was on the rise. And someone would meet those needs. That entrepreneur would get filthy rich. *Rich, baby. Rico, papa.*

The Crack Era and Its Riches

The inner-city poor were hungry to fill that economic niche. They were at high risk for unemployment. Unlike preceding generations of immigrants, they didn't have the manufacturing sector as the crucial first step up the economic ladder. The Reagan administration had also cut social services. And the 1980s was the decade of Greed is Good, when Wall Street executives and brokers were earning—fraudulently—staggering amounts of money.[80] They spent it too. Jets. Yachts. Fast cars. The high life. Everyone saw it.

Since its inception, the U.S., like other capitalist-based nations, reframed greed and gluttony as worthy, as the building blocks of the nation's prosperity and well-being. It was an entrenched "tough luck" ideology that made it noble to contrive ways of making money, even if "losers" were hurt in the process. The quintessential American pursued wealth, *punto*. Regard for the economic, mental, and health consequences of fellow citizens—that was not part of the equation or plan.

The urban poor, born and bred in the U.S., were just as willing to work and spend in their self-interest. And in the 1980s, they used crack as the vehicle for financial and material success. Unlike most businesses, legal or illegal, a crack operation was easy to start: cocaine was cheap, demand was strong, and monopolies were few. Mom-and-pop capitalists could open their doors to business with few obstacles. Crack businesses would hit the city streets, everywhere.

For instance, in Detroit, journalist William Adler traced the rise of the Chambers Brothers, a family-based African American crime organization whose founders had migrated north to escape from poverty in the rural South.[81] After switching from selling marijuana to crack, they struck gold, eventually making about fifty-six million dollars per year. In highlife style, they draped gold on their necks, and draped women on their arms—and even hired a procession of limousines to drive them back to their Alabama hometown. *We rich, Goddammit!* a lieutenant was caught saying on video-tape as he shook a laundry basket full of cash.

In New York City, a Dominican crack-selling organization, the Wild Cowboys, also made millions—over sixteen million dollars a year. In sepa-rate accounts, sociologist Robert Jackall and journalist Michael Stone note how the crew established crack businesses in parts of Brooklyn, Manhattan, and especially the Bronx. Some selling spots earned them over fifteen thou-sand a week; others, more than a million dollars per year. But protecting those earnings led to violence—the murder of both rival drug sellers and innocent bystanders caught in their line of fire.[82]

Not every crack organization was large, violent, or worth millions. Smaller operations made just enough for dealers to live large, in installments. For in-stance, in Washington Heights (upper Manhattan), Terry Williams docu-mented the lives of the "Cocaine Kids," those cool, slick, lyrical young Do-minicans that sold cocaine out of an apartment.[83] After they added crack to their business, their staggering profit hurled them into the high life, into bedrooms overflowing with women, into expensive jewelry and clothes— into recognition in the after-hours club, where they mingled with the kings and queens of the drug world. Crack made them "somebody."

The first (brief) newspaper account of Bronx crack came in late 1985.[84] By mid-1986, journalists were covering it as a serious problem.[85] As in other U.S. cities, crack had outstripped the Bronx demand for powder cocaine. Bronx dealers soon prepackaged chipped rocks into small and large perfume vials. They used colored tops—Red, Blue, Yellow, Gold, and so forth—to market their brands. They priced crack from three dollars for a tiny vial, to five dollars for a regular one, to ten dollars for a "jumbo." Although most never became "filthy rich," some made lots of money and ascended to the pinnacle of the neighborhood hierarchy. For many youths, they became role models, the guys who were "getting paid."

In my neighborhood, the crack business owners and employees were mar-ginalized urban youths and young adults, and they were everywhere: some sold on corners, some in building lobbies, some from apartments, and others in the public parks. Crack dealing, unfortunately, became a source of hope, a way out of poverty, a way into manhood, a way to be good at something when everywhere else we failed. Through crack, we saw the American Dream—with all of its material and hedonistic promises—within reach.

Bring It All Together

In sum, no one could have predicted this: that the building of a road through the tropics and mountains of South America would pave the way for cocaine. That cocaine would transform Colombia's gloom into riches, well beyond its deep valleys and rain forests—turning up as fluttering snow on balmy Caribbean islands, then as dewy, luscious raindrops running down the faces of enterprising but poor Black and Brown American men. No one could have predicted that this would partially give rise to not one, but two, drug epidemics—a blessing to some, a scourge to others.

No one would have tied these two epidemics to a rising conservative movement. Our nation's conservatives had stirred up fear, anger, and hate among White Americans, who were unsure of their place on the rungs of unsteady economic and racial ladders. The source of that uncertainty lay in the 1960s civil rights movements, in the open rebellion against injustice led by long-haired liberals, feminists, and people of color. The culmination—the fires, lootings, and shootings—would lock that conservative frame in place.

Yet someone should have known (and perhaps someone did) that this conservative frame would create a space where logic based on fear mongering triumphed, where reason, science, and dialogue were lost to irrationality, where a fear of marijuana use would result in greater cocaine use, where federal funds would push "law and order" to unprecedented heights while reducing critical drug treatment. Someone should have known (and perhaps someone did) that while their conservative words stirred voter fear and outrage, they would also ripen the conditions for a hardcore drug epidemic. Someone should have known—they must have known!—that inner cities and their poor would be ravaged the most.

Because by the time crack arrived in the South Bronx, there was no social barricade to block its entry. By then, the area was still recovering from a social knockout: from the massive White flight that had stripped it of political, social, and economic resources; from the power-hungry, intellectual monstrosity of a man—Robert Moses—who broke and then reconfigured it to feed his ego; and from the arson and abandonment that hollowed out neighborhoods and created a gigantic, rubble-strewn war zone. Crack just strolled right in.

And crack would wreak havoc in the South Bronx. It produced a world that pitted law-abiding residents against crack dealers and users, a world where neighborhoods suffered from violence while empty crack vials and worn condoms littered its streets. It also produced a world where Bronx families were torn—where crack-abusing loved ones tested the limits of trust and family, and where dilemmas arose as to the practical acceptance or moral rejection of much-needed crack earnings. Bronx communities were taken hostage, but its children were employed.

For the Dominican men that I studied, the deadly combination of South Bronx misery and a crack scourge would shape the rest of their lives. In fact, this combination would eventually lead to their self-destruction, to a state where they would live and die for the drug market's promise, would do anything, no matter how brutal, to keep its dream alive.

Crack was the central turning point of their lives.

TWO

Crack Days

GETTING PAID

Every other month, I get a brand new car,
Got twenty, that's plenty, but I still want more,
Kind'a fond of Honda scooters—got seventy-four
I got the riches—to fulfill my needs,
Got land in the sand of the West Indies
Even got a little island of my very own,
I got a frog—a dog with a solid gold bone
An accountant to account the amount I spent,
Gotta a treaty with Tahiti 'cause I own a percent
Got gear, out-wear—for everyday
Boutiques from France to the U.S.A. . . .
I got it made

Special Ed "I Got It Made"

THE START OF GUS, 1975—1990

Gus, who was twenty-five years old, was born in the South Bronx. His mother, Regina, had emigrated from the Dominican Republic with her first two children, Sylvio and Maribel. In the D.R., she was a small-time entrepreneur, selling homemade candy and cooked food from a street cart. After her husband died in a car accident, Regina moved to the United States for better work.

When she arrived during the early 1970s, Regina moved in with her sister, into a cramped apartment in the South Bronx. Like other Dominican immigrants, she immediately found employment in a sweatshop and worked long hours for meager pay. Here, she met Gus' father, a philanderer who, after impregnating her, fled the relationship, rarely to be seen or heard from again.

Alone with two children, and one on the way, Regina wanted to avoid deportation. So she arranged a marriage to establish her family's legal residency. After borrowing four thousand dollars, she married Daniel, an older Puerto Rican man, who disappeared after the business transaction.

Then she met Salazar.

Salazar was a Colombian immigrant who washed dishes in a small Latino restaurant on Jerome Avenue. A short, wide-ribbed, amiable man, he worked long and late hours for a dishwasher's pay. However, on the side, Salazar ran a cocaine operation. During the early 1970s, he was one of the thousands of destitute emigrants that fled Colombia for New York City. And he was one of the few who saw cocaine as a way out of abusive work conditions. So, through a network of Colombian compatriots in Queens, he started selling cocaine in the Bronx.

At first, it was slow going. Salazar only sold to friends in nightclubs and after-hours clubs. The disco era, though, improved his cocaine sales, and he moved the family from their cramped basement apartment on Elliot Place to an art deco–style three-bedroom apartment on 165th Street and Walton Avenue. Then crack cocaine exploded on New York City streets. Drug dealers now purchased more of his cocaine (to cook into crack), and he established his own crack spot. To top it off, he even earned money from competitors, who bought their product from him. So by the mid-1980s, Salazar was the King of Walton Avenue, making the most money out of all the neighborhood drug dealers.

Since childhood, then, the crack industry's high profit and violence were normal for Gus. For as long as he could remember, money, drugs, and guns had been a part of his world.

"They would always be talkin' about drugs in front of me," Gus recalls. "They probably thought that since I was little I ain't know what they were talkin' about. But I knew what they were talkin' about. I mean, I didn't really understand it. Like I knew they was sellin' drugs, but I didn't know everything they were doin'. I would see guns all the time too. They [Salazar and his workers] would like open their jackets, take them off, whatever, and they would have guns like in their waist. What I saw a lot was them always carryin' a lot of money. Sometimes they would like bring that shit to the house and just start countin' it."

As a teenager, I observed such moments when visiting Gus and his older brother, Sylvio. During playtime visits, we often had to close their bedroom door. Yet on bathroom breaks, I sometimes opened the door to see Salazar and others diligently counting a mound of money on the dining room table. Knowing that it was "business," I immediately averted my eyes and detoured into the bathroom. If I saw this occasionally, Gus must have seen it daily.

Also, Gus saw his older brother, Sylvio, drop out of high school to work with Salazar. Within a year, he had climbed his way up to becoming Salazar's partner, making tens of thousands of dollars per week. Soon neighborhood residents crowded around him, treating him like a local dignitary. Hat in hand, some asked for work in his crack business, and others, all cheers, just wanted his good favor. Gus wanted the same respect too.

"Salazar made a lot of money," Gus recalls, "and I saw how everybody was treatin' him. Even Sylvio, when he started workin' with Salazar, people was lookin' up to him. So imagine, bro, everybody lookin' up to them, and that's my brother and [step] father. I had to do somethin' too. Put it like this, it's like I wanted to prove to everybody that I was a man, that I could do it better than them. That's why I wanted to sell drugs, bro. But I knew that Salazar would be like, 'No,' if I went to him and told him to put me down."

So at the age of thirteen, Gus fell into a teenage drug-selling team that sold three-dollar crack vials. His partners were neighborhood Black youths whose families dealt small amounts of angel dust (PCP) and crack. Unlike their suburban counterparts, with better options for achieving status, Gus and his crew would use crack to earn masculinity and respect.

"I started sellin' crack with Tikki and Buggy, the *morenos* (Blacks) on my block," Gus recalled. "For every vial we sold, we got fifty cents. I was makin' like two hundred, three hundred [dollars] a day. For thirteen, that shit was good, man. We were buyin' all types of clothes and shit. We had money to eat, we was takin' people out to eat, payin' for their shit. That's when we started gettin' all these girls and shit, ha-ha. Imagine, I was only thirteen years old and was already fuckin'! I'm tellin' you, man, money makes a lot of things happen, bro. It definitely gets you a lot of ass at thirteen, ha-ha."

With the drugs came unsanctioned masculine violence. Middle-class teens proved toughness on athletic fields and rinks, and if violent enough, received university scholarships; South Bronx youths with drug market exposure proved their courage in other ways.

For instance, Tikki and Buggy gave Gus two guns, "a .22 [revolver] and a fuckin' old ass .38 [revolver]" for protection. "I used to carry the .38 every day," Gus recalls. "The shit ain't have no fuckin' handle or nothing, ha-ha-ha! We had to put the handle like with a piece of cardboard. We cut it and taped the cardboard to make the handle."

With that junkyard gun Gus caught his first criminal case at the age of fourteen. While attending school sporadically, Gus started talking to Eileen, a classmate. However, she was seeing a member of the Casanova Crew, one of the many New York City crews that emerged during the mid-eighties. Some Casanova guys warned Gus to stay away from her. But he paid no attention.

"So one day I'm out there," Gus recalled, "and this kid comes over and he's like, 'Yo, this dude wants to talk to you over there.' I was like, 'He wanna talk to me? For what?' He was like, 'Nah, he just wanna talk to you.' I was like, fuck it. And I just happened to have that .38 on me that day in school. So we was talkin' and he was like, 'Yo, I told you to stop fuckin' with Eileen.' Then he went to get somethin' in his car, like he turned around. When I seen him like reachin' into his car, I didn't even give him a chance and just shot his ass."

Gus shot him four times: "I shot him once and he fell. And then I ran up to him and shot him again three times." Then Gus ran. However, a couple of plainclothes police officers in a corner pizza shop heard the shots. They went outside, saw Gus running, and took to chase.

"They were right behind me," Gus recalled. "But I didn't know they was cops. So I turned around and shot the last two bullets that I had. I shot those shits. I didn't know they was cops. But the cops try to say that I shot at them."

At the age of fourteen, then, Gus attempted murder. Sadly, such violence was one of the few ways that he, and a growing cadre of marginal youngsters, could demonstrate their toughness. The government, in its own attempts to be conservatively tough, had reduced social safety nets for the poor, which made the neighborhood more vulnerable to drugs and violence. It was no surprise that the *probability* for deadly violence among youths like Gus increased.

The shooting also made Gus a neighborhood legend. From then on, I observed residents fear and respect him. And even fear and respect those close to him—for instance, me. Since I often hung out with Gus, teenagers within a half-mile radius linked me with his violence, greeting me as though we were long lost friends. Clearly, I knew that Gus' enormous shadow granted me this deference. Yet I didn't care. As a marginal teenager, any respect felt good, especially if it was linked to masculinity and violence. Tragically, then, I cheered on Gus' shootings and beatings. It made me "somebody" too.

After his arrest, Gus was detained at the Spofford Juvenile Center, a jail for juveniles awaiting adjudication and sentencing—a warehouse that only worsened marginal youths. Its most important highlight: fights. According to Gus, most fights arose to prove who was tough or punk.

"The kids," Gus recalled, "they all wanted to be gangsters. They used to talk about who was makin' more money on the street, like who was sellin' *more* drugs, all this bullshit. So a lot of fights started because somebody would say that somebody else was talkin' shit . . . or like somebody would hear somebody talkin' about this and that, or they see them actin' like we can't fuck with them. We would be like, 'I'm gonna test him. I'm gonna make him prove it.'"

In time, Gus adapted to the center's violence. For instance, when he sat in a seat, another inmate challenged his spot. Now he did this to others. When he changed the channel on the dormitory television, another inmate challenged his program choice. Now he did this to others. Rather than rehabilitate him, the juvenile facility enhanced his brutality.

After his release from Spofford, and then from Highland Residential Center (a medium-security youth facility), Gus enrolled in Walton High School in the South Bronx. But after a couple of months, he dropped out. At sixteen years old, he just wanted to earn serious money and saw little hope through school. So he asked Salazar and Sylvio for work in their crack business. He was older now, and they gave him a job.

From Monday to Saturday, noon to midnight, Gus managed their crack operation. Sitting in a stash apartment, he distributed crack to street workers and kept a daily record of drug and money transactions. During his tenure there, Pablo and I often visited him. He looked bored and lonely, with the long hours taking their toll. The job left little room for imagination: just counting crack vials, money, and scribbling numbers into a notebook. Eventually, he felt shortchanged, considering all the drudgery and risk involved.

"I was gettin' played," Gus said. "I was only gettin' like six hundred a week or somethin' like that. And I was always there from twelve [P.M.] to twelve [A.M.], bro, almost every day. Sometimes I had to stay later because of some bullshit or something . . . On top of that, if the cops came I would get busted by myself, bro. I was the only person in that apartment. Imagine, if I went down, they would charge me with all those drugs."

Later, Gus became the new cook and bagger, where he worked the same hours and earned the same pay. Throughout the day, he cooked the cocaine into a mound of crack; then, with a razor, he sliced it into tiny pebbles, later stuffing them into perfume vials. After a few weeks of this routine, crack market realities sank in. Although he was family to Salazar and Sylvio, crack, after all, was business. And the point of business was to maximize profit by reducing labor costs as close to zero as possible while squeezing more labor from workers. Yet Gus found spaces of resistance.[1] Like a legitimate worker fighting against oppressive work conditions, Gus orchestrated a scheme that raised his income by about five hundred dollars per day. As a talented cook, he often produced more crack than usual from the same amount of cocaine. He called this getting "extra."

"When I got nice at cookin'," Gus recalled, "I started gettin' 'extra' back. I would keep that extra. Like it would be a half-ounce extra. So I would bag that up, you know, like for myself and Scotty [a seller in the organization] and I would tell him, 'Yo, here, send these down the hallway, and sell these dimes [ten-dollar vials].' We were sellin' like twenty-five [vials] at a time— twenty-five were ours, twenty-five were Sylvio's, twenty-five were ours, twenty-five were Sylvio's."

Competitive, Gus wanted to out-earn Salazar and Sylvio, who together made about fifty thousand dollars a week. So he left the organization to go independent. From then on, he bought his own "coke," cooked his own crack, and vialed his own product. He then managed his crack operation outside the Black Gate, a building with a black iron gate at its entrance.

Now Gus made serious money, which allowed him to spend conspicuously. Still sixteen, Gus bought a late-model car, in which he sometimes invited me out for a ride. He drove us around the neighborhood, nonchalantly, rolling to a stop on every corner, dramatically lowering the tinted windows to greet the ride-less corner boys.

Yo, Whatup? he asked.

Yo! they always responded.

Then, pumping up the bass-laden volume, we rolled off to somewhere else, *Let's go here, let's go there . . . Yo, look at that girl, say somethin': Hey baby, you wanna a ride? No? But made you smile,* slapping fives, *ha-ha-ha . . .* then cruising back to the block, inspecting for smudges, for dirt, admired by the sidewalk crowd, who laughed at his every joke, who agreed with his every line. Then he was back to business—*Yo, I'll be back*—disappearing for one, two, or three hours, then reappearing and inviting some of us to a food joint nearby, sorting the knot of wrinkled dollar bills that paid for the sodas, burgers, and fries.

Then gone again, then back again, talking discreetly (but not too discreetly) to his crack workers nearby.

Then gone again, then back again, adorned in more gold, in fresher clothes, to go with a girlfriend for a movie, and later, for a dinner, and *mucho ma' tarde,* for a hotel or the stash apartment's bedroom nearby. Money, women, power, respect—Gus, to the young and old of the neighborhood, had it all.

Jason, a neighborhood friend who back then was a low-wage security guard, but was now a cab driver, recalled: "I remember he was makin' money and spendin' money. The nigga had a lot gold. He was almost like Mr. T on the block, ha-ha. He had a car, a brand-new Trans Am with a system and half. He had mad bitches. He had money. That's all I can say, he had money. And the nigga was young, man. The nigga was like only fifteen, sixteen. Whenever we went out, he always flipped [paid] the bill. He used to go out a lot with Sylvio and Salazar, like to a bunch of restaurants, to clubs, all that. Like I said, he was a young nigga too, spendin' more money than grown men."

Later, Pablo joined the crack operation, managing the day shift, from noon to midnight, while Gus managed the night shift, from midnight to noon.[2]

But because of increased police presence, Gus and Pablo moved their operations to John Mullay Park, two blocks down, on Jerome Avenue. Here, I observed them recruit boys to sell crack while sitting on park benches. This, Gus reasoned, would reduce suspicion.

"Because think about it," Gus explained. "If you see a kid sittin' like on a bench in a park, you not gonna think, 'Oh, they sellin' drugs out here.' They just kids chillin' in the park. But let's say somebody older was to sit on a bench all day, you're gonna think somethin's up. You're gonna think that he's sellin' drugs or somethin'."

One afternoon, Gus took a drive with Sylvio. They were cruising down Gerard Avenue (a block down from Walton Avenue) when a police car ordered them to pull over. While searching Sylvio's vehicle, the police found a handgun under the passenger seat, where Gus was sitting. Both were arrested. Although Gus knew nothing about the gun, he willingly took the charge. He already had two previous cases pending: a robbery and a drug possession.

The robbery charge was from the previous year. As crack use had risen, its committed users had gained a bad reputation. They were often unwashed and emaciated, and thought to be so immoral as to do "anything" for crack. For instance, as a teen, I once witnessed a young street dealer offer a dollar to a crack user if he would do twenty push-ups over a pile of dog dung. As the crack user got close to twenty, the young dealer pressed his foot against his back. The crack user strained and eventually fell upon the droppings. He got up and shamefully received his dollar while everyone laughed. The crack user became an object of ridicule, while his tormentor achieved status.

Similarly, I observed Gus secure status through the brutal humiliation of crack users. "Like when they [crack users] were walkin' by," Gus recalled, "we just like knocked them out. We used to make bets to see who could knock one out with one punch and shit. Sometimes I could do that shit, just knock them out with one punch . . . Nobody gave a fuck about that shit. A fuckin' crackhead, nobody cared."

For instance, one day, he and a friend attacked a "crackhead" carrying two pillows. Afterward, Gus' friend stabbed the victim and stole the pillows. The next day, the police arrested Gus and charged him with the robbery. Gus took the charge without revealing the stabber, a show of bravado and loyalty that awed everyone.

The drug possession charge resulted from a police stop while he was out on bail. After exiting Salazar's "legitimate" clothing store one day, Gus entered his car, drove around the corner, and was immediately pulled over by undercover police. According to Gus, they placed him in their unmarked car and interrogated him.

"[They] started askin' me all these fuckin' questions about Salazar," Gus recalled. "They were tellin' me a lot of shit like, 'You think we don't know what goes on in there [the store]? We know everything that Salazar does, that you do . . . ,' all that shit. They even started beatin' the shit out of me, right there in the car and shit."

Afterward, the police searched Gus' car. Under the passenger seat, they found an ounce of cocaine. Gus was arrested.

With the new gun charge, the prosecuting attorney gave him a plea deal: if Gus took the gun charge (which came with a one-year sentence), then the robbery and drug possession charges would drop. Gus accepted.

He was sent to Rikers Island, the infamous New York City jail.

HOW PABLO BECAME PABLO, 1971–1990

Pablo, who was twenty-eight-years-old, was born in the South Bronx. His mother, Carmen, had arrived there during the late 1960s and secured work in a belt factory. With her paltry earnings, she supported her two children and mother, who were still in the Dominican Republic. To earn more income, she served and cooked in restaurants too.

Shortly, Carmen met Reuben, a Dominican immigrant working as a painter. After establishing a relationship, they moved into an apartment on

145th Street and St. Anns, sent for Carmen's two children, and then conceived Pablo. Reuben, however, drank heavily and often had late nights with friends (my own father—his best friend—among them). One morning, he arrived home drunk to find that one-year-old Pablo had been playing with a razor and badly cut his foot. He argued with Carmen and, enraged, got into his car and sped away. Later in the afternoon, his car was found in a construction ditch. Reuben was dead. Pablo would often wonder about his own life had his father lived.

"If he was still alive, I think my life would've been different," Pablo confided. "I mean, you never know what could've happened. But maybe I wouldn't have gone through all the shit that I been through. Maybe he could've given me support or somethin', bro. I don't know, man. I just think about that shit sometimes."

After Reuben's death, Carmen secured a job in a restaurant as a full-time cook. She then built up some savings and bought a house in Camden, New Jersey. Unlike their previous home, in the South Bronx, this house was on a hushed residential street.

"It was mad quiet," Pablo recalled. "After six o'clock, not even a car passed by. Everybody was nice and everybody went to church like two times a week. It was like a real safe street."

"Who lived in that neighborhood?" I asked.

"I remember that it was about half and half, White kids and Hispanic and Black kids. I used to play with them a lot. We used to play a lot of tackle football in this park. I had fun, man. I'm tellin' you, I used to live in a real quiet neighborhood. It was real nice, bro."

Though Camden would rank as the nation's most dangerous city within twenty-five years,[3] for now it was safe—so safe that Carmen, who still worked in New York City, felt comfortable leaving Pablo and his older sister alone for weeks at a time. Throughout her life, Carmen always worked hard, and she always looked for opportunities to get ahead, investing in small businesses and real estate. But as a single mother with limited English and no access to affordable child care, she was forced to leave her children alone. For Pablo, it resulted in a terror-ridden childhood.

"Living in the house was hell," Pablo recalled. "That bitch [his sister] was crazy. She did all type of shit to me, bro. If she didn't like somethin' I did, she would make me do stupid shit, bro. Like, I had to clean the house by myself. I had to clean the basement by myself. I had to wash clothes by myself—all type of shit. If I didn't do it, she would get a fuckin' belt or stick or whatever and beat the hell out of me. If I came back dirty from school, I would get an ass-whippin'. I got scars to this day from that bitch, bro."

The expense of maintaining households in New York and New Jersey proved too much for Carmen. After a year, their house went into foreclosure and they moved back to the Bronx. By then, Carmen had received a large lump-sum payout for Reuben's death (she had sued the city successfully for its negligence during street construction). With the money, she purchased a *bodega,* or grocery store, in Manhattan's Washington Heights.[4] After a year, she sold the store and purchased another one in our neighborhood. "I used to work there like after school and then the weekend," Pablo remembered. "I used to hate it 'cause I was a kid. I wanted to do kid stuff, you know. When you a kid you don't want to go to work. You wanna have fun. I was workin' and I wasn't gettin' paid."

Pablo attended a local high school in the Bronx, several train stops away. The school had a football program and Pablo joined its junior varsity team. He immediately shone: as a middle linebacker, he was a sure tackler, and as a running back, he made everyone one miss. According to Pablo, the head coach in junior varsity told him, "They already talkin' about you in varsity. Everybody sayin' you're gonna be great."

By his junior year, Pablo had made it to varsity, and after the starting middle linebacker got hurt, he played in every game. Soon the game's loud-speaker constantly announced his last name: *Garcia!*[5]

"I wasn't the fastest or the strongest," Pablo recalled, "but I had a heart like a lion. I didn't quit. I hit people hard. In fact, to this day people I don't even remember see me in the street and they're like, 'You're Garcia. You could fuckin' hit. I almost quit football 'cause you hit too fuckin' hard.'" By then, he wanted to start at running back, a position held by a teammate who was heavier, stronger, and faster, but less skilled.

"I just got fed up," Pablo remembered. "I told the offensive coordinator, 'Listen, just give me the rock. Just give it to me! Then coach finally put me in the game. That day I did work. I was breakin' niggas' knees. It was the day that I was like, 'I could do this and nothin' could stop me.'" Within weeks, Pablo was a superstar. "I used to walk down the hall," Pablo recalled, "and, forget it, everybody knew me." His fame strengthened his work ethic. To spend time with him, I often had to visit his school's gym after practice or his home when he was groggy-eyed and sore.

His athletic shine did not extend into the classroom. As long as I had known him, Pablo struggled academically, always putting forth a monumental effort for minimal grades. He was not alone. In outright acts of resistance, other struggling schoolmates repeatedly skipped classes and brazenly hung out by the school's infamous concrete "Wall." If not for football, Pablo might have joined them.

"The coach said," Pablo recalled, "'You're not gonna play with those grades.' So I could never fail classes. Football motivated me to pass my classes so that I could play. I used to see the kids who didn't play sports hang by the wall. They never went to class. Not me, I went to my classes. In fact, I only graduated because I wanted to play football."

In the summer before his senior year, buzz circulated about Pablo making All City and being recruited by a top college program. And Pablo did not disappoint. In his first game, he made sixteen tackles and five sacks (according to Pablo, the latter is still a school record). Now Division I universities showed interest.

"Rutgers was after me like crazy," Pablo remembered. "They weren't that good, but it was a major college, Division I. I also had Michigan callin' me. I had Iowa callin' me. I had a bunch of schools callin' me to let me know that they knew who I was."

However, Pablo would have trouble getting into a Division I school. He had the strength, toughness, quickness, and intelligence to play football. But he lacked the furious speed to play middle linebacker or running back at the top collegiate level. At two hundred pounds, Pablo ran the forty-yard dash in only 4.8 seconds. Top football programs now featured players that weighed twenty more pounds and ran the forty in 4.5 seconds or less. "I remember the coach tellin' me at the time," Pablo recalled, "that if I was just a little faster, I could get into Oklahoma, a Nebraska, or an LSU. But I just didn't have the speed."

What mostly hampered his football prospects, though, was an ankle injury he suffered during a team workout. He would miss the rest of the season after playing only two games. Pablo was down. He thought this was his year to explode.

"I was depressed," Pablo remembered, "because I knew that I was gonna break every fuckin' record out there if it wasn't for fracturing my ankle. I was supposed to do it all that year. I knew I could do it."

Although he eventually returned to the field, Pablo played with a limp for the rest of the season. And since he missed many games, college football programs lost interest. "Like all the people stopped callin' me and askin' me how I'm doin'," Pablo recalled. "Before I hurt my ankle, they would call a lot just call to say, 'How you doin'? How's everything comin' along?' Then they just stopped callin' me."

Pablo felt that his coach had not helped matters. He knew that organized football was a world where social networks counted just as much as ability. And the coach was Pablo's only broker to the higher ranks in athletics.[6] With a phone call, and a positive word or two, Pablo felt, the coach could potentially open a space—not a Division I space, but maybe a Division II or III space—for Pablo. And outside the school, no one could provide that social capital.

"Like when the offers stopped comin'," Pablo recalled, "he [the coach] didn't really like help me. I remember the guy from LSU [Louisiana State University] was watchin' a practice and he said somethin' good about me. But my coach didn't say anything to help." Pablo thought about playing football at Nassau Community College on Long Island, which expressed interest. However, he wanted to play at a four-year college, feeling that scouts would pay more attention. So when an African American high school teacher—not his coach—asked him if would be interested in playing at his Down South alma mater, Pablo jumped at the chance.

"[He] was like, 'I've seen you play and you're really good,'" Pablo recalled. " 'What do you plan to do? You should play at my alma mater in Georgia. You'll really like it down there and they have a good football team.' He said that he would help me get into the school and get the information for me."

After getting the college application, the teacher helped him complete and mail it off. Then he waited. A few months later, Pablo received a letter of acceptance. He also received a partial football scholarship and was scheduled to be at the summer football camp.

"I felt good," Pablo remembered. "I felt like everything was right there. Like everything was ready. Like I had to go to work. Like I was on a special mission. It was my first time goin' away and I was happy as hell."

So Pablo was proud of going "to work," of having a chance at labor that was valuable, creative, and fulfilling—not the monotonous blue-collar and service work of his family's immigrant generation. Just as important: it was a manly work; thus, unlike Gus, Pablo had little reason to do street violence to prove his manhood. He had the playing field.

However, Pablo also had the misfortune of having attended New York City public schools. Most were in disrepair and overcrowded, and located in blighted areas with low property values and tax bases. So they could never match the resources of suburban schools.[7] Worse, they became a place where boys like Pablo were treated not as bright minds and potential leaders, but as inferior students and future criminals.[8] And Pablo must have sensed this. He had a single-minded focus on football, not school. Yet for football success, he would endure more educational shame and humiliation.

Like many student-athletes, once he got to college, he found that he was academically unprepared to "get by."[9] "College was hard," Pablo remembered. "It was harder than I expected. When I got there, I wasn't prepared for those classes, man. I had trouble in almost all those classes. I mean, we had tutors, but it was still hard. Most of the time, I just let it go. If I passed a test, I passed. If I didn't, I didn't. After a while, I was like, 'Fuck it.' As long as I was playin' ball, fuck it."

Pablo also felt an economic strain. To survive and pay tuition, Pablo relied on student loans and the government-sponsored Pell grant. However, he had to wait till mid-semester to get any cash. Also, his mother sent him no money even though she had sold her grocery store for profit and established numerous investments in the Dominican Republic. "Financially, I was struggling," Pablo recalled. "I would ask my mom for money, but she would never send me some. I couldn't understand that shit. I was trying to do somethin' positive and she wouldn't send me any money. I always like needed extra money to buy things like food from the supermarket, like to get a snack or somethin', or like to just have money in my pocket. I was gettin' by—just barely, bro."

With no family support, Pablo depended on the generosity of his teammate and best friend. "I was lucky I had a good teammate. I'll never forget him, bro. He was this Black dude named Jay. He always looked out for me whenever I needed money, bro. He even took me to his hometown in Georgia and everything. That was a real cool experience. I'll never forget that shit. I remember when I got to his house, I was like shocked. His family treated me like real family, bro. They made me feel really like at home. He became like my best friend down there, man. I use to stay with him for like holidays, for break, for everything. 'Cause I couldn't go home. I ain't have no money to go home."

When summer break arrived, Pablo wanted to spend it in the South Bronx. He was tired of staying alone in his dorm and wanted to avoid overstaying his welcome with his friend. So he called Gus to ask if Sylvio could send him transportation funds. Gus then told him not to worry, that he would send the money instead. Gus gave me the money, which I then wired to Pablo.

A week later, Gus picked up Pablo at the bus terminal. Pablo was stunned. Sixteen-year-old Gus was driving a "hooked-up" car. Also, whenever we ate, drank, or danced, young Gus picked up the tab. Within a few days, Pablo made a life-changing decision. "Gus paid for my shit to come back to New York," Pablo remembered. "I was like, 'How the fuck is this little dude gonna pay my shit to come back? How the fuck he got himself a ride?' So I came home in the summer and saw Gus makin' money and payin' for all my shit. I just made the decision. I was gonna make money, man. I said, 'Fuck it' and that was it. I mean, I had plans of goin' back to school. I wanted to play ball. But I had plans of makin' a little bit of money so that I could be alright when I went back. I just didn't want to be broke."

Pablo decided to sell crack. This was not his first encounter with drug dealing. When Pablo was a child, his mother kicked out his older brother because he refused to work or attend school. Later, when Pablo was in his early teens, his brother started showing up in brand new cars. "I didn't know exactly what he was doin'," Pablo recalled, "because I was kid. But I liked the cars he was in. He was always in a new one almost every time I saw him."

Even when he learned that his big brother sold drugs, Pablo passed no judgment. In fact, he saw that no one ever made a big fuss. "I thought that it was alright that he was sellin' [drugs]," Pablo explained. "Because my mom never said, 'You better not do that.' He used to buy her stuff too and she never said, 'No, I don't want it. Take it back.' No one ever said anything, bro. So I didn't think nothin' of it."[10]

Sylvio, though, objected. He wanted Pablo to stay out of trouble and pursue his football dreams. Pablo had a special status in our neighborhood; since most of us dabbled in sports, we appreciated his athletic prowess. So when he, in partnership with Gus, approached Sylvio to buy some cocaine, Sylvio said "no."

But by then, Sylvio had become a true capitalist whose only obligation was to maximize profits. Now, he made money for its own sake; despite making tens of thousands of dollars weekly, he could not turn down a chance to make a few thousand more. He sold Pablo the drugs.

"What made Sylvio give in was money, man." Pablo recalled. "Me and Gus was buyin' top dollar off that nigga. He was jerkin' me and Gus. He was gettin' his shit dirt cheap and then killin' us. That nigga Sylvio made a lot of money from us." Alone, Gus had made about five hundred dollars daily. With Pablo's help, the crack operation ran twenty-four hours a day. So Pablo soon made close to five hundred dollars daily too. Times were looking good. And like many neighborhood youths, I admired his newfound riches and accorded him respect on the money-making gridiron. Also, I basked in our close friendship and eagerly hung out with him as he directed his sales team, collected his money, and treated me to food and drinks. So I rooted for him to reach the financial stars, cheered his success in the drug market— wished that I could one day earn money like him.

But his glory days were numbered. A month after his start, he was arrested for steering a customer (an undercover police officer) to a crack seller. He pled guilty to a felony and was released on probation. His football dreams: Gone.

"The arrest was what sealed the deal, bro," Pablo recalled. "I knew that once I got a felony, I couldn't go back [to school]. I would lose my scholarship, the financial aid, all that shit, bro. I couldn't go back down there because of that shit. So I stayed here."

Shortly after, Pablo was arrested for the same offense and pled guilty. No probation this time. He was sentenced to one year at Rikers island, or "The Rock," the infamous jail where chaos reigned.

IN SUMMARY

Both Gus and Pablo were remarkably loyal to the U.S. achievement ideology. Thus, rather than frame their acts as a rejection of society, we should view them as an acceptance of society's economic, material, and masculine goals. What hardened their capitalist tendencies were their family's business leanings: Carmen was always searching for business investments, and Salazar and Sylvio were savvy drug dealers. Also, Gus' mother, Regina, used some of Salazar's earnings to operate small businesses in the Bronx, and, later, to construct apartment rentals in the Dominican Republic.[11] Thus, for their families, the search for *riquezas,* or riches, was important.

This is why I place Pablo and Gus within a U.S. achievement ideology that urges high profit and self-interest—that values money and consumption over non-economic or non-material goals. Therefore, like sociologists Steven Messner and Richard Rosenfeld, and Robert Merton before them, I found that *economic* crime originates within society, within what it tells people to want and achieve.[12] Combined with a marginal neighborhood, terrible public schools, little social capital, and the crack era, this increased their *chances* of being sucked into the illegal drug market. And as marginal criminals, they had a high risk for arrest, detainment, and imprisonment. This meant experiencing the brutality of a cruel jail.

Rikers Island.

THREE

Rikers Island

NORMALIZING VIOLENCE

Just to hear the name, it makes your spine tingle
This is a jungle where the murderers mingle . . .
'Cause in every cellblock, there is a hard-rock
with a real nice device that's called a sock lock . . .
They have a nice warm welcome for new inmates
Razors, and shanks, and sharp edged plates
Posses will devour punks with power
After the shower, it's rush hour
So watch your back before you get sacked
These a bunch of maniacs that's about to attack
If you're a hustlin' pro, keep a low profiling
'Cause you won't be smilin' on Rikers Island!

KOOL G. RAP AND D. J POLO
"Rikers Island"

IN MY NEIGHBORHOOD, stories about Rikers abounded, mostly about how jailhouse wolves welcomed new detainees by robbing them of their jewelry and sneakers ("Welcome to the 'Rock'"). The most attention-grabbing stories (which had us laughing nervously under the streetlight) were about how the wolves eyed the new guy, how he cried as he made his entrance, how he cried again as he went to bed. Sensing a lamb, the wolves dishonored him, made him the jailhouse sex. So, as soon as you entered the jail, the Rikers veterans advised us, you had to *hit the first motha' fucka you see.*

Later, both Pablo and Gus would tell their stories about Rikers. Gus, with characteristic bravado, enjoyed telling his stories. Pablo rarely brought them up. "I try to like block that Rikers shit out, to be honest with you," Pablo said. "It [the barracks-style jail dorm] was a big empty room with a whole bunch of bunks. I'ma say about two hundred bunks in one room. Between a hundred and two hundred. But I can't tell you specifically . . . They were two to three feet away from each other, and all next to each other, like bang, bang, bang, bang—like a fuckin' railroad. It was crowded, man, crazy crowded. I mean, any little thing, you hear niggas arguing on the regular. Shit poppin' off here and there. And fights happened whenever they popped off. It didn't matter if it was night or day, bro. That shit was crazy."

The Rikers violence and overcrowding described by Pablo didn't always exist. It didn't come out of nowhere.

1960S: THE CONSERVATIVE TURN
IN PUNITIVE POLICIES

During the mid-1960s, conservative politicians were appalled at the groovy social rebellion, urban unrest, and new federal initiatives that mandated equal opportunity and social treatment. For them, it was a world turned upside down, a world that unfairly rewarded minorities.[1] The period's urban crime and job instability also had many Whites feeling unsafe and insecure. And as sociologist David Garland notes, conservative politicians used that White ambivalence to their advantage.[2] They repeatedly pointed to media images depicting urban riots—where Black looters threw rocks and bottles, shattered plate-glass windows, and sacked neighborhood stores—to argue that minorities were by nature criminal and that liberal policies led to chaos.

Many White Americans, once sympathetic to poor minorities, shifted ideologies. They no longer cared about the root causes of crime or the unequal distribution of opportunities and resources. Now popular sentiment perceived poverty as a symptom of individual moral failings and wayward cultures.[3] Worse, "rehabilitation" became a dirty word. Conservatives likened it to "liberal coddling," or to how liberals supposedly removed individual blame from lawbreakers.[4] A fearful and uncertain public willingly absorbed these messages.[5] Getting tough on criminals became simple, common sense.

For the next three decades, law and order dominated the political, media, and public spheres. The government would severely reduce social service programs and create costly law enforcement agencies. Conservative politicians also gave the public what it convinced them they needed: brutal, military-style policing that featured special units with advanced weaponry and state-of-the-art aircraft.[6] And on the incarceration end: longer prison sentences, especially for drug offenders.

Specifically, how had conservatives accomplished this? Through references with hidden cultural and racial meanings. For instance, to criticize welfare policies, Ronald Reagan's presidential campaign referenced Linda Taylor, an African American woman allegedly earning millions through welfare fraud. To show crime toughness, George Bush's presidential campaign referenced Willie Horton, an African American convicted of murder who, while on prison furlough, kidnapped a White couple, raping the female. Though not explicit, race was the subtext—the stereotypical *Black* welfare cheat and the big *Black* rapist.[7]

Thus, conservatives nourished fear and anxiety among White voters and then promised protection.[8] The public protested little when harsh sentencing guidelines were enacted[9]—even during years, as sociologist Katherine Beckett notes, when drug use declined.[10] Subsequently, Democrats and liberals reinvented themselves as tough officials. Now they wanted to break down doors, arrest widely, and send offenders to prison for a long, long time.[11]

1980S: NEW YORK CITY GETS TOUGH

By the late 1980s, crack dealers had flooded New York City streets. I saw them. They roamed sidewalks impatiently and hung out on corners and stoops, eyes always looking, searching for customers and avoiding cops. Making it through these crowded sidewalks was like walking through a human maze, a dangerous stretch of wandering arms and legs and eyes that reached out, inviting crack's clientele. And crack dealers did not discriminate: from the law-abiding *abuelita,* or grandmother, to the bottle-throwing kid—everyone was a potential sale.

Blue Top! Green Top! Yellow Top! Gold! yelled the dealers as people moved about the street.

Heavy crack users sought the drug around the clock, and they hit the streets hard. They became thieves who burglarized homes and broke into parked cars. They became sex workers who sold sex in a crack house or on the street. They became street pitchers who sold drugs at the drug market's lower end.

The dealers chased profits in cutthroat ways. They encroached on a rival's dealing turf, withheld money from suppliers, and sold bogus drugs. All led to trouble as wrongdoers were hunted down. Guns were drawn, people were shot, sidewalks were bloody, and children were hurt—dead bodies surfaced everywhere. Now violence ruled the streets; there was no more public space.[12] Street crime and murder, which had fallen steadily for four years during the early 1980s, now did an about-face.[13] The political response, predictable: get tough on crime.

Under Mayor Edward Koch, the law-and-order approach took the form of special units and massive street raids. First, the tactical narcotics team (TNT) pretended to be drug buyers and made several purchases with marked money. Then the unit burst onto the scene, surprising dealers and buyers. After the arrests, dealers and buyers were herded into large jail buses and driven off. Several members of TNT would then occupy the area for up to ninety days.

I witnessed this spectacular show of force several times. And overall, the massive arrests barely dented crack sales. Jailed dealers were often replaced by up-and-coming youngsters. Targeted drug operations were displaced to nearby neighborhoods. And drug dealers returned to their old stomping grounds once the military-like occupation moved elsewhere.[14]

What the arrests did do was jam the courts and aggravate the already-deplorable conditions on Rikers Island. Even before TNT's massive drug arrests, New York City jails were abysmal. In fact, in 1983, a federal court mandated the city to release 611 detainees because of overcrowding. And back then, the entire jail system had fewer than ten thousand detainees.[15] In the mid-1980s, Mayor Koch was under public pressure to reduce crime. So he ramped up arrests. By 1988, the number of detainees would rise to over seventeen thousand.[16] By 1990, that number had rocketed to over twenty-one thousand. Rikers Island alone, in that same year, held fourteen thousand of those detainees.[17]

To accommodate this burgeoning inmate population, Koch created new Rikers jail space, some barracks-style buildings with dormitories.[18] Housing about 60 percent of Rikers detainees, the dormitories held about sixty metal cots in a large, open floor plan.[19] In theory, each prisoner had his required fifty feet of personal space. In practice, though, personal space was up for grabs. Violent detainees took over entire dormitories, controlling television and telephone access, while openly extorting and robbing too. The open design also amplified tensions: loud radios and talk agitated detainees, who literally had to walk over each other to get anywhere.[20] Worse, correction officers (COs) sometimes let the violence go unfettered, unchecked.[21] Mayhem reigned.

Pablo and Gus—and Manolo, who I include to triangulate their experiences—were about to enter the jail under its worse condition.

Manolo, a drug dealer who sometimes hung out with us (and who later tried his hand in a drug robbery), was detained at Rikers twice during the early 1990s.[22] "I remember you always had fights, like, one on one," Manolo recalled. "Like me and you had a card problem, or I found out you stole my sock or something, like we'll just go to the bathroom, no crowds or nothing, just me and you. Because if somebody took somethin' from you, you see, nobody got in your business. You had to resolve the problem with whoever took your stuff. Even if you lost, they gave you your shit back, 'cause then you won't be a punk.

"Usually, like when we didn't want somebody in the dorm, like literally, everybody ran the dude out. Like if we found out he was a rapo' [rapist] or did some shysty shit like that . . . like about twenty of us used to just like jump them. We used to just beat them down to make the COs take them out our dorm."

The worst violence concerned the dormitory telephone. Since jail provided little in positive rewards, ordinary objects like a phone took on powerful meanings. In fact, its possession became a way to enhance status. "The phones back then," Manolo explained, "were free from like seven in the morning to eleven at night. But there was always that *matatan* (killer) in the dorm that it was supposedly his, you understand? Whoever he wanted, he would let them use the phone. But most of the time, the regular COs would like have a pad there, with the time. And you would write your name at the slot, like the time you wanted to use it. Then you could use it."[23]

"So the dude that controlled the phone, did you pay him?" I asked.

"No, you didn't have to pay him."

"So what was the purpose of him havin' the phone?"

"Jail, man. Jail mentality. That was like *his* shit. That was like his drug spot on the street, you understand? That was his, that's it. The phone was his. Whoever wanted to use the phone more than him had to fight him."

"So how did he intimidate people?"

"[If] they were on the phone, he would just hang it up. He used to take the cord, put it in his pocket. [I start laughing.] You can't use the phone without the cord, right, Randy? Ha-ha. I'm tellin' you, jail was some real bullshit."

Manolo went on to describe his first day at Rikers Island, when he learned how the phone, as petty as it may seem, was so significant. "Like the first day at Rikers Island. Like when we went to that dorm, I got there with like nine guys. I got there with this Black guy, this other Black guy, and this Bori' [slang for *Boriqua,* or Puerto Rican], some other guys. Right away on the bus, the Black guy was like, 'Yo, whatever house I get to, whoever got the phone, that nigga better have his shit [shank], 'cause I got my shit [shank] boofed."

"What do you mean by 'boofed'?" I asked.

"It's like when they put a razor in a little balloon, with a little cloth, and they put in their ass. Then they go into the bathroom, squat, and—plah!— they take it out of there, they wash their hands, and go and resolve with whoever. . . . So when we got there, the Black dude saw this Bori' usin' the phone and he was like, 'Yo, if you don't want to get sliced in the face, you better hang up that phone.' Pah. The Bori' hung up the phone. Then the Black dude took off the phone and took it with him. He was like, 'Yo, who runnin' the phone?' Then this Bori' guy, who was layin' on his bed readin', was like, 'Me. What's up?' The Black guy was like, 'What you gonna do for the phone?' 'Let's go to the showers.' The dude got up and they went to the bathroom."

Later, Manolo remarked on Gus, saying something that was known to the entire neighborhood: that Gus became a violence specialist at Rikers Island. Clearly, Gus started his violence earlier. But he mastered it in jail. "Gus used to do all that shit," Manolo explained. "That's why Gus is all fucked up in the head."

"How do you know that Gus used to do that shit?"

" 'Cause I was with two guys in there that were with him when he was there. He was wil[d]in' out. They told me that if he slept in a corner and didn't want someone to sleep around him, he would make them sleep somewhere else. I'm tellin' you, Gus was doin' all that shit. Jail made him crazy."

"How did Gus get away with doin' all of that?"

"Tell me, Randy, who wants to mess with that crazy motherfucka? Ha-ha-ha!"

No one, I thought to myself as I laughed along.

GLADIATOR SCHOOL

Overall, Mayor Koch's ill-conceived solution to both the drug problem and the rising number of detainees led to terror in Rikers. At its best, the Rikers experience was always full of tension and uncertainty. Most detainees awaited trial, trial results, bail, or transfers to better state facilities. But when the city squeezed these anxious individuals into tiny spaces, disaster resulted. For instance, in 1987, there were 361 reported slashings at Rikers. By 1989, the slashings had almost doubled, reaching 654. The stats on reported stabbings were just as horrific: in 1987, there were 369; within the first five months of 1990—there were already 364.[24]

Despite these telling statistics and a jail population reaching epidemic proportions, in October of 1990, city officials approved the addition of 575 beds on Rikers Island.[25] How would they fit them in? Simple. By squeezing the existing beds even closer together.

Violence soared.

Upon arrival, Pablo witnessed the results. He remembered Rikers as a place where detainees always got "blown-up," or slashed and stabbed with illegal contraband. "Niggas just fuckin' went at it in there," Pablo recalled. "Niggas was just gettin' blown-up like crazy, bro, like when everybody was goin' to lunch or whatever, in the gym, liftin', in the cafeteria. I remember one time, dudes came runnin' into the bathroom and took these fuckin' shanks out their stash [hiding places] there. I was like, 'Damn, niggas got stashes in the bathroom.' Then I seen this dude runnin' with blood all over on him and some other dude runnin' behind him rippin' him."

Pablo also witnessed sexual domination. In this all-male setting, detainees had revived traditional gender hierarchies, but with spaces for men to do domestic roles. Within this system, homosexual men became the new subordinate objects. As "Maytags" (like the washing machine brand), they performed laundry services for a fee, or did chores for lovers. But their romantic and domestic utility sometimes resulted in power plays that were centered on courting rights. "But the funniest shit I seen was niggas in my dorm fightin' over fuckin' homos," Pablo recalled. "Niggas was callin' home and talkin' to their wifey and then niggas fuckin' with homos in there. Like I seen this dude callin' his wife and talkin' to her. Then later he went up to this other dude, bro, and was like, 'Yo, you better leave so-and-so [a male lover] alone.' Then he just started swingin', bro. I mean, goin' at it, killin'-type shit. I never seen some shit like that. Over a homo, bro."

Pablo and Gus developed their own survival strategies, which would inform their lives outside. Pablo's strategy was to remain a loner. Sensing that violence at Rikers stemmed from fights between pals and cliques, he kept to himself. Later in life, he would use the insight he had gained at Rikers to keep drug dealers and robbers uncertain about what he might do.

"If you don't really associate with other people," Pablo explained, "they not gonna mess with you. When you start bein' friendly with everybody, they then like think you soft or somethin'. You also, too, gonna eventually get into some type of problem with them. Or some gang bullshit. [That's why] I only talked to one dude who was from my grandmother's block. And I hardly talked to him at all. 'Cause once you start gettin' funny with niggas, niggas start sizin' you up. But if a nigga don't know what the fuck is goin' on in your mind, a nigga ain't really gonna fuck with you. [Pretending to be someone wondering about him] 'I don't know what the fuck that nigga's thinkin'. I don't know who the fuck is that.' And don't look like you fuckin' scared or nothin'. Act like you been there [and] niggas ain't really gonna fuck with you. But if you act scared, or niggas offer you somethin' and you take it, you showin' weakness right there. You gotta be like, 'Nah, I'm a'ight, keep it movin'.' They tryin' to see if you bite. If you take it, you're done."[26]

Gus took a different approach to the violence and instability at Rikers. Sensing that showing weakness resulted in victimization, he quickly jumped into the fray, getting down with some neighborhood friends. As their leader, he directed them on a string of strong-arms, where they stole jewelry, clothing, and food. Mostly, they preyed on detainees making purchases from the jailhouse commissary. "Once a week people used to go to commissary to buy food, soda, [and] junk food," Gus recalled. "We would wait till everybody shops to see who got the most food. They come back to the house [dormitory] and we would take their shit. I used to just walk up behind them and just choke them until they fell asleep. 'Cause once I learned to put people to sleep, we used to rob people for a lot of shit, like their jewelry, sneakers, shit like that.

"Like one time, I seen this dude with these new sneakers. I was like, 'Fuck that,' I'm takin' those shits.' He [the victim] was sittin' on his bed readin' or some shit. So, boom, he gets up and goes to the bathroom, and me and my boy go in there with him. As soon as he turns around to look back—bam!—I knocked [punched] the shit out of him. Right in the jaw, bro. You could hear the sound of that shit go, plap! The nigga was in a fuckin' daze after that. Then I grabbed him from behind, choked him. Just put the nigga to sleep and we took his shits."

"But why did you take his sneakers?" I asked.

"'Cause he was walkin' around like he ran shit, you know. Like he controlled the house. I was like fuck that shit. I'ma take his shit, see what he gonna do. You gotta prove that you a man in jail. You gotta show that shit." Since social position was determined by one's ability to dominate—whether physically, psychologically, or sexually—Gus became skilled at predation. In the process, he learned a valuable skill for violence: weeding out weak detainees and ambushing them.[27]

He also learned that violence had to be witnessed to garner respect from other detainees: "'Cause they [correction officers] don't leave you in the same place [after you stab someone]. You gotta have juice with COs [correction officers] for them to bring you back [to the same dorm]. 'Cause you wanna come back to where people saw you stab somebody, you know what I'm sayin'? Ha-ha-ha. They [the stabbers] don't wanna go somewhere else where nobody knows them! You gotta stab somebody else now! Ha-ha-ha!"

Gus didn't limit his violent encounters to weak detainees; he went after powerful detainees too. This move, though, sometimes backfired. For instance, after disputing with a detainee who controlled the television (similar to telephone control), Gus was sliced—in the face. "This Jamaican dude had control over the TV," Gus recalled. "He thought he could run shit, like tellin' people what they could watch, whatever. I was like, 'Fuck that.' So one day I tell this Puerto Rican kid that I'm gonna change the channel. He was like, 'Yeah, yeah. I got your back. Don't worry, just do that shit.'

"So, boom, we get our shanks ready and everything. I go up to the television, I'm like, 'Yo, I don't want to watch this shit. Change that shit.' The Jamaican dude starts talkin' mad shit like, 'Yo, what you doing, that's my TV . . .' and a bunch of other shit. I'm like, 'I'm gonna change this show. What the fuck you gonna do?' Then he goes runnin' to get his shank, and these other Jamaicans, like his boys, go run to get their shanks. I go run to get my shank, and, yo, can you believe this shit? The [Puerto Rican] kid broke the fuck out on me. He left me all fuckin' alone. So I'm by myself and have to face like four Jamaican niggas.

"The Jamaican dude comes back, and he got his shank, I got my shank. We start swingin' at each other. I'ma tell you right now, I was lucky, bro. Like these other Puerto Rican kids had seen what was happenin' and they got their shanks and we was all fightin'. But when we heard the COs, everybody started runnin'. The Jamaican dude turned around to run, but then he turned back around real quick and swung at me. Like I didn't expect it, like I thought he was gonna run. And that's how he got me—shaa!—right in my face. . . . But we caught one of them, me and this kid, and we stabbed him like fourteen times before the COs got there. Like in his legs, his back— Shaa! Shaa! Shaa! I'm surprised we didn't kill him."

In that knife fight, Gus was scarred for life. And in most places, that scar was a stigma. But on the street, that thick slant running down his jaw became his badge of honor. Gus was a gladiator that had survived the imperial Rikers coliseum. For instance, after meeting Gus, many guys would later ask me about his scar. After I explained its origin, they were in awe. *Damn, that nigga was gettin' down like that?* Later, when hanging out with Gus again, they showed extreme deference, agreeing with him on every point, laughing at his every line.

The scar impressed women too. Once, at a bar, I saw an attractive young woman slowly make her way toward him, stand by him, and then make small talk by referencing his scar, which she slowly traced with her finger. With a large gold-toothed grin, he briefly explained where he got it—*in jail.* At night's end, he took her home.

The scar, however, was symbolic of how the criminal justice system bred racial hatred. Surely, skin color always mattered to detainees. But the severe overcrowding in New York City jails increased tension over limited resources. And despite their common need for better mental, educational, and drug treatment services, many detainees waged war—not on the brutal institution that intensified their marginality, but on each other. The terms of this war were often linked to race. For instance, at Rikers, Gus colorized his status preoccupations.

"It's like in jail," Gus explained, "Black dudes think like they bad. Like they better than everybody. They all think they could run shit just because they Black. Man, think about it. All they do is complain about everything, bro. They want to have everything, but don't want nobody else to have it. That's why in jail, I ain't like those Black dudes, bro. They thought they could tell everybody like what to do. They actin' like they the toughest, whatever, like we have to listen to them. Fuck that shit."

On its face, it seemed like Gus challenged Black oppressors. Yet his stories show how it was *he* who wanted unchallenged domination, how he conjured up racist stereotypes when Black men contested him. Ironically, Gus had dark skin, thick lips, and wavy hair—and had African American youths as best friends. Yet in jail, Gus constructed his Dominican identity against them, portraying them as an inferior race.

Pablo, whose best friend in college was Black, also racialized his Rikers experience. In fact, he claimed that it was the first time he started disliking "Black dudes," adding a homophobic, emasculating twist. "After I seen them dudes fighting over a homo," he said, "I lost respect for the Black man.

'Cause the dudes that I seen fighting—I mean, killing each other, bro!—were two Black dudes, over a homo, bro. Yo, and that was some disgusting shit. They in there to do a year, bro, and they can't wait to get some pussy? They gotta fuck a dude, bro? I remember one time like a homo walked by me and got kind'a too close to me, you understand, almost touchin' me. And he kinda gave me a funny look when he did that shit. I was like, 'Yo, you better keep your fuckin' distance! The next time you do that I'ma fuck your homo ass up!' 'Cause I ain't with that shit, bro. But like I said, I only seen Black dudes doin' it. I mean, I could imagine Hispanics do that shit too, in prison. But I only seen Black dudes do it. I lost respect for them after that. They disgusting, bro."

Rikers evoked the worst racist rationalizations within Pablo. From then on he—and Gus—would use race as a status marker, alongside money and material items.

Just as terrible was how turbulent jail conditions encouraged nonviolent detainees to lash out. At Rikers, most detainees were charged with nonviolent offenses, like for drug dealing or drug possession. Others were there for innocently being at the wrong place at the wrong time (when TNT made a massive sweep, they arrested everyone in the targeted area). To survive, these detainees had to stand up to predators, which evoked their violence too. For instance, one day Gus and his crime partner decided to strong-arm a *punk*. "Like the kid was a punk, a punk, a punk," Gus recalled. "We knew he got like fifty dollars from his father, that his father had sent him. So, boom, he went to commissary and brought back food, rice, beans, all type of shit. He came back, we robbed him for all his shit."

And since they thought that the victim was a "punk," Gus and his partner later let down their guard. However, unbeknownst to them, the victim had secured a razor. "The kid got like a shank from these two Chinese kids we were extorting," Gus recalled. "So, boom, we were walkin' by the kid, and he just went Shaa! [swiped in the air] and got my friend, bro, real bad. He cut him down his face, like down from his forehead, bro—that shit [the slash] jumped [over his eye], like all the way down his cheek, down to his chest and stomach. One big fuckin' line from his forehead down to his stomach, bro. I was like stunned 'cause the kid was a punk. I ain't really think he had it in him to do that.

"Then I seen the kid later and I told him, [in a powerful tone] 'Yo, what the fuck you did that shit for? Yo, you wanna fuckin' die? That shit ain't stayin' like that.' He was like, 'Nah, I ain't want to do it. That shit ain't me, it ain't in my heart. But ya' took my shit. That was my father's last fifty dollars that he sent me. My father ain't have no more money, and he sent his last fifty dollars to me. Ya' made that shit come out my heart.'"

In his Rikers experiences, Manolo also saw this monstrous transformation within "humble" individuals, or those who went to Rikers wanting to do easy time. "I'm tellin' you, I seen humble, humble guys go to jail, right, and just fuckin' change. . . . Say me and you went to court together. You're okay, *tranquilo* [and say], 'Yo, I just want to cop out, I don't want no problem. I just want to do my time,' whatever. Then like two months later, we go to court again, and I see you, you all full of tattoos, you're fuckin' kickin' the door, you're yellin', 'Yo, CO!' You know, your attitude changed. Yo, I've seen that happen in jail, Randy. Like first you're readin' a book, you're not talkin' to nobody. Then you're like a Latin King or a Nyeta [two Latino prison gangs], and your arms full of tattoos. Yo, I'm tellin' you, man, jail was more like a mental institution. It made guys crazy."

Rikers, then, resembled an educational institution. Here, men learned how to survive a prison culture that, because of horrific overcrowding, was destined to promote violence. Lessons learned—keeping a low profile or victimizing to avoid one's own victimization—then transferred on to the street.

CORRECTIONAL FLAWS

On the corrections side, the guards were in a bind. Before Mayor Koch's dormitory expansion, individual jail cells had kept inmate violence in check and allowed COs more control. Now, the new dormitories had them patrolling large spaces, unarmed. Detainees outnumbered them about thirty to one. So when fights broke out, some guards let them take their course. Worse, if guards apprehended wrongdoers, they sometimes went too far, venting their frustration on them.[28]

In his dormitory, Pablo observed the detachment of some COs. When I asked him whether COs were around to stop inmate violence, he answered: "I mean, they ain't leave the dorms, but they always had somethin' to do. Like a dorm is so big, you could blow up a nigga in the bathroom, you could blow up a nigga in the rec' room. By the time they get there, they already blown up. If you want to get a nigga, you could get a nigga anywhere."

Pablo also observed how some COs gave up on keeping order. In fact, many allowed detainees to fight it out, creating their own order out of the chaos. For instance, one day when Pablo was on the phone with his mother, the phone controller hurried him. Angry, Pablo told him to "Fuckin' wait," and a heated argument ensued. A CO then suggested that they resolve the issue physically. "The CO was like, 'Look, I'm gonna leave for five minutes and both of you just get your aggression out. When I come back, the shit better be over.' That CO was always like that. Like if you have a problem, he would let you go at it. He was cool with everybody, man. He let you do your business. He was smart, man. He knew that he could get it [get attacked], you know what I'm sayin'?"

Might Makes Right. That was one of many lessons Rikers taught detainees. Pablo saw that to survive the overcrowded work conditions, the COs allowed detainees to use violence to establish their own hierarchy. He understood why they developed such strategies, ones that resulted from how the state had abdicated its responsibility to provide a safe environment.

HIGH SCHOOL REUNION

After two months of Rikers chaos, Pablo requested a transfer to a prison in upstate New York. After approval, he was bussed to the Watertown Correctional Facility, about six hours north, near the Canadian border. Watertown was different. Here, Pablo worked a full day as a beginning welder, then went to the gym, and later went to sleep in a dorm. Fights were infrequent and inmates did more "good" time.

"In Rikers, bro, there's no structure, really," Pablo explained. "They had you doin' stuff, but it's not like when you go upstate [prison]. Upstate your mind is more at ease. At least when you upstate you know you already sentenced. In Rikers, you don't know what's gonna happen next. You not really sentenced yet. For example, I ain't see no slashin', or I ain't see no fights, in Watertown. I mean, maybe one or two [fights], that's it. But Rikers was bananas, B. You could get shanked any minute. You see the fresh stitches on the nigga's face. Or you see the bandage or the butterfly shits [stitches]. You see a lot of niggas with that scar in their face like Gus. Rikers was wild, bro. Watertown was easier. You did easy time, like they say."

And in Watertown, Pablo felt respected and recognized. As soon as he stepped into the facility, he heard his last name shouted by various inmates. *Yo, Garcia! Garcia! There goes Garcia.* "What happened," Pablo proudly explained, "was niggas in there knew me from football. They were like a lot of niggas there like from high school that used to watch me play. So as soon as I went there, I had niggas that knew me from football that I didn't even know."

And while he bench-pressed one day, the most muscular inmate in the gym approached him. "He was like, 'Yo, you went to my high school. You're fuckin' Garcia! What the fuck you doin' here?' That shit was funny, bro. That nigga knew everything about me, bro. He was tellin' me about the game against Kennedy [High School], which ways I ran, the plays I did. So he knew me and we started lifting together. So we kinda bonded."

As Pablo recounted this experience, he smiled often, proud of how football still defined him. Yet he had little choice but to fondly remember this event. Otherwise, he would have to admit to the tragedy: that his first high school reunion took place not in a balloon-filled school gymnasium, but behind concrete prison walls.[29] The ultimate tragedy, though, was how the state had built a bridge to resolve social and economic inequality—a bridge that, according to sociologist Loic Wacquant, extends from poor urban neighborhoods directly to the state prison.[30]

For the next few months, Pablo spent his time lifting weights, playing "jail football," and welding for hours every day. After completing eight months, he was transferred back to Rikers and then released early. With his belongings stuffed into a clear plastic bag, Pablo took the two-hour bus and subway trip home. "If I woulda been there longer, I woulda got a welding certificate," Pablo reflected. "But I came home with shit, just a fuckin' plastic bag. If you ever seen a nigga in the train with clear bags, that means that he just came home. That was me, all alone on the fuckin' train with my shit in a fuckin' clear bag. I just came home."

To this day, I vividly remember seeing Pablo for the first time after he got home. He came to my apartment to catch up while we lifted weights. Physically, he was more muscular and powerful than ever. He bench-pressed two hundred and seventy-five pounds—my one-rep max—easily. But he had changed in other ways too. With a crazed look in his eyes, he spoke wildly in prison slang and used exaggerated body movements and gestures. He also could not stop describing prison and jail violence, especially incidents where detainees had been "blown-up," or slashed with razors. When especially excited, his eyes widened almost to the point of popping out of their sockets, which made him look scary. *What had incarceration done to him?* I kept asking myself as I looked into his feral face. *It had traumatized him—made him crazy, insane.* This was not the same Pablo I had known.

For Gus, jail, and later prison, solidified his preoccupation with toughness. In fact, it became his reference point for determining manhood. *You don't know if you a man,* he often told me, *unless you go to prison. If you could survive prison, then you could say you a man.* He proudly made that proclamation, beaming as he said the words. Like a proud U.S. Marine holding basic training as the ultimate manhood test, Gus used prison as the measure of a man. During those moments, I wished I could turn back time and change the course of events. While I knew that it would not guarantee outcomes, I knew that things could have been different.

I just knew it.

FOUR

The New York Boys

TAIL ENDERS OF THE CRACK ERA

IN A BROAD SENSE, Pablo, Gus, Tukee, Manolo, and I were part of what I call the "tail enders." We were squeezed between the crack era generation and the marijuana/blunts era generation.[1] ("Blunts" refers to marijuana in cigar wrappings.) The crack era generation had come of age during the early to mid-1980s, the onset and peak years, when it was more likely to produce committed crack users or profitable crack dealers.[2] The marijuana/blunts era generation was younger, coming up during the mid-1990s. Its young people witnessed the horrors of crack and repudiated its use, making their drugs of choice marijuana and forty-ounce beers.

As tail enders, we avoided using crack, but we didn't reject it entirely. Through crack, we still had a chance to get rich. We had observed its money-making face: the successful dealers driving "fresh" cars and dating "fly" girls. Still, just to get a foot in the drug game, the tail enders had little choice but to journey to small cities and rural towns across the United States.[3] And in the "sticks," these traveling dealers became instantly rich, selling their crack and cocaine for up to four times New York City prices. In most places, these migrant dealers were known as the New York Boys—a name given to them by town locals who resented their presence or feared their violence and crime.[4]

As tail enders, Pablo, Gus, and some others joined the exodus, migrating first to small-town Ohio and then to Georgia. Even Tukee (who asked me to be vague about his crimes) journeyed to a town near Philadelphia to set up shop. Throughout, I heard their stories of making *crazy dollars,* getting with *mad* women, and *blasting* people in rural towns. I also observed their returns to the South Bronx, when they lived the high life on their earnings. For the next year and a half, they finally were somebody. They were stars.

After Pablo's release, he was broke. During that time, I observed him get drugs from Sylvio on credit and desperately search for a crack-selling location in the South Bronx. But there were no empty slots. "Shit was hard for a minute," Pablo remembered. "Real, real hard. I couldn't find no place to put out some crack. Every place I went, that shit was taken, or I had to pay rent to some dude to sell my shit on his block. It was always something, bro."

Then Alex, a local dealer, recruited Pablo for a drug venture.[5] He had just been connected to some Black dealers from Ohio who needed a steady supply of cocaine. The operation was simple. Pablo or Alex transported the drugs through female couriers that accompanied them on bus trips. Once in Ohio, they supplied the dealers with the cocaine on consignment, or credit, receiving payment once it was sold. After Gus was released, they recruited him; he helped with the long bus rides. They would earn more money than ever.

"We gettin' our keys [kilos] for real cheap from Sylvio," Pablo remembered. "Then we sellin' it out there for like double [its price]. Those Black dudes [Ohio dealers] were movin' it too. They like controlled those little towns out there . . . Like all of us together was makin' like fifteen [thousand dollars], and then we split it, like between me, Alex, and Gus. So each of us was makin' like five thousand [dollars] a week. Now that's serious money, bro."

AFTERSHOCKS

Around that time, crack-related crime was spreading from urban areas to small-town U.S.A.[6] These manifestations were what I call drug epidemic "aftershocks." Like an earthquake, the crack epidemic had its powerful epicenter in large cities. The violent seismic shift created aftershocks, or a ripple effect of crime and violence, that shook places far away. Sometimes, the New York Boys created them. As outlaw capitalists, they could not rely on laws to ensure smooth business. So they projected a violent image to scare potential wrongdoers. Sometimes they did violence.

According to the Dominican New York Boys, their first aftershock came one night when Pablo and the Ohio dealers were out at a local nightclub. "Some dude got into an argument with one of the Ohio niggas [dealers] I was with [in the club]," Pablo recalled. "So, boom, we get outside, we walkin' and the dude is still poppin' mad shit, bro. He had all these other dudes with him talkin' mad shit. I was like, fuck that. We got to the car and I got my nine [millimeter handgun] and just unloaded that shit. I was like, Pah! Pah! Pah! Pah! Pah! I wasn't even aimin', bro. I just shot into their little group, whatever. Those motherfuckas started runnin', bro, ha-ha. That's when everybody in that little town knew who the fuck we was. Those Ohio niggas [dealers] was like, 'Yo, you crazy, man.' That's all they kept saying, ha-ha, that I was crazy."

This was the new Pablo, the "crazy" Pablo that had emerged from incarceration. Before this, I never thought that Pablo could do deadly violence. For instance, when he first started drug dealing, he and some others got into a turf dispute with some competing dealers. Armed, both crews squared off in the disputed park, where shots were fired and people ran for their lives. Later, Pablo explained how he never got a shot off because his gun "jammed." In secret, no one believed him. Me, I thought that he had been afraid to shoot and he used the "jamming" story to save face. Pablo was not Gus.

But in Ohio, Pablo used his gun multiple times—even risked committing a murder. And people noticed. "People was scared of us," Gus recalled. "Like they were givin' us more respect because they knew that we had guns and we would shoot them."

After about six months, though, the cocaine profits suddenly wavered. The Ohio dealers started coming up short with payments, claiming to have collection problems with their clientele. " 'Cause they started sayin' that shit was fucked up over there," Gus recalled, "that shit was goin' bad, that some of their clientele had left, the ones they got on credit, left. But they was buyin' new cars . . . goin' out for a week to Cleveland on vacation and shit, just chillin'. So we knew somethin' was going on 'cause we was the only ones that wasn't seein' no money."

Pablo saw the same: "When I met them niggas, they ain't have shit. A couple of months later they got their whole house furnished, big-screen TVs, new sofas, mad shit. Motherfuckas were drivin' around in Jaguars. One of those niggas had a BMW, the M6, a coupe. It was one of the most expensive BMWs. I was thinkin', 'How these niggas got better cars than I do?' I was the one who set them off."

Suspecting foul play, Gus wanted to kill them. "Gus wanted to do some crazy shit to them, bro," Pablo recalled. "He wanted to put those niggas out [kill them]. He kept sayin' that shit over and over, bro. But I was like, 'Yo, let's get them another way. Let's get somethin' out of this. 'Cause if we put them out, we not gettin' anything back.' "

So Pablo convinced the Ohio dealers to purchase, all cash, a kilo of cocaine at a much reduced price: twenty-five thousand dollars. This was fifteen thousand dollars less than what they usually paid. Agreeing, they gave all the money up front. Bad move. They never saw the South Bronx dealers again. And when they called Pablo to inquire about the drugs, he simply lied. "I was like, 'Yo, you not gonna believe what happened. Gus bagged [robbed] me. He took the money and bounced. I can't find his ass.' Then he [the dealer] was like, 'Yo, Pablo, that's all I had.' I was like, 'I can't do nothin' about it.' We left it at that."

SWEET GEORGIA

After duping the Ohio dealers, Pablo, Gus, and Alex returned to the Bronx, where drug market opportunities, they soon found, had dried up. Police had increased their street presence and crack dealers had saturated the drug market. Worse, their new street operations attracted few customers. The crack epidemic had passed its peak, and they started feeling the pressures of its decline. "Things were gettin' rough out here," recalled Pablo. "We weren't doin' shit. We was fuckin' scrambling to make money."

Then, good news. Tikki, the young Black dealer who had mentored Gus as a teen, needed someone with capital and a drug connection. He had a brother-in-law living just south of Atlanta with a large cocaine clientele. Gus, convinced of the operation's potential, asked Pablo to provide the startup cash. Pablo agreed and purchased a half kilo of cocaine, worth ten thousand dollars, from Sylvio and Salazar. Later, he brought in Alex, who had an immigration warrant, and Manolo, who was just doing poorly. The New York Boys were back.

After a few setbacks (Tikki and his brother-in-law were arrested and extradited to New York), everyone was making money. "We was buyin' a key [a kilo of cocaine] at eighteen thousand [dollars]," Gus recalled, "and we was sellin' it at fifty [thousand dollars]. We was makin' thirty thousand dollars profit, man. We was movin' it fast. And everybody was seein' their money in a week and shit."

Pablo liked being back in Georgia. "People were different," he recalled. "A lot nicer than in New York. More polite, I would say. And you felt like you was in a different world. Even the food tasted different. The air you breath down there was different . . . I was like somewhere I never been before, somewhere where I just read in books or saw in movies. . . . I wish New York [City] was like Georgia. It ain't. It'll never be."

For Gus, Georgia was empowering. He saw rural living as basic and slow and felt that Georgians treated him well. "It was like going to the Dominican Republic," Gus explained. "You know how it is, like when people find out that you're from New York, everything was easy. We dressed different, we did everything different. So you could imagine how they was actin' with us. I guess their way of livin' was slower than ours. Like the way we hustled, the way we sold drugs, like the way we lived, it was like brand new to them. Imagine, they weren't even smokin' blunts. Everyone smoked paper— bamboo and stuff. People were like, 'What you smokin'? Cigars?' We were the first people to smoke blunts down there."

Manolo's view of Georgia and its lax gun laws was almost libertarian; to him, Georgia was a world where individuals were on their own. "We were like free, you know what I mean?" Manolo explained. "Free, in terms of no one tellin' us to behave, nothin'. The police wasn't even tellin' us what to do. We were like cowboys out there. Literally like cowboys with our guns in our waistband. Everyone could see that we had them . . . We did whatever we wanted in front of everybody, bro, and nobody said nothin'."

The small-town nightclub scene was also happening. Here, the New York Boys spent a lot of money, flashing drug earnings and flaunting urban panache—and discovering that people either loved them or hated them. But according to Pablo, "Nobody ever crossed the line." And there was a reason for that. After closing time, drug dealers often filed into the nightclub's parking lot. Then they competed in friendly gun competitions, where individuals shot their guns into the sky. One night, after some town dealers unloaded their fifteen-round semi-automatics, Gus pulled out his new Calico M950, a hundred-round nine-millimeter gun. Then he unloaded that deadly weapon into the Georgia night.

"I mean, everybody stood quiet when they heard all those shots," Pablo recalled. "I know they knew then not fuck around 'cause they knew that what we got, they didn't have. They'll come up with fifteen-shot gun, whatever-whatever. But when they heard a hundred shots coming out of that gun, they knew not to fuck around with us."

Manolo also remembered a time when Gus created an aftershock with the Calico M950 in a nightclub. "One time we went to this club and Gus had an argument with a Black dude . . . and that *loco* [Gus] went to the car and came back with the Calico. He kicked the wall of the club or something and they turned on the lights, and when everyone saw that *loco* with the Calico, yo, that place was empty like in twenty seconds. He didn't even have to shoot. Everybody just ran and left . . . I'ma tell you right now, after that *loco* did that, no one messed with us."

The New York Boys also started buying handguns in Georgia and selling them in New York. Since they sold them for twice their retail value, they made several thousand dollars on each return trip. Gus once used his pregnant girlfriend, who had no criminal record, to purchase twenty-five hundred dollars worth of guns. "It was December, for Christmas," Gus recalled. "I took all the guns, put them in a box. I gift wrap the box, like a gift and shit, put that shit in the trunk and we all went to New York. It was me, Manolo, and my girl. No license, I had just bought the car. No license plate. Twenty-hour trip, with fifteen guns, everything illegal, ha-ha." Within a week of getting to the Bronx, Gus sold all of the guns, earning about three thousand dollars.

Overall, the New York Boys were having a blast—a roller-coaster ride of drugs, cash, partying, and adventure. "We was down there ten months already, steady," Gus recalled, "just sellin' coke and crack in Georgia, takin' some of the money, buyin' guns. We was buyin', no bullshit, like twenty-five guns a week and sendin' them up to New York. Then we would come to Atlanta like on Thursdays through Sunday and go to clubs and all that shit. So we sellin' drugs, got the money, bought guns, send the guns up to New York, sell the guns, bought the drugs, came back to Georgia, go to Atlanta, go to the clubs—just goin' around, goin' back and forth, goin' back and forth."

Thus, the Georgia experience was uplifting for these South Bronx Dominican men. It was where they made money, attracted attention, and felt liberated—far from the abandoned buildings that stood frozen in time. Later, they would all wish that they could have stayed. It was the best time of their lives. "We did everything," Gus reminisced. "We went to clubs, strip clubs, went fishing, go to the woods and shoot guns, smoke weed, barbeque . . . That time I spent in Georgia, man, that was like the most fun I ever had. Ever, ever, ever."

RACING AROUND GEORGIA: *ANGUSTIA RACIAL*

Yet Georgia had a downside. It burrowed deeply into race. The New York Boys would hate almost everything Black—hate Black people, hate their own African past. Not that I was unaware of Dominican racism. I had heard disturbing racist comments all my life at family gatherings and on the streets with friends. Hearing it straight, though—not in passing—was brutal. Often, these Dominican men sounded like self-righteous sixteenth-century Spanish colonizers bent on oppressing their African ancestors.

Their racial constructions offended me, deeply. I have a son whose skin is brown, with coarse hair. So during their racist commentary, I became angered, getting the urge to force a mirror to their face and say: *Look, you too have Black reflections!* I wanted them to visualize their irrationality, how they hated people who looked like them. But as a sociologist, I had to intellectually step back and *momentarily* bracket my in-the-moment anger and frustration:

I knew that Spanish colonization had long ago planted the racist seeds that would later sprout among Dominicans on the island, in Europe, and in the United States.

I knew that these Dominican men had been inculcated with a racial hierarchy, one ranging from *blanco,* to *indio,* to *trigeño,* to *habio,* to *negro,* to *haitiano,* with more categories within.[7]

I knew that they learned how being *negro* or *haitiano* entailed the worst stigma, a stigma that the Dominican Republic's infamous dictator, Rafael Leónidas Trujillo, had brutally ingrained.[8]

I knew that this was why they worshipped Whiteness and took great pride in a child's light eyes, a girlfriend's dead hair, or a mythical great-great-grandmother from Spain.

I knew that while U.S. society wanted to prove Blackness for hateful reasons—hence, the "one drop of blood rule"[9]—these Dominican men wanted to prove Whiteness to reach a fictitious higher racial and moral plane.[10]

I knew that this was the racial construct that these Dominican men had brought to Georgia and why they were shocked when Georgians thought that they were Black men. "They thought we were like Black and White," Gus recalled. "When we told them we were Dominican, like from the Caribbean, they never heard of that shit. People were confused as hell down there. They were buggin' out when we spoke Spanish. You could see it in their faces, bro."

Manolo and Alex experienced the same confused reactions from people as they partied their way through the Atlanta nightlife. Manolo had limper hair and lighter skin than Gus, but a thicker nose and lips. Alex also had lighter skin than Gus, but coarser hair, which he oiled into curls. Atlanta Blacks saw them as African American. "When I went to Atlanta, everybody thought we was Black," Manolo recalled. "They thought we was redbone, Alex and me. I was like, 'Yo, we Dominican.' They never heard of that shit."

"What's a 'redbone'?" I asked.

"Like you Black and White, but you're more White. Like Jeeter [a famous Yankee shortstop], he's a redbone. His dad is Black and his mom is White."

They were perplexed at southern race relations. For instance, Gus never identified as *negro,* but always as *indio.* So when confronted with southern-style racism, he was confused. "We from New York and we like heard of the South and the Ku Klux Klan, all that shit," Gus explained, "but when we saw those Klan niggas parading, bro, that shit was crazy. But I didn't grow up with that shit, so I was just curious. I was like, 'What the fuck is this?' In a way, I didn't really know what I was lookin' at. I'm seein' this parade, but I wasn't thinkin' that this is what our country is tryin' to fight. I didn't know what to make of that shit."

For Gus, the racial turning point occurred when he and some Black clients drove to a small town an hour south of Atlanta. Here, he experienced southern racism face to face for the first time. "We was in this place called Warm Springs," Gus recalled, "and we pulled over to eat.... So there was this catfish place down there, bro. We went in there, and it was like—yo, you know like in the movies when like everybody just stops and looks and there's like silence? That's what happened to us, bro. We walked in and everybody just stopped whatever the fuck they were doin' and just looked at us. We were like aliens in there, bro. Nobody said anything to us. We went in and sat down and they just ignored us. That shit never happened to me before, bro. I was like, 'Damn, motherfuckas is racists here.'"

From then on, Gus framed his interactions with Whites through Blackness. Now he felt the sting of racial hatred that he himself had inflicted on Black men. "Then I was like, 'Damn, because they think I'm Black, so they ain't payin' attention to us.' Like pumpin' gas, like when the [White] attendant didn't take care of us, I would think it was because they were racists. A [White] cop pulled us over, I would think it was racist. We didn't get served right [properly] at a restaurant, I would think it was racist."

Yet Gus would become ashamed of his newfound Black consciousness. His repeated use of the phrase *I would think* in the above account shows how he saw himself as having been mistaken, that racism really mattered little. In fact, he reasoned that southern Blacks tricked him into framing the world through a Black mask.

"Like they had a place called Cove Road," Gus recalled. "Some grown Black men told us never get out of our car like if our car broke down there. Wait for someone to help us. Don't go lookin' for help. That shit is funny, bro. It's like we didn't have that fuckin' fear up here. Down there, we would act the same way, until people made it clear to us that shit wasn't the same down there. So little by little, we started becoming like more conscious."

Years later, he would echo the sentiments of conservative Whites who portrayed Blacks as delusional for discussing modern-day racism. He would complain that Blacks exaggerated racism, blocked racial progress, and that Whites were the victims of reverse discrimination. "The fact that we learned about how Whites were racists from the Blacks down there made us think they were all racists," Gus explained. "But the majority of the White people were nice down there. Yo, I never heard White people call Black people niggers down there. But when Black people talked about White people, they called them crackers. So Blacks were just as racist to White people, than White people were to Blacks."

The irony was that Whites perhaps shared the same feelings toward Gus. When he ventured outside the Dominican community, his dark skin and urban fashion could have him easily identified as African American. Yet he ignored this point. If not, he would be conceding that he was the nation's despised Black other.

The New York Boys were also perplexed by southern Black culture, especially with southern Black hospitality. Before Georgia, they based their racist generalizations on interactions with Black criminals. But in Georgia, they immersed themselves in the general Black community and experienced an overwhelming Black decency. Desperate, they would tweak their racist stereotypes to make sense of their experiences.

For instance, Pablo reasoned that southern Black decency came from church attendance, a logic that still demeaned northern Blacks. "The Black person from the South had more manners," Pablo explained. "Like they would say 'Hi' or 'Good morning' without you knowin' them. You know what it is? It's that Black people in the South, they go to church. They were raised in the church. So they have more morals, a little bit more than the ones in the North. The ones in the North never seen the inside of a church, bro. So they don't got manners or respect like the ones in the South."

Manolo also denigrated northern, inner-city Blacks in his attempts to explain Southern Black decency. Specifically, he invoked the urban Black Other, who personified evil and crime. "Those southern Black people, they're good people, Randy," Manolo explained. "They're not like those [Black] assholes from Brooklyn or the Bronx. The way they treat you, you know, they offered their homes, whatever they have *te lo brinda'* [they offer it to you]. They not lookin' out to rob you or to do somethin' [bad] to you, like the ones from up here.

"For example, we used to bring food [from New York] and take it to this chicken place and this Black woman [the owner] used to cook what we wanted. We used to bring rice, beans, *plátanos,* everything, and she used to cook it, bro. Because the food out there—yo. They eat pork chops, bro, fried. I mean deep fried. Everything with flour and fried. But, yo, she did it, bro. . . . People out there were real nice. They weren't like the Black people up here."

The irony was that Pablo and Manolo ignored how outsiders could racialize their crimes and label Dominicans as violent, evil, and deceitful. For instance, the devious Manolo: he once shredded soap bars into a mound of flakes, blended it with flour, and sold the mixture to a White dealer in Alabama as a kilo of "cocaine." And Pablo (who called Northern Blacks uncivilized): after his girlfriend's drunk father arrived at her home one night, an angry Pablo beat him down, and as he describes it: "I choked the shit out [of] him so bad that I almost killed that motherfucka. I just got tired of that nigga setting a bad example for my daughters."

There was also an alarming nuance to their racism. They were especially hateful toward Black women. That they volunteered this information showed how their racism was entangled with gender.[11] And as I listened to their gendered racist remarks, I wanted so badly to point out the contradictions. Mostly, I wanted to show how they reproduced the oppression of their dark-skinned mothers, grandmothers, and sisters, whom they claimed to hold so dear. However, I did know that, as children, they were ingrained with Trujillo-inspired messages of *mejorando,* or "improving" their race. In fact, I was the object of those teachings as a teenager visiting their homes: first, their mothers teased me about girlfriends, warning me not turn out gay, or *un maricón.* Then, within that gender "education," they taught me race: I had to marry a White woman, they said, to avoid the *problemas* of having a Black child, especially a girl.

Even at that age, I was fascinated with their mothers' contradictions. All of these Dominican mothers had children with dark-skinned Dominican men. All of these Dominican mothers encouraged their sons to pursue women not resembling them. The result: their sons promoted a racial hierarchy that oppressed Black women the most. So when faced with dating them in Georgia, they balked.

"From my own family," Gus explained, "I was hearing that Black women got fucked up hair, that your kids are gonna come out all fucked up, that Black people are ugly, all that shit, bro. And I always heard Salazar call Black people monkeys all the time. I don't even know why he was sayin' that shit. We all come from Black people. If we wanted to, we could like all trace our heritage to Africa. Look at our skin color. And I know that shit, bro. But maybe hearin' all that shit from my family and Salazar got it ingrained in me, like when I was a kid. Maybe that's why I didn't like Black girls. It was weird to me. I wanted to fuck down there [in Georgia], but not Black girls."

Pablo, who had brown skin and tightly curled hair (what he derisively called "nappy" in women), also recalled a racist upbringing. But unlike Gus, he would not admit to its irrationality. Thus, when caught desiring the Black female body, an ashamed Pablo pleaded drunkenness. "I prefer, to be honest with you, the lighter the better," he said. "I could deal with brown skin, but as far as black skin, nah. And not that brown, brown skin either. I'm talkin' about between caramel and white skin, bro. That's as far as I go. I guess it was that shit growin' up. You always heard that you can't be with a Black woman because of her hair and because she had dark skin . . . I guess that's why I don't like Black women. I might'a said that I should bang that Black girl because there was no light-skinned chicks out there [here, he referred to how Gus sometimes joked that he was attracted to Black women]. But I probably said it because I was drunk. But as far as me pursuin' them, nah. That's a negative, B."

Manolo also expressed a gendered racism, denigrating Black women the most. He preferred to have sex with White or Asian women—and even if these women had sex with Black men (which stigmatized them), they were still preferable over Black women. "One time we went to a club and we got this *blanquita* [White girl or woman] and her Philippine friend and they left with us," Manolo recalled. "We drove an hour and a half to that dusty ass town because they said they had women there. We got there and met the White girl and the Philippine girl. But all the Black dudes there had already hit them [had sex with them]. We had like sloppy twenties, ha-ha. We had our plates dirty, but we ate anyway, ha-ha. We didn't care, ha-ha, we just didn't want to mess around with *prietas* [Black women or girls]."

Manolo did admit to having had sex with Black women, but only oral sex: "Before that we only had some Black girls who sucked our dicks. [Then realizing its offensiveness] I don't go to bed with Black girls, Randy. I'm sorry, yo. I'm racist in bed. God forgive me. I can't sleep with a Black girl. So when we saw the White girl and the Philippine girl, that's why we took them. I'm just racist in bed. I'm sorry, yo."

Though I was unsure of the claim's reliability (Pablo and Gus told me stories of Manolo having sex with Black women), its utterance still reinforced Black women's racial and sexual oppression. Deeper and deeper, his words etched Western notions of beauty; deeper and deeper, he etched the longtime sexual degradation of Black women—both on the island and in the United States.

For sex, they claimed to rely on their Puerto Rican female drug couriers. Like Dominicans, Puerto Ricans had a mix of African and Spanish,[12] but, at least in our South Bronx neighborhood, they had generally whiter phenotypes. "In the beginning," Gus explained, "we were gettin' like Puerto Rican girls like from Marcy [Avenue in the Bronx]. Like we would have them transport the drugs down there to bring it to us. And even before she came down, we would be like makin' dibs on who would bag her [have sex with her] when she got down there. That's how bad shit got. And we were doin' that shit because we didn't want to fuck Black girls."

Eventually, though, they gave in. By this point, they were earning lots of drug money and wanted to demonstrate their hypersexual masculinity. True, they could pursue White women, who were plentiful. But White women showed no desire for them (they were, after all, Black Others). So the New York Boys began to pursue Black women—but ones with signs of Whiteness.

"After awhile, it was like 'Fuck it,' we got with the Black girls," Gus explained. "Like the Black girls, they were with it. We were like exotic animals to them, bro. But it took them awhile 'cause like they wanted us, but they ain't know what to make of us. Like we would go out to the clubs and they were always like [in a southern drawl], 'Y'all the New York Boys?' But I started fuckin' with a lot of Black girls after awhile. And I ain't gonna lie, I had a main girl down there. She was Black. But she was redbone Black."

Pablo also secured a steady Black girlfriend. He first saw her in a nightclub and approached her, thinking she was not Black. "The minute I got inside the club, I saw a chick with a huge ol' ass," Pablo explained. "The bitch looked Puerto Rican, bro. She was light skin and had good hair. No nappy hair, B. Her hair was dead. In fact, the whole fuckin' family was light-skinned with good hair. I thought they was all Puerto Rican, bro. When they told me they was Black, I was all fucked up. I'm tellin' you, that family, not one of them had nappy hair. Not one."

Thus, these men experienced *una angustia racial,* or racial anguish—as they struggled to be racially superior men.[13] They lived out the contradiction. All of them could pass for Black. All of them could have the same racism hurled back at them. However, racially, they saw themselves as disappointments, and to overcome this, they derided Black women and pursued women who were Whiter than they were. So their economic pursuits were entangled with that racially divisive, gendered refrain: *Para mejorar la raza.* To improve the race.

REMEMBERING PABLO, "THE MAN"

On his returns to the South Bronx, I remember Pablo as a Prince. He had gold spread across his fingers; bracelets dangling off his wrist; and a thick gold chain that rested admirably on his muscled chest. I remember his sporty German car, which he only drove after dark. After he lent me some jewelry and a couple of hundred dollars, we drove it to pick up our dates, making me feel like a big shot for the night.

I remember him at dance clubs, where he was The Man. There he was, arriving at the nightclub in a white limo, surrounded by us all. There he was, ordering bottles of champagne to attract the women nearby. There he was, drunk, with his eyes half-lidded, now talking to the women, offering them some champagne, some lies . . . Then: *Yo . . . where's Pablo?* There he was! He was at the dance floor's crowded center, pumping his body against "this girl," then snake-like, dropping to his knees to do his trademark move: leaning back slowly, he touched his back to the ground. *Pablo, you the man! Ha-ha!* Then he and she chose each other for the night, and they were gone.

At the time (before I attended graduate school), I thought Pablo had it all. So did his entourage, or the neighborhood guys escorting him to nightclubs. Most were law-abiding and never sold drugs, but given their marginality, they welcomed the high life. Pablo was like a professional athlete or Hollywood star, surrounded by his admirers. And, while the celebrity garnered the attention, the celebrity also footed the bill. The entourage—we tagged along for the ride.

For instance, Jay was an old neighborhood guy, now an accounts manager at a hospital, but back then, he was a high school dropout and a low-wage "shipper" in a warehouse. He remembered marveling at Pablo's lavish spending in nightclubs. "He always had money in his pockets. Like when we went out, he pulled out his money and was always buyin' bottles, like six, seven, eight bottles of Moet. We were drinkin', we had all these girls around us. He was tippin' the bartenders, the waitresses, givin' them mad money. He was just spendin' money like, 'Easy come easy go.' I remember we would leave from his house and he would have like five thousand dollars on him. I was like, 'Damn, how could he spend all this money?'"

Pablo also paid for our club entrances and transportation. Here, he was exercising a hidden, masculine power that I mistook for generosity. He was the adult covering our expenses, as though we were children. Sometimes he spent over five hundred dollars on us—before we even got inside the club. Beannie, a high school dropout who was now a cabdriver, recalled: "He would pay all of our way. Entrance, everything. I remember one time he had rented a limo and me, him, and George went out to this club, and they had this big line and everything. Yo, he paid a hundred dollars [to the bouncer], and we got in. Yo, that line was crazy long, bro. He was always doin' that so we could skip the line."

At the time, we were struggling academically and in low-wage jobs. Someone like Pablo was our superhero, someone who, if only for a moment, made us forget about our unfulfilling lives. For instance, there was George, now a supervisor at a medical center, but back then a part-time youth counselor. When I asked about his feelings while hanging out with Pablo, he admitted: "With Pablo, I felt secure. Like in case I didn't have money, I knew that he had money. So I didn't have that anxiety like, 'Oh, I can't spend all my money,' or anything like that. Like every time we took a cab, he was like 'I got it, I got it.' He would just give the cab money and walk away.

"Yo, what killed me was that he would just spend his money and wouldn't even look to see how much he had left! Ha-ha. Me, I had to count my money every time I spent money. I had to be like, 'Oh, I spent forty [dollars], now I got twenty left.' Like I always had to calculate to make sure that I didn't spend it all. I had to make sure that I had enough for the cab, for food for the diner afterward, ha-ha. That's why he was one of the first people you would ask to see if they were goin' [out to a nightclub]. He was gonna pay for everybody."

The nightclub. This is where I observed Pablo act out what sociologist David Grazian calls the nocturnal self.[14] For Pablo, it was doing the nightclub's ultimate manhood: a hard-drinking drug dealer who spent big money while women adored him. The props and wardrobe were there: his money, clothing, liquor, jewelry, and muscles. He just had to pull off his masculine act.[15] Most of the time, he did it convincingly. For instance, Ralph, who had dropped out of high school and worked in a belt factory, recalled: "Women just went to him, you understand. Pablo was big [muscular], he had the money. He had all these clothes, a lot of gold chains. I remember he used to leave [from the club] with a different woman all the time. Look, one time, he left with one of the girls from this club, that he just met, bro, and she stood with him like the whole week. He bought her a whole wardrobe and everything."

Yet his manhood act had an ugly side. His repeated masculine success made him feel so powerful that he no longer wanted to perform. Now he expected women to accept him with no effort on his part. If they refused his advances, he showed a brute masculinity, one with no discretion or disguise. This made everyone feel uncomfortable. For instance, George recalled: "He had money, you know, and he felt like the women should talk to him because he had money. He felt like he was 'the man.'"

"How did the women act around him?" I asked.

"Some of them thought he was annoying, while others flocked at him."

"Annoying?" I asked.

"Well, Randy, he would get physical, okay. You remember that. He would grab their arm or their hand and pull them, hold them, while he's talkin' to them. And you could see them, like they had one hand pushin' him away, and their head is leanin' back, like, 'Get away from me.' And they're like noddin' their head, like, 'Yeah, yeah' [while he's talking to them]. Then they would push him away. I didn't like that that much. If you're 'the man,' you shouldn't have to force it. He had the money. He was spendin' it. He was always buyin' women drinks, so they knew he had money. I just don't understand it."

Jay remembered when Pablo struck one of his girlfriends. "Yo, I remember, one time one of his girls was there with him. He was drunk, bro, I mean wasted, drunk. He was dancin' with her, he bought her a bottle [of liquor], drinkin', all that, bro. Then we leavin' the club, and he tells her to bounce [leave] with him. She said she couldn't and then all of sudden he just smacked the shit out of her. Yo, he smacked her so hard that she fell and he even fell on the floor with her. I was like, 'Yo, what the fuck you doin'!' Me and Ralph had to get him off of her and put him in a cab . . . Look, Pablo had money, he had jewelry, he was rentin' limos, he was big—why he have to do that? You just get with the next one [woman]. It's not like he didn't have women, bro. Personally, that hittin' shit, he ain't have to do that."

Although I never witnessed Pablo hit women in a nightclub, I saw his physical aggression—the pulling and grabbing—whenever a woman refused his advances. Back then, I too had trouble understanding this, especially since he had no problem meeting women (at one point he had over half a dozen girlfriends). In hindsight, I saw that charm, wit, and dancing were no longer central to his masculine act. His success led to a delusion of masculine grandeur, that all he had to do was step on a stage to get instant female applause. Thus, like superstar athletes, he started expecting women to want him, with no presentation on his part. He was Pablo. The Man.

Almost always, Pablo targeted marginal women. With one exception, all were high school dropouts, some of them young mothers who were on public assistance or unemployed. Thus, in the relationship marketplace, where people choose mates based on resources and abilities, these women were less desirable to stable, legally employed men. Their best economic hope was someone like Pablo. Like them, he was a product of larger social, economic, and residential inequalities. And though he dressed sharp and spent lots of money, he could not hide his core marginality. He was, after all, a crack and cocaine dealer. So they pursued him. His masculine ego soared.

For instance, with amusement and pride, Pablo recalled how these marginalized women put up with his masculine antics: "I remember I had four or five chicks in the club one night," Pablo recalled. "I remember Tanya was there, Tina was there, Maribel was there, and there was one more, I forget her name, I know she had a big ass . . . she was light-skinned with a huge ass. That night, I ended up breaking out with Maribel and she knew all those bitches were there.

"I remember I took her on shopping spree one time, bro. Yo, that shit was funny. She picked out the other girls' gifts! It's like I had went to buy all those bitches Christmas gifts and I took her with me. And she was cool with it, bro. She was like pickin' out their gifts, ha-ha. She got the best gift, though. She got these big ass custom-made earrings. They were made out of gold, had diamonds, all that shit. I spent like fifteen hundred dollars on those shits."

Pablo knew he could play on both their economic hopelessness and their limited access to financially stable men. Through occasional shopping sprees and costly dinners, he won their affection and started using money as his main masculine plan. He would later conflate the women's survival tactics with a stereotype—that all women could be bought. For instance, in a frustrating debate I had with him, Pablo claimed that *all* women would offer sex if the "money was right."

"I tell you why," Pablo explained. "I met this chick one time [in a club], and just fuckin' around I told her I would give her five hundred dollars if she came home with me for that night. Guess what? She came home with me . . . but I got my five hundred dollars worth, bro, ha-ha. I made that bitch do everything, bro."

"So you did it once and now you're saying that all women would do it?" I asked.

"That's right, they would all do it," he responded.

"Bro, you got it wrong," I told him. "In sociology, we would say that you're generalizing from one case to an entire population. And you can't do that. Just because you found one woman who did it, that doesn't mean every woman would do it."

"Well, your sociology shit is wrong," he retorted. "Every woman would do it. I'm tellin' you, from my experience."

"Suppose someone just met you," I countered, "and found out you were a drug robber. Would it be right for them to say that all Dominican men—all of them, bro—are drug robbers?"

Long Pause. Then: "Nigga, I don't care what you say with your sociology," he answered. "We're not talkin' about men. We talkin' about women. From my experience, they would do it. Like I said, I got experience in that shit. You don't."

This exchange lasted about another five minutes. And no matter how many times I unraveled his logic, Pablo remained stubbornly sexist. The hard part was explaining how his relationships were with marginal women, who could only turn to someone like him. I simply did not want to devalue these women, who were already oppressed on many levels. They were minorities. They were poor. They were uneducated. They were stereotyped as unfit mothers who were greedy for government handouts. Since their standpoint was mostly ignored,[16] it was easy to vilify them—one more time—for drifting toward men like Pablo. And I knew that he would lift my observation from its context and drop it within his sexist frame.

Yet I knew that much of his sexism resulted from his dealing success. This was when, at the height of superstardom, he would spend thousands of dollars for a night out. This was when the most marginalized women flocked to him, when he was The Man on the block. This was when he made the link between money, respect, women, and manhood, a link that remained strong from that point on. From now on, everything had a price tag—even success, friendship, and love. The moment was that strong.

RUNNING FROM GEORGIA

After about ten months of partying and dealing, the New York Boys felt impervious to law enforcement. So they moved from the "boondocks" to the middle of the small town. Though this brought them closer to customers, it made them more conspicuous. They cared not.

Then on a foggy morning, on Valentine's Day: raid. The police would find a machine gun, cash, a scale, and notebook with scribbled drug transactions. Gus, Pablo, and Alex were arrested. The dealers had been warned the previous day about a possible raid. But feeling invincible, they paid little heed.

"We had an inside scoop and we just didn't listen," Pablo explained. " 'Cause some guy, this customer we had, he knew people connected to law enforcement out there. The police told him that they were lookin' for three Haitian guys—'cause they didn't know what Dominican was—for three Haitian guys from New York. They thought we were Haitians, real light skin Haitians, ha-ha. He said that they were gonna bust those Haitian guys during the week. But what we did? 'Ah, fuck them niggas. Let them come. Whenever they come they ain't gonna find shit.' But they arrested us. And it was all because we moved to town. You don't shit where you eat. And that's what happened there."

A week later, the New York Boys were out on bail. Alex went back to New York and was arrested within a week on a gun charge. Gus and Pablo, who had lost a lot of money, needed quick cash. Together, they bought twenty-five guns to sell in New York. Driving on I-95, they made it through the middle Atlantic states, then into New Jersey with no hassle. But just as they were set to enter New York, the New Jersey State Police pulled them over. They found the guns in the car's trunk. Pablo and Gus were arrested.

In jail, Pablo pretended to be a college student with no bank account (hence his seven thousand dollars in cash). Claiming no knowledge of the guns, he was released. Gus, though, claimed gun ownership and took a plea deal of three years. As he later said, he did his time in New Jersey easily, "standing on one leg."

FIVE

Crack is Dead

1994–1997. THE HUSTLE AND BUSTLE of the Bronx drug world had quieted, almost disappeared. Beepers and cell phones replaced brazen street dealers. Profits were down; corporate-style earnings, gone. New crack dealers were in for a big surprise. No customers. Crack had stopped its rumble, settled into a deep sleep.[1] Times had changed.

While Gus was doing his prison bid in New Jersey, Pablo made one bad business move after another. He was not alone. Most of the crack dealers I knew were also doing poorly and complaining about low sales. Yet the heroin dealers in the area were experiencing a surprising sales boom. Now neighborhoods that had been afflicted with crack were featuring long lines of haggard dope fiends, sometimes starting from a dope spot and wrapping around a corner.[2] As a struggling crack dealer, Pablo turned to the heroin action. But he had gotten a late start.

The heroin market had become saturated during his Georgia days, and he struggled in his efforts to launch a neighborhood operation. Determined, he tried to enter the infamous heroin market in the St. Ann's section of the South Bronx. However, its powerful Puerto Rican owner demanded two thousand dollars daily for the right to sell next to his workers. And for two weeks, Pablo barely made the daily rent. He was out.

New plan. With his brother Geraldo, Pablo tried to enter the heroin market of El Barrio, or Manhattan's East Harlem. However, when I visited Pablo there, I often sensed tension between his Dominican workers and the established Puerto Rican dealers. One day, the barrio dealers pulled out their weapons and confronted Pablo, ordering him to leave. Pablo exited, trying his luck in other neighborhoods, but always failing. Times were hard.

"Everything I did wasn't working," Pablo recalled. "I mean, I had little deals, whatever, whatever. But it just wasn't the same like before. That dope [heroin] shit, forget it. I was just losin' money. Like for example, you have to pay people to pack[age] it up. The bitches I had doin' it had to wear masks on their faces 'cause that shit gets into the air and gets you high. I had to pay those bitches to do it, and I wasn't even makin' money yet. Then you had to pay rent to a big Willie [a powerful dealer] to put your shit in his spot. I was just losin' money, left and right."

Now Gus. After three years in prison, he was back in the Bronx, looking to get on his feet. But the crack-cocaine market was depressed. Like Pablo, he tried to ride heroin's comeback. He partnered with a Colombian dealer, and within a few days, he had some clients wanting heroin. However, the quality of the dope was poor and Gus lost his clientele. He then partnered with an African dealer who sold better heroin and promised a higher commission. But he never realized the full profit potential. He was soon arrested for assaulting an off-duty correction officer—over a parking spot. He was found guilty and did an additional eight months for the parole violation.

Upon his release, Gus experienced the same dead streets, going weeks without consistent drug work. He peddled drugs here and there, sometimes connecting a seller and client, sometimes doing deals on his own. But it was a changed drug world, an uphill struggle, where it was hard to get a drug operation rolling.

"Dope [heroin] was the big thing now," Gus remembered. "But it was hard to get into because the Colombians and the Africans was the ones who had control over it . . ."

"How about settin' up a dope spot on the street, like puttin' workers out there to sell for you?"

"Nah, man, that shit was too hard," Gus responded. "You already had niggas [dealers] who had their dope spots for years, man. They got their customers already, people know who they are. You know Pablo and Geraldo tried that shit and all they did was lose money. Shit just got hard."

In all, drug market opportunities shifted during the 1990s. Unlike stockbrokers, who had advanced forecasting methods, these men had no warning that the crack market was ending. And when they tried to sell "dope," they faced ethnic and territorial barriers: Africans and Colombians had established wholesale heroin distribution niches, and Puerto Ricans, who had never given up heroin dealing, controlled its distribution on the street. The Dominicans were now ethnic outsiders to the lucrative drug market.

But what had happened to the crack market?

WAS IT THE COMMUNITY OR FUCKIN' GIULIANI?

The study participants blamed their crack woes on tougher policing. Like many Americans, they got their information from politicians and the media, which credited harsh drug policies for the demise of the crack market.[3] Also, this conservative idea meshed well with a drug-dealing ethos— might makes right. The Dominican drug dealers did the math: they counted the rising numbers of police officers who stopped and frisked them; they counted the family and friends who were being imprisoned or jailed. They came to agree with the message being disseminated by New York's top politicians: that Mayor Rudolph Giuliani and Police Commissioner William Bratton, with their "zero-tolerance" policing, had cleaned up the streets of New York City.

Giuliani and Bratton had implemented the zero-tolerance approach, which targeted "quality-of-life" offenses, in the mid-nineties. They reasoned that a focus on minor offenders, such as street pissers, liquor drinkers, subway fare beaters, and sponge-carrying squeegee men could deter more egregious crimes. How? Upon frisk and detainment, police officers might find an illegal knife, a gun, or an outstanding warrant for arrest. So society avoided a potential crime, police took a bad person off the street, and a cautious criminal now left his illegal weapon at home.[4]

As New York City's crime dropped, the link between zero tolerance and crime reduction became the conventional wisdom among journalists, politicians, and observers from around the world.[5] The view would also trickle down to the streets. For instance, though arrested under the watch of Mayor David Dinkins and Police Commissioner Lee Brown, Pablo blamed Mayor Giuliani for his crack market failures, and conflated community empowerment with tougher policing. "The streets died, bro, when Giuliani came to power," Pablo said, resignedly. "He put cops everywhere, all in the streets. . . . [before] it was fun out here. You coulda' done any crime you wanted and you could'a probably got away with it. But now? *Olvídate, loco.* Everybody's quick to call the police. I remember before you could practically shoot somebody, and nobody know who did it. Now? Everybody seein' everything. They don't mind their fuckin' business . . . Giuliani, that fuckin' bastard. We didn't want Dinkins in power, for what? For that Italian motherfucka that don't give a shit about nobody, bro. He's probably related to Mussolini. We got a fuckin' dictator in power, ha-ha-ha!"

Gus also perceived the demise of the crack market as the work of Mayor Giuliani, mistakenly giving him credit for "Operation Take Back Our Community" and confusing this community-policing program with zero-tolerance policing, which came later. "It was 'Operation Take Back' that fucked everything up, bro." Gus explained. "They started puttin' more fuckin' police officers everywhere, bro. They would even have like police officers in vans and shit, drivin' around lookin' for niggas to harass. For any little reason, bro, niggas was fuckin' stoppin' and friskin' you. That motherfucka Giuliani started all that shit, bro. That's when all that shit [drug dealing] ended."

Tukee concurred. As we sat on the hood of a car one afternoon, he recounted how the police had stormed his apartment several months earlier. They had searched for drugs, but only found a gun and the legal substances used to adulterate heroin. Tukee used this experience to explain poor drug market conditions. "They did that shit overnight," he explained. "They can't do that. Fuckin' Giuliani, that motherfucka . . ."

[Gus arrived with some weed. He and Tukee began smoking.]

"That cop said I got caught with two ounces of coke," Tukee continued, "and that shit was vitamin A or C or some other . . . and he knew it. Yo, I'm in a room, that nigga was like, 'We got it!' I was like, 'What the fuck do these niggas got?' Ha-ha-ha. I was like, 'They found a gun.' They came back, it's like, 'No! Found drugs!' I was like, 'What fuckin' drugs?' A-w-w-w, man. Ha-ha!"

"Bingo!" Pablo said, imitating a police officer.

"Them niggas closed off the whole block, like [it was] some real bullshit," Tukee continued.

"What was it that they found again, Vitamin A?" I asked.

"Vitamin A, C, and sugar," Tukee responded.

"What the fuck you had that for?" I asked.

"It was Manito[l], bro, to cut some dope," Tukee answered.

"But they can't take you in for that," I said.

"Nah, but they put you through the hassle, bro," Tukee said, angrily. "Fuckin' pigs. They put you through all that shit, they knowin' they ain't got shit. It's all this fuckin' bullshit now."

While on the street, I observed how zero tolerance raised their resentment toward police officers. For instance, one night, some officers visited the bodega a couple of times, demanding that the store's owner lower its music. Whether a neighborhood resident called the police and complained, I was unsure. But these men seethed, seeing this incident as police encroachment on their space.

"Yo, what the fuck happened to the music?" Pablo asked Dee, who worked in the store.

"Cops crazy," Dee explained. "Niggas got up and went in the store and said lower the music, bro. Turn it off, as a matter fact."

"What?" asked Tukee, disbelieving.

"Yeah, Five-O is fuckin' buggin' out here," observed Pablo.

"Yo, why they actin' like that?" asked Tukee.

"I don't know what the fuck is up with these niggas [police]," Pablo exclaimed. "Yo, how the fuck you gonna say lower the fuckin' music?"

"Oh my God, bro," Tukee said, in disbelief.

"Yo, he said lower it more," Dee added. "That shit was like at real low already."

"Yeah, I couldn't even hear it from here, kid!" Pablo agreed.

"Then he [police officer] was like turn it off," Dee continued.

"He's pussy, though," Tukee said, referring to the bodega owner. "'Cause that's me, that's my store, that shit is stayin' on, man. Man, you don't like it, do something about it."

"Yeah, get the fuck outta here," Pablo added. "I hate those fuckin' motherfuckas [police officers], bro."

"You see I be goin' in there and raisin' it up," Dee explained. "But they [the owners] be on some bullshit. They be lowerin' that shit when I come outside. He don't even talk to the cop right, you know what I'm sayin'?"

"It's that these niggas be scared, man," Tukee explained. "Ya don't know how to talk to cops, man. Fuck po-lice, man. I'll tell you something about po-lice, nigga. You show them niggas that you know shit, those motherfuckas can't do shit to you. I know how to talk to the po-lice, B. Those fuckin' bitches."

At one point, I also believed that tougher policing reduced street dealing. During the early 1990s, I noted more uniformed officers standing on corners or walking through neighborhoods. Some were mean to us, disrupting our stickball games and ordering us to go home. But others were friendly, taking the time to talk to us about sports or the city's civil service exams. Later,

I learned that it was Mayor Dinkins and Police Commissioner Brown's policies that heightened their presence. Like Gus, I linked their community policing to the later zero-tolerance policies and tied both to the decline of the crack market.

For the most part, I was wrong.

Surely, higher police presence could drive outdoor drug markets indoors. But crime statistics suggested something else. In his penetrating analysis of NYC's dramatic 1990s murder rate drop, sociologist Andrew Karmen pointed to several important developments that related to the decline of the crack market:[6]

First, NYC's street crime, drug-related crime, and murder rates had been dropping under Mayor David Dinkins' watch, *before* Mayor Giuliani entered office.

Second, major cities across the nation—all with different policing styles—also experienced crime drops during the 1990s.[7]

And third, in the 1990s, young offenders tested positive for cocaine much less frequently than in the 1980s.[8]

These developments suggested that the crack epidemic, which brought a 1980s crime wave, started to contract and lose youth appeal during the early 1990s. However, since crack's demise was most obvious during the mid-nineties, zero tolerance *seemed* to have quelled it. So when these Dominican men failed to land a viable crack-selling location, they blamed the police. When a tidal wave of customers failed to flood their crack spots, they blamed the police. When anything failed—they blamed the police.

But there was another factor. During the late eighties, urban residents endured extreme suffering as they watched loved ones get trapped in crack's seismic quake. Some were beaten, shot, stabbed, or raped. Some were arrested, imprisoned, or jailed. Others were killed. Only a handful emerged unscathed, untouched. Enough was enough. The community took a stand. It lobbied the city to eliminate crack dealers from its neighborhoods.[9] Some public officials listened, realizing that tough policing alone did little to stop crack's rumble.[10] The focus then went to shielding youth from the lure of crack.

For instance, along with more community policing, Mayor Dinkins and Commissioner Brown added youth programs to their new policing initiative, the Safe Streets, Safe City Act. Also, NYC's Black police association, the Grand Council of Guardians, created a community policing program called "Operation Take Back Our Community." Both allowed high-risk youth to attend after-school programs in crime prevention, conflict resolution, and academics, while providing late-night recreation during weekdays and weekends.[11]

More important, the new generation of urban youth sought liberation. As urban anthropologist Ric Curtis observed, many of them had witnessed crack's effects on brothers, fathers, sisters, mothers, uncles, aunts, and neighbors.[12] They also saw a small cadre of committed crack users who would do anything for crack. Youths labeled them "crackheads," a green light to ridicule them and beat them, unprovoked.[13]

Crack-using women bore the worst stigma.[14] In fact, their denunciation reached the rap industry, a cultural institution that warned us of crack market perils. Like the streets, the rap songs often framed drug market males as heroic victims, while framing drug market women as crude, immoral, and calculating villains. The controversial Brand Nubians reflected this misogynistic trend, producing a rap hit, "Slowdown," directed at women:

> *Your ways and actions are like those of a savage,*
> *If the price is right, then anyone can ravage ...*
> *So don't come around trying to make a profit,*
> *At the expense of another man—Stop it,*
> *'Cause, you see, you're a freak show of the town,*
> *Know what I think you ought to do is—Slowdown.*[15]

Such stigmatizing images had the effect of making hardcore drugs look unattractive to urban youth. Their drugs of choice would no longer be crack or cocaine,[16] but marijuana and "a forty." The marijuana would be smoked in a "blunt," which was made from unrolling a cheap cigar (often a "Phillies Blunt"), emptying the tobacco, and then rerolling it with marijuana. "A forty" referred to a forty-ounce bottle of inexpensive malt liquor beer. Soon these practices and sentiments formed the marijuana/blunts generation, a generation of youth rejecting crack's use, violence, and lure. *Crack? Get the fuck outta here.*

The crack era was dead.

I AM A STICKUP KID, POST-1997

By 1997, Pablo and Gus were at an impasse. They were a part of a small cohort of displaced crack dealers struggling to survive within the drug market. They had invested their prime years in the crack game, when most young people were preparing for the legitimate labor force. So they knew how to manage drug spots, negotiate drug deals, and act around drug dealers— everything that had little use in a service economy demanding more subservience, less masculinity, more education, less resistance, and more middle-class etiquette.[17] The likelihood of their finding legal work that offered the money and status they had enjoyed in Georgia was zero. They would try to stay in the game.

Pablo donned his New York Boy hat again. He partnered with a dope dealer, Elias, who sold heroin in New Bedford, Massachusetts.[18] Elias initially hired Pablo as muscle, to keep a close watch on an untrustworthy worker in New Bedford. The amount of heroin the worker received was not producing the expected profit. Pablo soon discovered why the worker was coming up short. He claimed that he could only make fifty bags from the amount of heroin given to him. But when Pablo bagged up the heroin, he produced seventy-five bags. He concluded that the worker was stealing twenty-five bags a day, which was over two hundred dollars daily. Pablo confronted him:

"Yo, I know what the fuck you doin'," Pablo recalled telling him. "'You better fuckin' start baggin' up more fuckin' bags.' Then the nigga starts coppin' a plea, talkin' about how he's puttin' more in each bag by mistake, that's why he could only make fifty, that Elias is fucked up for havin' me watch him, all that shit, bro. I just told him that from now on, shit better be straight."

After Elias' worker was arrested for having a sexual relationship with a minor (a fourteen-year-old White girl whose mother had called the police), Pablo demanded equal partnership in the dope business. Though hesitant at first, Elias agreed. The deal was that Elias and Pablo would alternate staying in New Bedford: Pablo would sell dope one week, Elias would sell the next. With this arrangement, each earned about twenty-six hundred dollars in profit during his assigned week.

To avoid detection, Pablo paid a woman to do his dirty work. "I used to tell her where to go and give her the names of the people," Pablo explained. "I would say, 'Go to this side of town, that side of town, meet this person, that person.' She did everything. Instead of twenty-six hundred dollars, I was getting only two thousand 'cause I was paying her six hundred to do all that shit. But I ain't give a fuck. There was nothin' on me. If anything, all that shit was on her. But this nigga Elias was a stingy bastard. He did all that shit by himself. That's why he got popped [arrested]."

So Elias was eventually arrested. Worse, Pablo lost his dope connection. He had no more drug-dealing opportunities, no matter how he hard he tried. Pablo was up against the wall. It seemed like the end of the line. He needed an opportunity to hang on to his version of the American Dream.[19]

Pablo would find that opportunity in stickups—robbing drug dealers for their drugs and cash.[20] He had gotten his start during his New Bedford days, when he was recruited by a drug robbery crew that was a man short. Jackpot. He earned eleven thousand dollars on his first robbery. Then, after his New Bedford dealing ended, he was recruited for another robbery, where he earned eighteen thousand dollars. "After that shit," Pablo explained, "I was like, 'Fuck dope, fuck coke, fuck all that shit.' All that shit is a fuckin' headache. Dealin' with customers, Five-O [police], snitches, you ain't makin' money, shit is slow . . . I was like, 'Fuck that shit. From now on, stickups.' Boom, get your money quick. I'ma stickup kid from now on."

Because of his reputation, Gus was recruited for a drug robbery too: a suitcase snatch. An informant revealed the route of a drug dealer who walked daily with two kilos of cocaine. With an accomplice, Gus approached the dealer and successfully robbed him. He earned seventeen thousand dollars. Ecstatic, he flew to the Dominican Republic and splurged, spending the money in a couple of months on drinking, dancing, women, and drugs. He was soon back in New York for another drug robbery. This time, he earned twelve thousand dollars and went back to D.R. to spend it again on drinking, dancing, women, and drugs. Then he came back for another drug robbery, where he earned six thousand dollars. Then another: seventeen thousand dollars. Then another: four thousand dollars.

For Pablo and Gus, the stickups were a godsend. No more drug selling on the streets. No more packing vials, no more cutting and blending the lactose with the coke. No more headaches because of being short on the count. No more watching and checking the sidewalk crowd. No more double-locking doors, no more sneaking a peep through curtained windows. No more worries about those clean-cut guys, the *parecen* DTs, or undercovers, wearing the sports jersey, cheap jeans, and sneakers. No more dealing with corrupted wholesalers, the *sucios* who were always trying to peddle cheap powdered coke. No more long trips to New England or down South, to those new worlds where the journey doubled the risk of arrest. No more worries about those dirty *joloperos!* The stickup kids *que no tienen madres!* Who will slice you, maim you, shoot you—kill you—*for your shit!*

Nah, no more worries.

Pablo and Gus were now the hyenas of the drug world, the same stickup kids they had once worried about as dealers. Now *they* roamed in packs. *They* caused fear and panic among dealers. *They* searched for opportunities to take hard-won drug earnings. It was best not talk about a drug stash around them. They didn't care. They would just take it, whether it was from friend or foe.

They put their hopes in drug robberies as their last chance at capitalist success. It was a long shot, but their American success clock was ticking, and they were running out of time . . . it was too late to go back to school . . . it was too late to undo a criminal record . . .

Stickups—that was the only way to go.

In short, for these Dominican men, the end of the crack era was crucial. It was the moment when they faced extreme doubt, defeat, and frustration. It was the moment that put them on a path toward more violence and self-destruction. It was the moment that made the sum of their experiences—in their neighborhoods, families, and schools—equal a brutality that most people could never fathom. It was, overall, the moment that would become the barometer for the rest of their lives.

They were stickup kids now.

FIGURE 1. *Flag football.* Not all neighborhood youths participate in the local drug market. These teenagers are playing organized flag football in John Mullay Park.

FIGURE 2. *Mural backdrop.* A neighborhood child. The backdrop is the zoned elementary school featuring a mural of child-inspired racial and gender harmony. This stands in stark contrast to illegal drug market behaviors of the stickup kids, who hang out across the street.

FIGURE 3. *Pablo with gun*. Pablo shows off an illegal handgun, an important tool in drug robberies.

FIGURE 4. *Randol Contreras against the wall*. The author is hanging out in front of a dilapidated building in his early teens. During this period the South Bronx was seriously blighted and the crack era was just getting its start.

FIGURE 5. *Randol Contreras with guns.* The author displays his yearnings to be a successful crack dealer during his late teenage years.

FIGURE 6. *Art deco building.* This beautiful art deco building lines much of the neighborhood sidewalk. Now serving impoverished residents, it once housed the borough's middle class.

FIGURE 7. *Grand Concourse*. This row of art deco buildings on 167th Street is characteristic of most of the Grand Concourse Boulevard, once the pride of the Bronx.

FIGURE 8. *Elevated no. 4.* The no. 4 train rumbles nearby on the elevated tracks that pass over McClellan Avenue. Its constant presence blends into the neighborhood sights and sounds.

FIGURE 9. *Stairs.* Some of the neighborhood's young men use the public stairwell as a hangout. The scattered litter shows how all of the stairwell is used for recreational eating and drinking.

FIGURE 10. *Public stairwell with people.* Local residents use the public stairwell as shortcut to higher residential areas. The pedestrian traffic is constant during early mornings, late afternoons, and evenings.

FIGURE 11. *Gas station.* This gas station is a few hundred feet from the public stairwell and gives the neighborhood its distinctive gasoline-based aroma.

FIGURE 12. *Neighborhood 3.* This is the northern portion of the neighborhood, where most of the stickup kids live. It starts a long incline and bend, which takes residents to the topmost residential areas.

———

PART TWO

Doing the Stickup

Here's the deal,
we shatter his grill,
and drill fuck him,
oral torture,
No doubt,
the shit is holocaust,
In two minutes tops
he's guaranteed to cap and give up all the morsels
It's settled,
Blitt up,
put on your medal,
foot on the pedal,
we got a half-hour
before the plan sours
like Amaretto,
Far from the ghetto,
A rebel of chance,
The devil in pants,
Out for fast cash,
Level advance,
Takin' a chance . . .

Big Punisher "Fast Money"

SIX

The Girl

MELISSA SHUDDERED VISIBLY AS SHE reflected on her drug robbery role. "Afterwards, I was like, 'Arrggh!'" Melissa said, breaking into a laugh. "I kissed a *viejo* in the lips and all that. Arghhh!" Sensing her disgust, I asked if she would do it again.

"Yeah," Melissa said, smiling.

"Why?" I asked, surprised.

"Why not? For the money. It's easy and fast." We laughed.

I was in Julio's apartment, listening to Melissa's accounts of Saturday night's drug robbery. We sat in his bedroom, which was neat, but with old linoleum covering the floor. Melissa, who spoke in a low, calm voice, was the "The Girl." Her job was to seduce the dealer and lure him to an apartment. Once the crew began interrogating him, Melissa's task was done. This had been her first time doing a drug robbery.

Melissa was introduced to drug robberies by Julio, who had a *compadrazgo* tie to Pablo (they were God brothers) and had kept in touch through the years. Julio sold marijuana part-time to supplement his income as a doorman in Manhattan. The opportunity for a large windfall came when Gus asked him about "a girl" for a drug robbery. Julio immediately suggested Melissa, a neighborhood girl who smoked weed all day, "got a fat ass," and was definitely "down for that type of shit." In exchange for recruiting Melissa, Julio asked to be included in the drug robbery. Gus agreed. And after spending several minutes with her, he felt she was just right for the job.

Melissa, who was nineteen years old, was born into a poor Dominican immigrant family. During the late 1970s, her parents migrated from the Dominican Republic and settled in the South Bronx, renting an apartment a few blocks from Fordham Road. Her father secured steady work as their apartment building's superintendent. Melissa's mother remained unemployed and received public assistance, a stay-at-home mom to four boys and a girl. Melissa was the youngest child.

Melissa grew up during the 1980s, when the neighborhood was saturated with drug dealers. Even today, Melissa complained, "there's too much drugs and violence. You always gotta watch your back or be afraid that you're gonna get shot one day." Her parents, she said, tried to protect her from the drugs and violence by giving her a curfew. During the day, she came home about every two hours to "*calentar la casa un chin*" (warm the house up a bit).

Yet Melissa would be drawn into drugs. First, her father started selling drugs from their apartment. "He had all the drugs stashed in the house, like in closets, and money," recalled Melissa. "I used to see people standing outside the house [apartment] a lot and that was the only explainable reason he had all this money. Like in zip-lock bags he had his stash, the pounds of weed, or whatever else he had."

Second, Melissa's home was also a meeting place for her brother's drug-dealing business. As a child, she watched her brother hurry friends into his bedroom and then close the door. Later, though, he allowed Melissa into the room, which served as his office. "They would be having weed and the money," she recalled, "and they used to count the bags and the money in my brother's room."

Finally, she recalled that her father used cocaine, heroin, and marijuana. And sometimes, "when he used to smoke joints and stuff like that, he'll be like, 'Oh, Melissa throw this out for me.'" Obediently, she took the "roaches" (a tiny portion of the joint that was left unsmoked) and threw them away. But around the age of nine or ten, Melissa began experimenting with the roaches. "I used to be like, 'What's this?' And then I started taking some. I started smoking it."

By the age of twelve, Melissa was "smoking heavy," which led to cutting her junior high school classes. She and some friends attended hooky parties, where "everybody was drinking and smoking . . . and fucking." In high school, her truancy worsened. After homeroom, she and some girlfriends would cut to a friend's house, spending their days smoking weed, watching movies, doing "petty shit."

One day, her older brothers set up a family meeting and revealed a crisis: her father had AIDS. "They told me I gotta finish school, my father's dyin', my mother has nothin'. We gonna have to support her. That's when I realized that I gotta shape up. That's when I went to all my classes." Still, Melissa continued skipping school through a rotating cutting system: "Like, let's say fourth period was English," Melissa explained. "I wouldn't go to it for three days. Next week, I'll make sure to go to that class, and I'll cut another class, you know, just to even it out."

I asked her why she felt the need to keep cutting classes. "Because I'm a pothead!" she blurted out. "I had to smoke all the time, and one period at lunch wasn't enough for me."

After graduation, Melissa delayed entering college. She wanted a job to relieve her school "stress." However, she detested supermarket employment, which she had done during high school. As a woman, she felt uneasy when her employer stared at her and made lewd remarks. "The manager, he was a pervert," she recalled, "'Cause in the summer, or like when it got hot, I used to wear like little tank tops or little skirts. He'll look at you like with that deceiving look, like if he's undressin' you with his eyes. I felt uncomfortable. Or like the little comments I know he'll say to other managers that I'll overhear."

She also didn't like the job. Like most children of immigrants, Melissa compared herself with native-born Americans as to work conditions and status. She hated the long hours, the repetitive work, and especially the rude customers. "I hate workin', standin' up all those hours, the labor," Melissa said. "I was too smart for that, I thought. That's why I quit. Because I got tired of just standin' there, and packin', and dealin' with people's shit. People [customers] would just say the stupidest shit and get me mad. Sometimes I just wanted throw the food at them. But you couldn't do that. You had to take whatever they gave you."

Still, Melissa was unqualified for better work, and she returned to the supermarket. After a few months, however, she quit again: "Same thing that happened last time—the people, I couldn't deal with them."

Frustrated, Melissa yearned for the money she had once earned as an underground stripper. During her junior year, her cousin, a veteran dancer, recruited her to dance in a Yonkers housing project. "She knew mad people and I had a nice body," Melissa recalled, "so, I was like, 'Fuck it. It's a lot of money.'"

Mostly, she danced in a "ghetto-ass little laundry room" and entertained a variety of men—drug dealers, lawyers, doctors, transit workers, and public housing employees. She earned between twenty-five and fifty dollars a dance, depending on the customer's job.

"My cousin would be like, 'Oh, he's a doctor, charge this nigga this. This one you charge this, this and that.' And I'll be like a'ight. I would be dancin', strip, whatever, and I would get on top of them, and excite them, and whatever. The song stops—bye-bye."

Each song made up a dance, and for ten to fifteen dances, Melissa earned between two hundred and four hundred dollars. So in a couple of hours, she almost doubled the income she earned as a low-wage cashier. The money was so good, she explained, that she had trouble hiding it. Her mother soon became suspicious over her expensive jewelry and clothes. *You sellin' drugs?* she asked Melissa. No, Melissa answered, she was getting showered with gifts from boyfriends. "I used to always be like, 'My boyfriend, my boyfriend.' She [mother] used to be like, 'How many fuckin' boyfriends you got?'"

Her cousin moved to California, ending Melissa's lucrative dance career. Now she had no idea of what to do. I asked Melissa if she thought she would ever strip again.

"Hell yeah, I liked the money," Melissa answered, "Yeah, I would do it again, in a heartbeat."

I asked Melissa why she liked to strip.

"Because it's easy and niggas is suckas [suckers], that's why," she laughed, "and I could get them for money, that's why."

"So, that's what makes you feel good, gettin' them?"

"Yeah, and the money is fast," she laughed. "Who doesn't like fast money?"

In the end, Melissa was well suited for "The Girl" role in a drug robbery. She had grown up seeing her father, brother, and friends sell crack, cocaine, and marijuana. She had grown up in a poor neighborhood and had internalized American materialism. She had experienced sexual objectification and later used her body for income. And she saw men as "suckas." So when Julio introduced her to Gus, it was a godsend.

"I really needed some money," she recalled. "Gus knew how to get some money—some fast money. I already knew I could use my body and myself to get that money. They wanted to use me as the girl to go get the guy and to get him into an apartment."

Melissa was now The Girl.

Saturday afternoon. After some driving and walking around a targeted dealer's neighborhood, the crew finally spotted him. He stood in front of a building, talking with a younger friend. According to Melissa, she left the car and walked over to them, pretending to be a weed customer.

"I told him," Melissa recalled, "like, 'I smoke a lot of weed, but later on I want to buy an ounce with my friends, and maybe you know somebody else that could get better weed because I know the weed's good out here.'"

The dealer hesitated, saying, "I'll see what I could do. Come back later." Melissa was surprised. She assumed he would make immediate sexual advances. Instead, "he was really fightin' me," Melissa recalled, "and was like, 'you just come out here and I'll be out here at this time.'"

Melissa then invited him out, saying, "I'm gonna go home and get dressed and smoke with friends and come back. And we probably go to Studio 84" (a local nightclub on 145th Street and Broadway). "But you're so young," the dealer said, "Guys are gonna see you with an old guy. You shouldn't even come out here. Just come over here when you want drugs." Melissa countered, "*Papi*, age does not matter." The guy was "real old, like forty-five or something like that," and he kept insisting that "age does matter."

Melissa persisted. "I was like, 'I'm nineteen, I got my own apartment, I finished school, I work. Nobody does for me. I know I'm a woman, I'ma independent woman. And I'ma let you know, I could take you out as a matter of fact. You don't gotta spend on me.' He still didn't go for it. He was like, 'Okay, whatever.'"

Melissa encountered more problems: the dealer's younger friend started making advances toward her. "He was fuckin' my whole shit up," Melissa recalled. "He was young and he was tryin' to kick it to me. Then the old guy started sayin' that I should be with him [the younger man]. He was like, '*Vete con el. E' tu edad.*' [Go with him. He's your age.] Then I started tellin' him that I didn't like him. I told him [in her broken Spanish], "*Que el no me interesa. El ere' feo. Yo quiero ti [sic].*' [He does not interest me. He's ugly. I want you.] Then he was like, 'You like older men?' I was like, 'Yeah, little kids can't do nothin' for me.'" Again, Melissa invited him to the dance club, insisting that they meet later. "And that's when he gave me his beeper number." The dealer finally gave in.

Afterward, Melissa walked down a couple of blocks and met with Gus, Julio, Jonah, and David, who were watching. They then drove to the Bronx apartment where they planned to trap the dealer. Melissa had to remember the address—she was going to pretend that it was her home. Later, Julio dropped off Gus and David in the park. He then drove Melissa to their neighborhood, where she could finally smoke some weed. "I was feelin' hype," she remembered, "and I just needed to smoke some weed before I went back over there. Yeah, I was a little bit nervous."

Now nighttime.

Melissa met with the dealer, noting that he was dressed for a night of dancing. "He was all dressed up," Melissa said, laughing, "and I still had on the same jeans and shirt." The dealer looked at her clothing and asked, "What happened?" Lying, Melissa explained that she was locked out of her apartment and could not contact friends. The dealer then took her to a small social club with no dress code so that Melissa would not feel out of place.

As they sat listening to the music, Melissa tried to get him drunk. "I was like, 'if that's what I'm gonna drink, you gonna drink that too. Fuck that. If I'm gonna get fucked up, you gonna get fucked up too.' So for every drink that I drank, he had two drinks. Then I was making him buy rum, doing rum shots and everything. I'll be like, yo, *'Papi, bébete un chin de 'to'* [Papi, drink a little of this]. *Y yo me tiro encima de el* [and I'll throw myself on him], and he'll drink."

After a few rounds of liquor, they started dancing *merengue*. The dealer took this opportunity to press his body against her, to whisper in her ear, "I want to get to know you. I like you a lot. I'm glad we gettin' to know each other more." Melissa recalled, "That's what he kept saying, that he wanted to get to know me and that he wanted to make me his wifey."

As a former stripper, Melissa was not uncomfortable with his closeness and whispering. But when he pressed his lips on hers—"I *kissed* him," Melissa said, with disgust. "I was real fucked up and I kissed him back. He was kissin' me and I was like, 'Yeah,' I was kissin' him too."

I asked Melissa if she felt uncomfortable with people watching them.

"Well, I was feelin' nice and I wasn't really payin' attention to anybody around me like that. But thinkin' about it now . . . now I have a problem with it. I feel disgusting!"

As the night wore on, Melissa started feeling a bit too "nice"—she lost track of the time. "It was already like five [o'clock in the morning] or something like that and we were supposed to go back to the apartment like at three something." Melissa then told the dealer that she had to work the next day, so she had to leave. But she invited him to stay the night, and he agreed, forgetting her story about being locked out of her apartment. They took a cab to the Bronx.

When the cab arrived at the building, Melissa saw Gus talking to someone in a car, then hurry through the back entrance. Melissa and the dealer also entered through the back, walking into the lobby and then taking the elevator. In the elevator, the dealer was "all lovey-dovey, hugging me and all that," Melissa recalled, laughing. After getting off, Melissa walked to the apartment and unlocked the door.

"I go in first. He's walkin' in behind me. And that's when Gus was behind the door and the other guy was on the side of the door. And they grab him and say some shit to him. I just kept walkin' towards the living room and was like, '*Okay.*' They started hittin' him and I could see them askin' him all these questions. They had him on the floor."

Suddenly, Melissa felt sorry for the dealer. In a concerned voice, she said, "I was like, 'Damn, they gonna fuck him up. They gonna beat the shit out of him.'" She then felt "real nervous" and sat on a sofa to calm down. Here, she got glimpses of everyone involved—especially Jonah.

"And one of Gus' friends," Melissa recalled, "the guy, Jonah, he was doing coke that night. He was real crazy. And the coke that he had, he had it like in a big white paper or something, in a cardboard paper, and he was just sniffing it like that. And his hair was all loose. I was like, 'Oh my God. This nigga's crazy. He's getting all coked up.'"

As the minutes passed, the scene became a whirlwind of interrogation, torture, and drug use: "I was gettin' mad nervous. I didn't know Gus *like that*. He's doin' whatever in the room, to the guy, with David, in the bathroom, like torturin' and whatever, to get information out of him, and I'm in the room, this nigga [Jonah] is coked up, Julio's downstairs in the fuckin' car. And I was feelin' mad bad for the guy ... [the dealer] he was like, 'Ar-rghh!' He was screamin' in the bathroom ... And they were burnin' him or something. He was screamin'.'"

Later, David entered the living room. "You alright?" he asked Melissa, caressing her shoulder. "Don't touch me," snapped Melissa, "I'm alright." Unable to deal with the situation anymore, she told Gus "bye" and left. Her job was done.

Throughout the years, I observed how drug dealers were a cautious bunch. They always worried about the people they encountered daily: the "thug lookin'" guy who glanced at them as they walked past on the street. The clean-shaven stranger who met their eye as they scurried in and out of elevators. The mail deliverer. The Con Ed meter reader. The Jehovah's Witness who wanted to discuss the true meaning of happiness, the gospel of Jesus, God, the oncoming Armageddon.

But not the girl. The girl—especially an attractive one—took on a different meaning. The girl meant potential sex in a bedroom, an alley, or rooftop. The sex meant demonstrating manliness to peers. The manliness meant respect and status on the streets. All of it meant a rise in rank in the drug world, a world of men. Thus, as Melissa approached the dealer, smiling, she and the robbers assumed that the drug dealer would welcome the opportunity to have sex with her, to add distinction among his peers. Simply put, these drug robbers set what I call a *masculinity trap,* a play on a male's manhood to victimize him.[1]

Pablo and Tukee explained the logic of the masculinity trap. "All niggas think about is pussy, bro," Pablo explained. "Look, man, I heard someplace that men, they think about sex about every eight seconds or something like that, bro. You know what's every eight seconds, bro? I think that's almost like a thousand fuckin' times every hour! Trust me, Ran, niggas will open the door to get some pussy. And then to say that they fucked some bitch they just met, and that the bitch was a dime [a ten] at that, forget it, bro, they gonna open that door."

"Bitches be makin' niggas do a lotta shit," added Tukee. "They make niggas talk about shit they have, all the shit they movin'—'Look, baby, I got this, this, and that over here, in my house, in my man's house, you know what I'm sayin'?' They talk about all that shit—shit they have in they house or shit that they gonna get, like how much dough they rollin' with, all type of shit, B."

"Bitches even make niggas talk about shit they don't got," joked Pablo.

"For real, B, ha-ha-ha," Tukee said, laughing. "Niggas be movin' only two ounces [of cocaine] a week, and they be like, 'Yo, you know what I'm sayin', I be movin' two kilos, three kilos a week—'"

"'I'm movin' ten kilos, twenty kilos, ha-ha-ha!'" Pablo added, laughing hysterically. "They be some broke ass niggas talkin' shit when they not supposed to. Especially to some stupid bitch they just met. That's why them dumb niggas get bagged [robbed]."

"All she ['The Girl] gotta do," Pablo explained, "is say something like, 'Excuse me, I got a leak comin' downstairs and I think it's comin' from up here.' Then it's over, bro. They gonna open that door wantin' to get that ass." I feign skepticism, telling Pablo that it seemed too easy: an attractive woman knocks on a door, says that there's a leak coming down into her apartment—that will make a drug dealer open the door?

"Yo, one time we had this fuckin' bitch knock on a door," Pablo explained, "and that's what she said. All she said was that there was like a leak or a lot of water or something goin' down into her apartment, where she lives downstairs. Randy, believe it or not, niggas opened the door, bro. And right there, boom, we just went in."

As in Melissa's case, the masculinity trap is easier if the girl approaches a dealer among male friends. Now his "boys" are watching—which pressures him to act sexually aggressive.[2] The crew usually baits the masculinity trap with the "marijuana line." A lone woman buying marijuana from a street peddler is perceived to be open to sex: she is bold (no male accompanies her). Dealers call her a "freak" or a "hoe" [whore], or as Pablo saw it: "she's a whole lotta fun"; Tukee: "that bitch is open" [to anything]; Gus: "easy pussy"; and Manolo: "What else wouldn't she do?" Stickup kids, then, count on dealers to sexualize a female's simple query: *You know where I could find some good weed?* And if the query extends to an invitation (*You wanna smoke with me?*)—jackpot.

REPRODUCING MASCULINITY

However, as I thought about The Girl, I struggled placing her within the context of the larger drug market. Because when I reviewed the literature on women and drugs, I found a range of images:

Images of women selling sex-for-crack—the haggard women strutting on the empty boulevard, leaning and peering into car windows to negotiate price and job; or the women visiting crack houses, the corrupted urban bordellos, performing oral tricks, on one girl, two girls, on a crack-smoking John.[3]

Images of servile women introduced to the drug scene by the men in their lives—women bound to boyfriends, lovers, husbands, and pimps; women holding money, hiding drugs, making sales, buying drugs, waiting for the crack, the coke, the dope, waiting for their turn at the pipe, the needle, the snort.[4]

Images of women copping drugs for cautious buyers—for the addicts on the "DL," the down low: the White boys from midtown, downtown, across the bridge, across social spheres and ladders, or the Janus-faced cops side-stepping the law.[5]

Images of lowly entrepreneurial women—the vulnerable freelancers at the bottom of the pack, suffering the glare of envious men who take her stash and beat her brutally, claiming that the drug scene belongs to them (the men), that women have no place in this underground world (the street).[6]

Images of powerful women who refuse to "behave": women who abuse drugs, sell drugs, shoot guns, batter and taunt men—women with much status and *respeto* on the unforgiving streets.[7]

The Girl, though, was all of them at once. She was clever, using her smarts to manipulate men. She was crucial, securing a dealer to get robberies under way. She was unique: only she could play the role. Yet male robbers trivialized and cheated her. So it was an image of a brave, intelligent woman who was nevertheless deceived and exploited by men.

But there was more than just men trying to keep more of the money. It was also about men keeping a masculine edge. For instance, Pablo admitted that after using a girl to enter an apartment, he lied to her about the score. "I don't tell them what's really involved," Pablo said, with a slick grin. "I let them think something else. I'll gas them, I'll lie to them. Like, for example, one time I said, 'My girlfriend is in there with this guy and I just want to beat him up.' And the girl just went and I didn't even have to pay her. And the door opened."

Neno also admitted to short-changing a female crew member. Like his criminal counterparts in other settings, and even males in the mainstream, he saw women as gullible and easy to cheat.[8] For instance, he informed me that he once lied to a female accomplice about a robbery's profit and paid her only a tenth of her agreed-upon share. I then asked him if he shortchanged her because she was female. "Look, I'll do it to whoever," Neno explained, in Spanish. "But a woman is easier, she doesn't know anything about this business. You tell her anything and she'll believe it. Because a woman is like that. Women are *boba* (stupid). They're like children. They believe anything you say."

"What if she doesn't believe you," I asked, "and she finds out that you lied?"

"I don't care if she knows. What can she do to me? I'll just keep telling her that she doesn't know what she's talkin' about. What can she do to me?"

Gus also shortchanged The Girl by convincing her that the role was unimportant. He would do so despite knowing that society, not biology, accounted for the demeaning qualities attributed to women. "Most women don't question that their role isn't that important," Gus explained. "But a man would think, 'Hold on. I knock on the door—without me, they can't get in.' A woman, it's not in her character like to question that. Like they would go by like what we would tell them—'Yo, go knock on the door'— they not even gonna see that it's important."

"So what is it about women that . . ."

"I mean, it's just not natural for men to look at women as equals. That's basically it."

"So why aren't they looked at as equal?"

"They're women. It just goes back to how we were brought up to look at women, whatever, you know."

"So how are women? Like what is it about women that makes them less than men?"

"It's just how society looks at things. Like let's say you go somewhere to fix your car or whatever, you see a man mechanic and a woman mechanic. You automatically go to the man. The woman could be better qualified, but it's just how it is."

I also observed how female accomplices were often the girlfriends of male dealers or robbers (for instance, Gus and Melissa became intimate after a drug robbery). Thus, I asked Gus about why girlfriends sometimes risked a lot despite getting little in return. "Women want to make themselves feel needed," Gus said. "So they would do stuff just to show you, or prove to you, like they worth it . . . like Melissa, like if I told her to go do something for me, like go knock on a door, or whatever, she would—for free. That's the difference between men and women. Women deal with a lot more emotion, more than men. I mean, I wouldn't take a risk of spendin' whatever amount of years in jail just to prove to somebody that I'm worth it, or that I'm needed, that you need me."

Clearly, Gus exercised a double standard.[9] I knew that he often did jail and prison time for friends. Apart from this, he ignored how women might take on the role of The Girl for financial reasons: earning a thousand dollars, or even its half, in a day, was more than one or two weeks of legitimate pay for women working at low-skilled, low-waged jobs.[10]

For Melissa, drug robbery money was fast and easy. But I knew how the men felt toward her, so I wondered about her future. I later found out that she had applied to Monroe College, a business school in the Bronx. In fact, she was supposed to be attending, but since she missed the first two weeks of classes, the college dropped her for the semester.

After explaining that Monroe was the only school to accept her because of low grades, she revealed her true ambitions. "I wanted to go John Jay [College of Criminal Justice, CUNY]," Melissa said.

"Why?"

"To study criminal law."

"Why do you want to study criminal law?"

"Because I realized that I wanted to do something better for myself. I could go to school and I can work as my like, do what I wanna do. I wanna be a cop, so I can work at a precinct. And because I'm in school and takin' that up, I could do something better with myself than just stayin' around the house and smoke weed, and lettin' time pass."

On the one hand, she desired a stable, unionized, high-paying job. On the other hand, she had had the taste of what seemed like fast money and sometimes thought it was her best chance at success. Also, to this point in her life, her best advantage was her body. She had successfully strip-danced and played The Girl—work she saw as giving her power over men.[11]

Unfortunately, Melissa eventually gave up her law enforcement ambitions. Instead, she went on to more stickups—and even tried her hand at other crimes, like street robberies. "Gus brung out the badness in me," Melissa explained, laughing. "You know the excitement and shit, 'cause I ain't really fucked with no guns or anything, touched them, until I met Gus. He used to show me all these guns and teach me to shoot. And I used to get hype and go, 'Yeeeaaaah!'"

So with the help of a cousin, who knew a "perfect" target, Melissa planned her first street robbery. But she needed a gun. "So I went upstairs to Julio's house," Melissa recalled, "and I told one of his friends that Gus told me to tell Julio to give him his gun. And he went inside the hamper and got the shit and clocked it back. I was like, 'What's that little red button for? He's like, 'That's the safety. Red is fire, that's when it's off the safety. And black is when it's on the safety.'"

Now with a gun, she pursued the target. On the planned day, the target walked past an alley and Melissa slipped out behind her. "So, I was walkin', me and her, had the gun out, and just said, 'Yo, give me your shit!' I put the gun against her back and she just got like nervous and was like, 'Here, here, here. Take everything!' I wasn't gonna shoot her. I had the safety on anyways. I didn't know what the fuck to do, so I hit her over the head with the shit. I was like, 'Pah!'"

According to Melissa, she took the victim's leather jacket and Gucci bag, and then took off down the street, where she met up with her cousin. After taking a cab to Melissa's home, they were upset at finding only eighty dollars in the purse. "I expected at least like two hundred, three hundred dollars, some credit cards I could scheme on," Melissa said. "Something that's worthwhile to do, you know what I'm sayin'? . . . I didn't think of the consequences at the time until afterward. I was like, 'Damn, man, over some petty shit. I got a .380 [handgun] on me. I don't even know how to use the shit. Five-O [police] would'a came, I would'a been stressed.'"

In the end, the street robbery was a one-time affair. Being The Girl was easier, with more income and less risk of arrest. The question, though, lingers. Did she enter the criminal world to experience the thrill? Partially. Clearly, Melissa enjoyed crime and got thrills from deceiving men for cash. Yet as her biography shows, the answer is more complicated. It involved her South Bronx community, her family and poverty, and her underground networks. And in terms of drug robberies: her body. Sexism, Melissa once observed, was "just a part of life that unfortunately us women gotta go through." And her insight—a result of larger gender inequality—influenced her to do drug world crimes.

In a perfect world, it was the wrong choice. But in a world where race, class, and gender worked against her, it was an unsurprising one. As with the men, I would not interfere with her life or try to block her criminal path.

Just silence.

A CAUTIONARY TALE IN A GENDERED WORLD

Of all the men, Pablo was the most extreme in his hypermasculinity and misogyny. Over the years, he grew to hate women and repeatedly harked back to a time when women *knew their place.* He wished he lived in Afghanistan, where he could have many wives and women were under constant male surveillance. *Over there, if a bitch acts up, the bitch gets stoned.*

Ultimately, Pablo's disturbing beliefs made me question our relationship; if I had just met him today, I would never have had anything to do with him. But I had known him since childhood, and he used to be my best friend. Also, I knew something about the origins of his patriarchal ideas. He was raised in a traditional household, where I observed his uncles, mother, and sister encourage him (and me) to be a *mujeriego* (womanizer) and to blame a woman if she was beaten by a man.

I also knew that female subordination went beyond the Dominican community. Pablo and the others aspired to an overarching hypermasculinity—an extreme expression of masculine domination, heterosexuality, competitiveness, and sexual prowess.[12]

Despite knowing this, I could not pretend to wear a white lab coat that transformed me into an emotionless or expressionless blank state. Sometimes their words compelled me to challenge them. These heated exchanges would prove to be the most revealing, especially as to their sexist rationalizations. One day when we were talking, Pablo observed:

> *You wanna know what's really wrong with kids today? . . . It's the mothers, bro, that's what's wrong with them. Mothers ain't like they used to be. Before, they knew their place. They were always home takin' care of the kids. Now, forget it. They goin' out all the time. They hangin' out with their friends. They gettin' too much freedom, bro. Man, that's why I wish I could live in Afghanistan. Arab motherfuckas over there could have like ten wives, bro, and they all live in the same house. He be fuckin' a different one every night and they can't say shit about it. And women there can't be like the ones here, in New York City. They stayin' home and takin' care of the children. If not, they'll beat their ass, whip the shit out [of] them, bro.*

In response, I asked if he would like Whites to harken to a time when Blacks were slaves and "knew their place," especially since he passed as Black.

I'ma tell you right now, Pablo responded, *I could'a never been a slave. I would've fought back, bro. I woulda been killin' White people. I would've killed my master, bro. If I didn't kill his ass, I would've fuckin' killed myself. I wouldn't be able to live like that, bro.*

So why do you oppress women? You say that you hate oppression, that you would fight back and even kill yourself before living under oppression.

I don't know what the fuck you talkin' about, bro, he responded. *The Bible says that women have to serve their husbands. That's what I'm goin' by. Read the Bible, bro.*

But didn't the Bible also allow people to have slaves? So that means if you get enslaved, it's cool because the Bible doesn't say anything against it.

Still, women have to respect men . . .

Look, man, I said, *you're just bein' a hypocrite. For you, oppression is okay as long as you benefit from it. But when you're on the losing end, then you're against it. If White people or police officers are oppressing you, then you're like, 'Fuck that shit, I'ma fight back. Fuck those motherfuckas.' But when you're oppressing women, then you say that it's the way it should be. Man, listen to your logic. You're bein' a hypocrite, bro.*

Pablo paused. Then he said: *Nah, bro. The Bible says that the woman was made from a man. God took the rib out of Adam and made Eve out of him. So think about it, a woman is lower than a man. If the Bible says it, bro . . .*

Pablo also had two main girlfriends, Lydia and Neida. Neida, with whom he had a one-year-old daughter, was his second girlfriend. One afternoon, I sat on a leather sofa in Neida's apartment and complained about how my clunky tape recorder hardly fit into my jeans pocket. Pablo, who sat across from me, then pulled out a micro-cassette recorder, saying that I could borrow it for my fieldwork. After observing me test the micro-recorder, Neida told me how Pablo secretly taped the happenings at Lydia's, his main girlfriend's home. Surreptitiously, he had placed a micro-recorder inside Lydia's television and taped her conversations. He did so because he suspected Lydia of cheating on him. After the tapes confirmed it, he beat her badly.

As Neida spoke, I looked over at Pablo. He went back and forth between a sheepish grin toward me and an angry face toward Neida (he had never told me about this). But she was on a roll. She saw my regular tape recorder lying on the dining room table and told me to turn it on. Like the guys, she said, I had to hear her story too. Excited, Pablo said, *Go ahead, man. We finally gonna get this shit straight. I want you to listen to what she has to say. And then I want you to tell me who's right and who's wrong here.*

Briefly, I thought about Pablo being there. But since Neida often complained about Pablo in his presence, I thought I could pull off a smooth interview. I was wrong. The interview would end in violence.

Neida and I sat at the dining room table. I turned on the tape recorder. "You know what he used to do?" Neida started, needing no cue.

"What?"

"He used to record me, then he used to put Stephanie [a girlfriend from Massachusetts] to hear them [the tapes] and then he used to put Lydia to hear them. But he used to erase those parts that he didn't want them to listen to."

Pablo, I realized, augmented his masculinity through technology. Not that he was alone. Gus repeatedly showed me a radio transmitter that could pick up telephone lines within a set radius. Although he had gotten it for crime purposes (which never panned out), he mostly used it to listen in on Melissa's home phone conversations. When I visited him in Julio's apartment (which was in the same building as Melissa's apartment), he sometimes turned on the transmitter and tried to catch her on the phone. *I know everything's she sayin' about me,* he would brag. *She be complainin' to her friends about me when she's mad and I be listenin' to that shit. Now I could have my arguments ready even before I see her.*

But Pablo played at another level. Neida revealed that he misrepresented his relationships by having girlfriends listen to edited recordings. So although the "truth" was in the tapes, it was a revised truth that benefited him. Moreover, his sophisticated surveillance no longer required his presence to exert masculine control. To borrow from Michel Foucault's metaphor of the Panopticon prison,[13] Pablo displayed a *panoptic masculinity.* Now he dominated women through the threat of technological surveillance; now women self-regulated for fear of that constant surveillance. So it no longer mattered whether Pablo secretly recorded them. Just the possibility forced his girlfriends into "good" behavior.

As Neida noted: "Now she's [Lydia] acting like a goody-goody. Doing everything like the perfect wifey. She's scared as shit that Pablo might find out that she's cheatin' again. But Pablo doesn't know what she's feelin' inside. She could want in her heart to play [cheat on] him again with whatever guy she was seein'. The only way Pablo could make sure that she's not playin' him is to record her. But like I said, the only reason why she's not playin' him is because she's scared. He even told me that she hardly talks on the phone anymore and she does little things for him now. She's just scared."

Then she talked about how Pablo's longing for "Afghanistan" was not just a fanciful dream—how he almost made it happen in the South Bronx. "You know what he said to me one day?" Neida asked me. "That he would love to have a house, have Lydia live on top, and have me live on the bottom. And then every other day, he would live one with Lydia, and then one with me. Like Mondays for Lydia, Tuesdays for Neida, and we'll be a whole big happy family. . . . sometimes I feel bad for him. He wants to be with his kids, I understand that. But he gotta understand that we're not in fuckin' . . . where was it that he said? I don't know. [To a smiling Pablo, sitting on the sofa] Where was it that you have to be born? Erub? No, Arab, some shit like that. Was it Arab? Because they have seven wives, and they be all happy, and they don't get jealous. You know, I was so fuckin' into him, I was so blind, that if he was to tell me, 'Okay Neida, let's go, let's move, all three of us, with the kids and everything,' I would do it. At that time I would've. Not anymore. Hell no!"

I was surprised that Neida was ever open to his "Arab" plan. But then, Neida's options were severely limited. She was born in the Dominican Republic and came to the South Bronx during her early teens. After becoming involved with a big-time Puerto Rican dealer, she dropped out of high school. He lavished money and gifts on her, and after she had two children, he set her up in a nice apartment. But after his arrest and conviction, she was lost—alone with two children, no education. Given her marginal background and the stigma of having three children from two different fathers, someone like Pablo gave her the best chance at approaching a "traditional" family.

"It's more because of my kids," Neida explained. " 'Cause I don't want my kids to see one man now and another one tomorrow, and another one after tomorrow, and another one . . . And my daughter's too small. And whoever I get involved with, she's gonna grow to love that person that is not her father 'cause he gonna spend more time with me, you understand?"

Later, the interview's methodological problems surfaced, which implicated my tape recorder and masculinity in her powerlessness. Here, Pablo demanded that she tell the "truth" on "tape," and Neida responded by suggesting that I had planned to use the tape recording against her.

"You just want me to talk 'cause you got me on tape right now," Neida said. "That's why you want me talk. It's that you don't see: I don't care. You could do whatever you want with the tape. I really don't fuckin' care."

"Look Neida, I'm not givin' this tape to nobody," I said, feeling uncomfortable. "I'm serious. I'm not givin' this tape to Stephanie [Pablo's former fiancée] or Lydia."

"I don't care," Neida continued. "Before it bothered me, but it doesn't fuckin' phase me anymore. I don't fuckin' care."

"Do you want the tape?" I asked Neida. "I'm serious. Do you want it? I'll destroy the tape in front of you and make sure that Pablo's doesn't get it."

"It doesn't bother me," Neida said. "It's like I'm at that point that I don't care. He could stay with Lydia for what I care."

Throughout the interview, Pablo's anger grew as Neida repeatedly referred to Lydia's cheating. And when his mother, who disliked Neida, became the topic, my gut told me that something was about to happen, that the interview was going wrong. Yet I let it continue.

"I know I love my mother," Pablo stated. "He [Neida's imprisoned husband] didn't love his mother according to you because his mother had to 'swallow it.' That's what you said. That'll never happen to me. I only have one mother."

"You got it all wrong," Neida responded. "His mother didn't like me 'cause she was Puerto Rican. So she wanted his [Puerto Rican] ex-wife to be with him."

"But his mother didn't like you because you are the way you are." Pablo returned. "Isn't that a coincidence that two different people from two different worlds—two mother-in-laws—don't like a certain person? Isn't there something wrong with somebody?"

"Your mother likes for people to kiss her ass," Neida rejoined.

"I guess these two different people are nuts," Pablo said.

"Now listen," Neida said to me. "His mother was everything to him [Neida's ex-husband]—"

"I'm not gonna put you never on top of my mother," Pablo interrupted. "My mother is always gonna be my mother."

"I don't care," Neida said, boldly. "I don't want you to, let's get that shit straight."

"I'm happy you don't care," he responded.

Angry, Pablo then shot up from the sofa and over to Neida, and with precision, punched her repeatedly on the sides of the head. As he hit her, she stumbled out of her chair and fell to the floor on her knees. His rapid blows continued while he yelled out, "I love my mother, you fuckin' bitch! You'll never come first in front of my mother!"

"Yo, Pablo, chill, man!" I shouted as I squeezed my way through the tight dining room space. I then tried to grab him, but he easily pushed off my arms, turned, and walked quickly out of the apartment. Standing in front of Neida, I was at a loss.

I froze.

Seconds later I asked Neida if she was okay even though I could clearly see that she wasn't. She said nothing. She now sat with her back against the wall, sobbing softly, with tears running down her face. Her children. They were still in their bedroom. The door was shut, but I wondered if they had heard the commotion. They didn't come out. Good.

I asked her one more time if she was okay. She just stared at the floor. Again, I was at a loss. I went from looking at her, to the bedroom door, back to her, and then on impulse, I raced down the six flights to see if I could catch up with Pablo. As I made my way out of the building's entrance, I could see him walking briskly through the park.

I didn't bother calling him. *Pablo.*

Still haunting me to this day, this was my most disastrous ethnographic moment. In fact, I omitted it from my original manuscript—I was so ashamed.[14] First, I dismissed the potential consequences of interviewing Neida in Pablo's presence. Second, although I sensed Pablo's swelling anger, I let the interview go on. Then, I did nothing to help her.[15]

Regretfully, I let neighborhood experiences dictate my actions. Several weeks before, Julio had been struck in the head with an aluminum baseball bat after he encouraged a young woman to leave her abusive boyfriend. Later, the thick bandage on his bald head would serve as a potent reminder and a warning to would-be "heroes," wanting to save the day.

SEVEN

Gettin' the Shit

AROUND 5:30 A.M. A PITCH-DARK apartment in the South Bronx.

Gus and David, each with a gun, wait silently on either side of the apartment door. Several moments later, the building's hallway light shines through as the door opens from outside. Melissa and the dealer enter, shutting the door behind them. It is dark again. Gus suddenly smacks the dealer across the neck, grabs him with both hands, and pulls him down to the floor.

"Yo, don't move, motherfucka!" Gus says, angrily.

"Que lo que pasa? [What's happening?]" asks the bewildered dealer.

As David holds a gun to the dealer's head, Gus blindfolds the dealer and binds his arms and legs with a metal hanger wire. Together, Gus and David then drag the dealer farther into the hallway, away from the door. Gus pulls a knife from his pants pocket.

"Look, I'ma ask you what you do and dependin' on the answer you give me, depends what happens to you," Gus tells the dealer. "I'ma ask you what you got on 145th Street. Tell me what it is and nothing's gonna happen to you. If you don't tell me, I'ma cut your ear off. You understand the shit?"

"Yes, I understand," replies the dealer.

"A'ight. What you got on 145th Street and Broadway?"

"What are you talkin' about? I don't got nothin' there."

"On the fifth floor, on 145th Street and Broadway, what you got in the room?"

"I don't have nothin'. I work for a store. That's all I do."

Gus grabs the dealer's ear and slices off the lobe. Blood spurts. To keep the blood from flowing onto the floor, Gus and David drag the dealer to the bathtub. The torture has begun.

This scene was recounted to me several times by David and Gus. It would ignite a brutal drama that would last till the next afternoon. That event (and others like it) embody what sociologist Paul Goldstein calls "systemic violence."[1] It resulted not from drug cravings or drugs effects, but because of the drug economy's outlaw style of regulation and capitalist greed. Territorial disputes, retaliation, rule enforcement, debt collection, drug robberies— all are examples of what sociologist Timothy Black calls "urban cowboy capitalism."[2] And in New York City's 1988 homicide count, Goldstein and others found that systemic violence accounted for three-fourths of all drug-related homicides and two-thirds of all crack-related homicides.[3] They also found that one-fifth of crack-related homicides involved drug robberies in which either a dealer or robber was killed.

This chapter and the next provide meat to Goldstein's concept in a way that crime statistics and police reports can never do. They analyze drug robbery dynamics through the experiences of perpetrators and victims, which criminal investigators often guess their way through.

GENERAL PRACTICES

Although each robbery is different, there is a general plan—subdue the dealer through force or the threat of force, then ask calmly (for dramatic effect) or harshly (for a scare) about the whereabouts of the drugs and cash. And after receiving the standard dealer silence, or *I don't know,* induce pain. Then, if needed, induce more pain.

But let us start at the beginning.

Ain't Fuckin' Around

As criminologist Bruce Jacobs notes, surprise is essential to enacting drug robberies.[4] Catching dealers off-guard freezes them and allows robbers to define and control the situation.[5] I would add that personal history and experience influence how robbers surprise the dealer. For instance, Pablo, Gus, and Tukee, who were familiar with jail, prison, drug market, and street violence, surprised victims head on, with a gun. That is why they often used The Girl to get inside a drug stash apartment. While she knocked, and the dealer peeped, the robbers, with guns in hand, squatted on either side of the door, out of sight. As the dealer opened the door, they sprang forward and rushed inside to subdue him. Gus usually led and immediately hit the dealer with his gun.

"I just go in real fast and shit," Gus explained, "not to give them enough time to think what's happening. They're like, 'Oh shit.' Like when the nigga opens the door, boom, I jump up and run inside real fast. I always grab the nigga that opened the door and hit him with my gun right away. I smack him with my gun in his head."[6]

I asked why he hits the dealer.

" 'Cause I always do that shit," Gus said. "I just hit him so he could know not to fuck around. 'Cause if the first thing you do is grab the nigga and hit him, he's gonna know not to fuck around and shit. We ain't fuckin' around."

Pablo agreed: "You just go in and fuck everybody up. They have to know you ain't fuckin' around, that if you gonna have to hurt them, you won't even think about it. Once they see that they got fucked up and see that everybody else is gettin' fucked up, they ain't gonna try no funny business. They gonna be like, 'Damn, if they fuckin' us up now and we haven't done nothin', imagine if we try to do somethin'.' "

Sometimes they eased up on dealers, slowly, smoothly, and announced the robbery without a hint of rage. In this way, robbers avoid the screams, the yells, the pleas, all the unwanted noise that might arouse neighbors. Pablo explained: "When you see that they [the dealers] goin' to their door, you come up to them and tell them, 'You know what the fuck this is. Don't act like you don't. You know what the fuck you do.' But you got your gun out and you got niggas with you with guns. So they don't fight back."

"Do you have to say much?"

"Do I have to say much? '*Cojelo suave.* Take it easy. The quicker the better.' Then the nigga cops a plea—'Yo, don't kill me, bro. I don't have nothin'.' That's when you start fuckin' them up. But you try to be as quiet as possible. Too much commotion brings static and you don't want the extra heat. And gettin' inside the apartment is easy. He's gonna have a bunch of niggas with guns on him. But I heard stories about that dick that tries to be Superman. There's always that dick. But when I do my shit, they always listen. When they got guns on them, believe me, you don't gotta do much talkin'. The gun speaks for itself, ha-ha."[7]

Tukee also preferred this approach, believing that controlled violence reduced the risk of arrest. "I just stay calm, B," Tukee explained. "Just put a gun on them and be like, 'Yo, just take me inside [the apartment]. Then boom, they take you inside, you make them lie down, use duct tape, tie them up, and start askin' them questions. Now don't get it twisted. If I gotta fuck a nigga up, I will. But I'm not into that screamin' or yellin' shit. 'Cause if somebody hears you, then the fuckin' pigs [police] gonna be knockin' on that door. If you do it right, they [dealers] gonna see you not fuckin' around. If they act up, 'A'ight, gotta kick you now. You still actin' up? A'ight, gotta get the iron.' Once they see that you ain't fuckin' around, you don't gotta make that much noise."

On the Sneak Tip

Topi, Neno, and David used a different general approach. They had different criminal backgrounds than Gus, Pablo, and Tukee, and less experience with one-on-one violence. They were born into poverty in the Dominican Republic, where they became petty burglars and never spent time in adult jail or prison. For instance, Topi, who was now twenty-one years old, grew up in a run-down Dominican barrio and hung out with school truants. Mostly, they smoked weed to pass time, but sometimes stole from local vendors or burglarized homes. Eventually, his mother sent him to live with an aunt in the Bronx, hoping that he would cut his drug use and do better in school.

However, he attended a locally zoned high school and returned to truancy and smoking weed. After learning of his renewed delinquency, his aunt sent him to live with family in Puerto Rico. Here, he claims to have cleaned his act up and returned to the Bronx with good intentions. But after finding work as a supermarket delivery boy, he became reacquainted with a childhood buddy who now did street robberies. Topi would quit his job.

"Imagine," Topi recalled in Spanish, "I was going up to a fifth floor, a sixth, without an elevator. I worked to go up stairs. That's what I did all day, go up stairs. And when I went up, they told me, 'Thank you. Here's fifty cents, here's a dollar.' Some of them didn't even pay. I left that. I was earning more money robbing." Later, he started hanging out with drug dealers and using their inside information to break into drug stash apartments.

Neno, who was eighteen years old, and David, who was nineteen years old, were slightly younger than Topi. Like Topi, both were raised in poor Dominican barrios, where they hung out with school truants, smoked weed, and burglarized homes. Also, their families sent them away to reduce their delinquency. For instance, Neno's mother sent him to the Bronx to better his education. However, he struggled academically and eventually dropped out.

"Tengo una cabeza dura," Neno said in Spanish, saying that he had a hard head. "When I was in school, I had trouble understanding the lessons. It just didn't enter my head. I sat down in class and looked at the teacher, and I don't know, it didn't interest me. That's why when I got here [to the Bronx] I enrolled in school, but then I started hanging out and missing class. School's not for people like me."

David made a stop in Puerto Rico before coming to the United States. His mother sent him there to live with an aunt, hoping that he would stay out of trouble. The plan backfired. "In Puerto Rico," David explained, in Spanish, "it was the same thing. I started hanging out with guys who were smoking weed. I stopped going to school. Sometimes we would steal from the markets or steal from people when they were not home. I was sent to Puerto Rico to change. But imagine, I started doing the same again." Afterward, David was sent to live with family in the Bronx. But there he dropped out of school and, along with Neno, joined Topi on drug robberies.

Their burglary backgrounds shaped their general drug robbery approach.[8] They preferred to enter stash apartments through windows, risking a three-, four-, five-, or six-story drop. To accomplish this, they learned how to use mountain-climbing equipment. One afternoon, Topi and Neno took me to a neighborhood rooftop to describe their method. As we walked across the roof, Neno pointed to a furnace pipe coming through the black-tarred, gravel-like tiling. They used the pipe as an anchor, he said, to secure the rope they used to lower themselves. I asked Neno if he thought the pipe could bend.

"That doesn't bend," he said. "It comes from all the way down there, from the basement. So, imagine, that's a strong pipe that doesn't come out of place. Well, it doesn't bend because I don't weigh much, and Topi less—that one, he's a flyweight, ha-ha-ha."

Focusing on a building nearby, I pointed to a window and asked Topi to describe how he would enter it. "You take the rope, tie yourself good, and go down."

"But how do you go down . . . you just let yourself drop?" I asked.

"You have to use your legs," he said, "like if you're walking down backwards." He crouched slightly, took a few backward steps, and stopped short of a good example. "But it's easy," Topi continued. "With that rope, you can go up and down like nothing."

"Do you look down?"

"You can't look down," Neno said. "If you look down, forget it, you'll get scared, you'll get panicked. How do I tell you? You always have to look down, but you have to keep the window in your mind. You look down to see the window, not the ground. If you always have the ground in mind, that's where you'll end up."

"How many people go down by rope?" I asked. "Does everybody go in through the window?"

"Only one enters through the window," answered Neno. "Everybody else is waiting outside the apartment."

"Where?"

"Outside the apartment, in the hallway. I have three or four guys waiting until me or Topi go down from the roof and enter the window and then open the door for them."

"But there are people [dealers] in the apartment, right?"

"Yes, there's always somebody inside. But you grab them, put a gun on them, and you tell them to keep still or you're going to kill them. And then you go real fast and open the door."

"But can't they escape while you go open the door?"

"No, they can't because they're already panicked, they're nervous. They won't move after you show them your gun."

"But Topi, didn't you let a woman escape one time while you went to open the door?" I asked, knowing that he had "fucked up" once.

"Yes," Topi said, grinning.

"What happened there?"

"What happened was that I went through the window and I found a woman naked—naked, naked. It looked like she was going to take a bath. I told her to lie down on the floor or that I was going to kill her. And she got panicked. 'Don't kill me, I haven't done anything.' And I told her to shut her mouth and lie on the floor. And I left her there, in the hallway, naked, just like that, while I opened the door. And when I open the door, I hear her running and then I hear a door close—Pah! *Anda el diablo,* she locked herself in a room. I tried to open the door and it wouldn't open. And all the guys are telling me, 'Open the door!' So, I kicked the door—"

"And his foot went right through the door, ha-ha-ha," interrupted Neno.

"And my foot got stuck in the door," Topi said, grinning.

"And when we come to see," continued Neno, "the woman had gone out the window and was going down the fire escape—naked! Ha-ha!"

"Naked, *loco,*" added Topi. "We had to leave."

As I peered over the ledge, I was amazed at their daring. They had no formal training in mountain climbing and were *determined*. Later, though,

I thought of how the powerful lure of money and materialism had them risking life and limb. I also thought of how they fulfilled themselves through danger. Yes, as Jack Katz would say, they sought thrills; yes, as the cultural criminologists would say, they performed criminal "edgework."[9] Lowering oneself from a rooftop, sneaking in through a window, stepping into the unknown, taking the chance of being seen or heard, risking injury or death, and then escaping in the nick of time—that was thrilling. The economic undertones were there; but window-entry robberies gave them spectacular transcendence. For the moment, they recuperated their social losses and controlled their crisis-ridden lives. They were "somebody" in one more way and, if they survived, one more time.

To cope with their risk taking, some drug robbers used copious amounts of drugs. For instance, Neno, Topi, and Jonah were always high, and right before drug robberies they smoked more weed, sniffed more coke, and drank more liquor. In fact, Neno and Topi would be in a stupor when presumably they needed pinpoint clarity. This, though, is how they dealt with the tension and fear that welled up inside them.[10] There was a cost, however.

One day, I found Gus and Neno sitting on a stoop by the public stairwell. With them were three guys, two of whom had participated in a recent drug robbery with Neno. Everyone was smoking weed, looking relaxed. Except for Neno. He was unusually sober despite taking hits off the blunt. I assumed that his sobriety had to do with his arrest during that robbery and recent release from jail.

After some small talk, everyone slowly branched out to other groups on the block, leaving Gus and me alone. I asked Gus if he wanted a beer. He nodded his head and I went to the *bodega* to buy a Heineken for him and a Corona for myself. On my way, I walked by Neno and an older guy talking in hushed voices. When I got back, he and Neno were standing next to Gus, arguing heatedly. Both of them had been in the botched robbery.

"When the police got there, I didn't even know they were coming!" Neno shouted in Spanish. "Nobody told me anything!"

"Don't tell me that!" the guy shot back. "You were high. Both of you [referring to Topi too] were so high, you didn't even know what you were doing! That's why they got you. You didn't even know what was going on!"

"Look, I've done this when I've been higher so don't start talking shit," Neno said. "Nobody told me anything. That's why the police grabbed me."

After an uncomfortable pause, Gus asked if the lookout had walkie-talkies. The older guy explained that he did, but that Neno and the lookout were high. At first, when they entered the apartment through a window, the lookout cell-phoned twice to warn about police in the neighborhood. However, each time he called back to say that it was a false alarm. The lookout then called in a third warning, this time telling them to put the guns in the sack and have them pulled to the roof. The police were already going up the stairs. *They got us arrested!* someone yelled out in Spanish. Everyone then raised themselves to the roof with the mountain-climbing equipment.

"If I didn't jump to the other buildings, I would've been caught!" the older guy said excitedly.

Neno then blamed the lookout for his arrest.

"Don't blame anyone else," yelled the older guy. "All of you were high and weren't functioning! We're lucky that all of us didn't get caught. Dammit, all of you guys were all high and talking loud on the cell phone like if you lived in the apartment, like if it was yours. These guys were acting like nothing! Let's thank God we all didn't get caught."

THE VIOLENCE

After getting inside the apartment, the drug robbery is dizzying and explosive: the furious search for people, in the bedroom, in the closet, behind the door, *get everybody, get everybody;* the demands to know if anyone else is inside, anywhere inside, *don't lie, don't lie;* the punches to the jaw, the kicks to the stomach, *don't move, don't move.*

And after subduing the dealers, robbers begin the questioning.

Let us pause.

That is what drug robbers often got, silence. Or if a dealer responds, it is to plead ignorance, to cry foul, to beg mercy, to insist on being left alone. This is why, more often than not, drug robberies get bloody and grimy, with robbers resorting to torture. For instance, when I asked Gus about why he cut off the dealer's earlobe, he provided a glimpse into how drug robbers transitioned into torture.

"You tell them, 'Look, I'ma ask you what you do.' If you don't tell me what I wanna know, I'ma cut your ear.' So, when you tell 'em that shit, you gotta do it. Or they gonna wanna start fuckin' with you, 'Ah, this nigga's bullshit. He told me he was gonna cut my ear off and he didn't cut it.' So, I asked him what he had on 145th Street and Broadway. He said that he doesn't know. I didn't even ask him again. I just cut his earlobe off. But I mean, that was like the second option. That's not the first. Like, we let them know that we will do something to them. But we don't go straight into that. 'Cause if we ask you, and you tell us, everything goes down right. You just saved a lot of trouble."

As for torture, the setting often shaped the process. Apart from a gun, drug robbers rarely carried torture tools, instead using everyday household items to do violence. If a knife is nearby, they might slice off fingers. If an electrical appliance is nearby, they might electrocute. And if a hammer is nearby, they might hammer fingers, legs, or heads—or anything until the dealer gives up the goods.

For instance, Tukee, in a rare criminal admission, described an incident where a frustrated robber found a torture tool in the kitchen. "One time, there was this dude [dealer]," explained Tukee, "who just ain't want to talk. This dude I was with was like, 'Fuck this.' He went to the kitchen, got this big ass knife, came back, was like, 'Look, tell us where the shit's at, or I'ma cut your finger off.' The dude didn't say nothing. 'A'ight.' [We] put his hands on the table, held that shit . . . Shaaa! Chopped off one of his fingers, like the tip of it off. The nigga [dealer] started screamin', blood was shootin' out of that shit [finger]. My boy was like, 'You better talk or I'ma cut all your fingers off.' The nigga [dealer] looked down, saw the little part of his finger on the table, then he started talkin'. If he just would'a told us from the get-go, he woulda still had his finger. Stupid motherfucka."

Lalo, a drug robber who sometimes came to the block to learn of potential scores, also described the use of household items for torture. "We had the guy in the bathtub," Lalo explained, in Spanish, "and we were hitting him with the gun so much that his head was swollen. But damn, the guy kept sayin' he didn't know anything. I grabbed a bottle of Clorox and told him, 'Let's see if you talk. If you don't talk, *maricón,* I'm going to pour this Clorox into your eyes. You want to go blind?' Then the guy was like, 'That's not right, I don't even have anything.' And I poured it into his eyes. And real quick he started saying, 'Stop! That's it, stop!' Ha-ha. The bottle was empty [now], but he didn't know that. I was like, "Talk or I'll keep going. You're going to go blind, cocksucker.' And he told us everything."

However, the most profound torture tool is the iron. The iron is often the savior for drug robbers, and if they find one in a dealer's apartment, it's all over: after heating the iron, robbers place it against a dealer's flesh, which produces immediate results. "The worst torture is an iron," Pablo explained. "You gonna give up everything. You gonna give up even your own mother. Because from what I seen, the worst feeling is an iron burnin' your back up, kid. I haven't met a man that could take the iron, ha-ha. And usually these guys, where they got their stuff [drugs] like in a house—they got TVs, sofas, beds . . . they gotta make it look like a house, in case Five-O [police] comes, or the super[intendent] comes to fix something. And most of the time they chill in them. So they got to have an iron. You don't even have to bring one."

Thus, the iron, in the drug robber's world, is legend. It resurfaced in successful robbery tales as the technique that would always turn the tables on a dealer. Gus provided such an account, where he and others interrogated and beat a dealer in the living room. After the dealer refused to talk, Gus went into a bedroom closet, found an iron, and confronted the dealer.

"So, boom, I had the iron in front of the nigga's face," Gus said. "I was like, 'Yo, just tell me where the shit is at. If you don't tell us, I'ma fuckin' burn your ass.' He ain't say nothing. So I told my boy to put duct tape over his mouth 'cause I knew the nigga was gonna be screamin'. I didn't want nobody to hear that shit. We take everything off, his shirt, everything, bro. And while we doin' all this, we got the iron like heatin' up, gettin' that shit hot. Soon as it got real hot, I put that shit on his back. Shaaaa! Nigga was screamin', bro. Screamin', screamin'. But you couldn't hear him that much 'cause of the duct tape. I took the iron off and saw this big ass red mark turnin' like purple, bro. I was like, 'Fuck it.' I put that shit on him again. Nigga couldn't take that shit, bro. These niggas [the other robbers] had to hold him down, he was movin' so much. I took the iron off and waited a while. When I saw that he like calmed down, I took the duct tape off [his mouth], and asked him again to tell us where the shit is at. Right there he told us."

There were many more torture tactics—like heating an uncoiled metal hanger wire on a stove and then placing it in a dealer's ear. But again, the torture mostly depends on the circumstance: if a dealer is dragged into a bathtub to avoid bloodying the floor, the robbers may fill the tub with water, which makes electrocution an option. If a dealer happens to be ironing clothes when he is subdued, burning becomes an option. In short, drug robbers use their imagination with household items to make a dealer surrender the goods.

HARDHEADEDNESS

So far we see that dealers often refuse to give up the drugs or cash despite facing torture. A simple reason explains a dealer's hardheadedness, or resistance:[11]

the consignment system. In the drug world, dealers often receive drugs on consignment, a system where suppliers provide drugs on credit and wait for dealers to sell the drugs to get paid.[12] However, it is a dreadful credit system: no legal recourse exists and it works within a capitalist frame.

For instance, let's say that a kilo of cocaine has a retail value of twenty thousand dollars. A dealer receiving the kilo on credit and selling it keeps a thousand dollars (profit) and returns the remaining nineteen thousand dollars to the supplier. The deal is done. Likewise, a dealer receiving ten kilos on credit and selling them keeps a profit of ten thousand dollars (one thousand for each kilo) and returns one hundred and ninety thousand dollars to the supplier (nineteen thousand dollars for each kilo). Again, the deal is done.

However, if robbers steal the ten kilos of cocaine from that dealer, not only does the dealer lose a profit of ten thousand dollars, but the supplier loses one hundred and ninety thousand dollars. And if a sneaky dealer lies, says he was robbed, then he can earn a lot of money. After selling the "robbed" product, the dealer can earn up to the entire retail value as profit, two hundred thousand dollars. *Diablo, 'mano!*

But there is a chance that the dealer's supplier needs that sum to pay his own provider. There is a chance that, despite having enough disposable cash, the supplier does not want to absorb the loss. And there is a chance that the supplier holds the dealer accountable, not caring whether the robbery tale is true or not. To drug dealers, robbery tales are suspect, regarded as *pura mierda*. It is not unheard of for drug dealers to try to escape payments through cries of having been "stuck up." But typically, a dealer eventually pays— through selling drugs for several months with no profit, through broken limbs, bruised bodies, or, sometimes, through lost lives. *Muerte, papa.*

One night, Sylvio talked about why drug dealers resist drug robbers during a stickup. "Depending on who's the supplier, they take more than half [of the drugs] on consignment. So let's say you have five hundred thousand worth of material. It's more than likely not all yours. It's the Colombians' or the Mexicans' or whoever. They wouldn't buy that stickup line like it was something normal. They would think you fuckin' with them. And those are not people you would really want to fuck with. Regular common street thugs, you can handle. These guys, they don't take no shit."

"You're sayin' they won't believe you?" I asked.

"No, they won't believe you at all. They want their money, that's it. Or you gotta pay with something else."

"Like, have you heard of stories?"

"Yeah, I heard of stories, you know, guys comin' by, and they say they got stuck up and these guys all of sudden they disappear. You never hear from them again. So I wonder what happened to them. Some of it's true [that they get robbed]. Some of them they just take all of it on consignment, five hundred, three hundred thousand dollars and they just go to [the] Dominican Republic, go wherever they from, Jamaica, and that's it. You know, this is what the guys that own the material [drugs] are worried about."

So even in the face of a gun barrel pressed against their temple, or a heated iron waiting to be placed on their back, drug dealers are courageously stubborn. The potential consequences are enough to keep them from giving up their drugs and cash.

Gus provided an example. He told me of a job he had recently gotten as an enforcer for some upper-level Puerto Rican drug dealers. These men had supplied a dealer with forty kilos of cocaine—a million dollars worth of drugs—on consignment. The dealer later claimed that he was arrested by police, who then released him and kept the drugs. The Puerto Rican dealers did not believe him. So they paid Gus and his old prison-mate twenty thousand dollars to get information out of the dealer. The duo then held the dealer hostage in a basement. They tortured him for three days.

"I had bought a little welding torch," Gus recalled. "So I was askin' him, I was like, 'Look, this is what's happening. These people want their money or they want their drugs. You decide if you gonna give it to me or not. Don't worry about it. I got all night.' And when I'm talkin' to him, I'm fuckin' with the torch, you know, lightin' it and everything. Yo, kid, I started burnin' this nigga just a little bit, you know, just passin' the flames, burnin' his hairs, fuckin' with him, smackin' him. Nigga won't talk. I start burnin' him for real. I'm puttin' holes in his chest. The nigga passed out on me twice, put it like that. I had to hose him down with a water hose in the basement, twice.

"I told him, 'Look, these people givin' me a hundred thousand dollars to do this to you. If you pay me, I'll stop. I don't got nothing to do with what you owe them.' He was like, 'Yeah, I know that this is your job. And you're doing a good job.' He was tellin' me that shit, ha-ha. He was like, '*Tu 'ta ciendo un buen trabajo*. But I don't got no money.'"

"So, what they made us do after they found out that he ain't have no money or nothing on him, they made us tell him to call his wife in [the] Dominican Republic and sign [off] like all his property. I'm tellin' you, his house is worth like eight million in pesos . . . he had a business that's worth like seven million [pesos] . . . I mean, all his shit was worth mad money. And he had to sign all that shit over to them."

Gus' account also showed why a dealer might endure horrible torture even if he knew he was going to give in eventually. Because if a dealer claims that vicious robbers robbed him, but has not a bruise or scratch, then a supplier might think that the robbery tale is a lie. *Pura mierda.* No puffed-up eye, no swollen jaw, no burn marks on the back—*yup, he took the shit.* A dealer, then, might undergo torture to have a good explanation for the missing goods.

Drug robbers understand a dealer's resistance. But they also need the goods. So, after drug robbers question a dealer, the next step is torture. However, a problem emerges—deciding on length and intensity. To succeed, drug robbers must not quit when dealers hold out. Otherwise, they won't profit. As Jack Katz notes, robbers need "a true hardheadedness,"[13] or stubbornness, to complete a robbery.

But, again, a dealer could be just as hardheaded, showing a dangerous commitment to keeping the drugs and cash. For a victimized dealer, life after a robbery—always running, always owing, always dodging death—might be worse than experiencing immediate pain. So the robbery could turn into what sociologist Erving Goffman called a "character contest,"[14] an emotional contest between robber and dealer. If a dealer demonstrates resolve through severe pain, then a robber must intensify the torture. However, a robber must check his emotions.

The dealer cannot not die.

PLAYING BY THE RULES: *NO LO MATEN*

To understand why drug robbers must avoid killing, we should briefly return to the end of the robbery that started the chapter. After a night of torture—of beating and kicking and electrocution—the dealer had not surrendered the whereabouts of the drugs and cash. Gus decided to grab the dealer's keys and go to the drug stash apartment. "I just didn't want to deal with this nigga," Gus recalled, "'cause we was gonna end up killin' him."

Overall, it had become an ordeal to continue torturing without receiving information. The crew even insisted to the dealer that they knew he sold drugs and where he lived. They just needed exact information on the whereabouts of his drug and money stash. The crew, though, already knew that he kept about three hundred grams of heroin and forty-eight thousand dollars in cash in his small, rented room. But how?

Like most drug robberies, this one began through betrayal. The dealer's partner, who had inside details, provided information to the crew. And after getting the drugs and cash, the crew planned to split the profits with the partner. Then the partner would pretend astonishment at the dealer's loss. *What happened? Who did this? They took what?*

But if the robbers held inside information—if they knew the exact location of the drugs and cash—then why did they torture rather than grab the apartment keys from the start?

There are rules to this game. As in a boxing match or a gang rumble, the drug robbers and traitorous partner established guidelines to reduce physical and emotional loss. One rule is that drug robbers must pretend ignorance of the drugs' location. This protects the betraying partner from a victim who later suspects foul play. Because if robbers went straight to the stash—the loose floor tile, the hidden sneaker box, the small tear in the sofa cushion—without jumping any hurdles, then they clearly received inside information. Sensing treachery, a dealer might seek retaliation against a partner.

"Because his friend was the one that told us where everything is at," Gus explained. "So, the only people that know where that shit is at are the ones that work there. So, we have to make him tell us where that shit is at 'cause then he was gonna suspect everybody that knows about this shit—he's gonna think, 'It's me, the other kid that works with me, and my man that I brought up here one time.' So, you know, I had to make him tell us where it was at."

Neno, this time in English, concurred: "Like the person who gives me the job could tell me where it's [the drugs] at exactly. You know, 'The nigga got the shit under the bed.' Sometimes they tell you exactly where it's at, but you can't take it like that 'cause then they could get in trouble, you feel me? So you have to do it the right way. 'Cause if I go and get your drugs without you tellin' me nothing, then you gonna be like, 'Who said something? I ain't say nothing. It's my drugs.'"

Another rule in most drug robberies is *No lo maten*. Do not kill him. Despite the betrayal, a partner wants the dealer to stay alive. Often, they establish strong friendships with co-workers: they eat in familiar ethnic restaurants;

drink and dance in nightclubs; talk and joke on the streets; and compare notes on the cars, clothes, and women they bought, either for friendly competition or a good laugh. In other words, dealers create strong bonds.

But business is business. Money supersedes all. The name of the game is high profits at whatever cost.[15] And dealers understand this, which is why they use guns to keep the money-grubbing sharks at bay. And setting up a partner? That's part of the game.

Yet betraying partners often show concern. They order robbers not to kill their partner, a sign of some humanity.[16] So robbers might beat them repeatedly with their fists, bloodying and bruising faces; they might burn them with an iron, creating bumpy, pockmarked scars; they might chop off fingers and slice off ears, laming and stigmatizing them for life—but *no lo maten.* Maim him, scar him, but *no lo maten.* Break him, shatter him, but *no lo maten.*

No. Lo. Maten.

For instance, Topi explained how betraying partners gave a green light to torture, but warned to stop short of a killing. "They always say to not kill the guy [dealer]," Topi said, in Spanish. "Because they are friends, you know. They look for ass [women] together, smoke weed together . . . they're friends. Like one time, this guy told me, 'You could do what you need to do because the guy [the victim] is a lion. If you let him, he'll eat you alive. But he's my buddy. Do what you need to do. But don't kill him. You're going to have to hit him a lot, but don't go over [the line]. Do not kill him.'"

This rule created a problem for Gus, David, and the others in the robbery described at the beginning of the chapter. After torturing the dealer and receiving no confession, the crew moved toward more life-threatening harm. At one point, Jonah struck the dealer repeatedly across the face and the blindfold came off. The dealer stared into Jonah's face. Angry, Jonah yelled, "*Sí, sí! Mírame la cara! Mírame la cara bien, mama huevo, que yo se que te voy a matar!* (Yes, yes! Look at my face! Look at my face well, cocksucker, because I know I'm going to kill you!)

But they could not kill the man.

"The guy that gave this [robbery] to us is his friend," David explained, in Spanish. "And he told us, 'If you are going to hurt him, hurt him. But try not to do too much shit to him. *No lo maten.*'"

EIGHT

Drug Robbery Torture

AFTER READING THE ACCOUNTS OF violence presented here, readers might have one of two alarmed reactions. The first: *These men are sociopaths who gain fulfillment through inflicting physical and emotional harm. Even if they are drug market participants, there must be a self-selection process. Not anyone can inflict pain so ruthlessly, so mercilessly. They must have been born that way. These men are monsters.* (This was the response from some non-academics in casual talks about my work). The second: *Like most minorities, these men are bound up in an inner-city culture of violence. Thus, violence is socially inscribed in their bodies, their minds, becoming their social nature. These men are social monsters.* (This is how some ethnographers felt I portrayed the study participants in an early draft.)

Both responses are understandable given the social morays against violence. However, both responses frame violent individuals as totally separate from mainstream moral bonds. This makes it hard to understand drug robbery violence sociologically. Even sociologists, who are trained to find the "social" in human interaction, will have trouble not passing moral judgment or keeping the "pathological" at bay. So I risk reinforcing racial and ethnic stereotypes, even if drug robbers hold only a small niche within the drug market.

To counter this tendency, I now analyze drug robbery violence within a broader social context. Like all violence, drug robbery torture is bolstered by the social—the societal logic, group dynamics, and emotions arising from the immediate event.

As the previous chapter showed, drug robbers accept torture, a cruelty that torments and degrades human beings. Yet society condemns torture, ranking it as one of humankind's most hideous acts. To resolve this moral tension, drug robbers socially construct a logic that justifies their torture. This move resembles, in spirit, the one by state-sponsored torturers, who turn an act so ethically wrong into one so morally right.

Though not drug robbers, state torturers from the United States to the remotest regions of the globe inflict bodily and psychological harm. Their waterboarding simulates drowning. Their electrical shocks sting muscles, breasts, and testicles. Their punches and kicks and limb twists and separations rupture organs. And they have a delayed or time-release mental torture component: once let go, victims face stigma as "traitors" and trudge through life knee-deep in shame.[1] All these forms of torture leave the victim in agony.

The moral mystery is how state-sponsored torturers do not seem to experience guilt. They stand in contrast to most people, who cannot do violence or even witness torture (which is why, except for the occasional moral reversal, modern torture occurs in concealed quarters, not public squares[2]). The question: What allows state-sponsored torturers to go against the moral grain?

The social.

As torture scholar Ronald Crelinsten observes, state torturers reside within nation-states that conjure up torture rationales for their citizens.[3] They do so by constructing a new reality in the nation-state's relationship to a certain national, racial, ethnic, or ideological group. Through powerful propaganda, the nation-state stigmatizes the target, rendering it as godless, threatening, and subhuman. This "reality" is then cemented through media control, political rhetoric, and reinterpretations of the law.[4] All stir up anger and fear among citizens, who now see the target group as evil; torture can then be justified within prevailing moral rules.[5] Just like that, state-sponsored torturers are morally cleared.[6]

Clearly, different aims exist between state-sponsored torture and drug robbery violence. David Luban, a distinguished scholar of law and philosophy, argues that historically, nations that torture often have five aims: to degrade, to terrorize, to punish, to extract incriminating confessions, and to gather intelligence.[7] Drug robbers perhaps only aim for the last: to gather information on money and drugs.

Yet South Bronx drug robbers are embedded in a societal logic that justifies their torture. It is the state-sponsored capitalist ideology that pervades the nation. The goal of capitalism—in its cocktail version—is to accumulate monstrosities of wealth and capital through competitive enterprise. It is a race in which winners amass the most capital, and losers are eventually forced from the competition. A befitting phrase is "survival of the fittest," a jungle metaphor connoting that the strong rise to the top, while the lesser fall to the bottom, perishing from existence.

A more objective phrase might be "greed is good."[8] On the premise of pure self-interest, capitalists go to great lengths to accumulate profit for its own sake. And with it comes the belief in amassing material status items—the ownership of more mansions and ranches, more expensive boats and cars, more jewelry and jets, more and more and more.[9] Those with the most income and wealth are respected and idolized. Those with nothing are put down as pathetic and low.

Capitalism's hidden reality, though, is that the competition is rigged, that those with the most capital have the resources to not only maintain but also multiply their financial, social, educational, and residential resources. This is why our nation's richest 10 percent own 63 percent of the nation's wealth, earn 42.5 percent of the nation's income, and hold 78 percent of all corporate stock.[10] Almost everyone else is, decade after decade, losing ground.

To keep the lead, capitalists socially construct a "reality."[11] Through the media, schools, and government, they put out the message: *as long as one is willing to work hard, regardless of social station, they can strike it rich.* They ignore their own mostly upper-middle-class backgrounds as they whip out rags-to-riches stories, for example, the atypical down-and-out minority, who, barely surviving, finds a way to skyrocket to success.[12] In an ideological sleight of hand, the finger is now turned on the poor, who are depicted as riddled with moral, cultural, and personal flaws.[13] Most people then come to believe that capitalism is fair, that outrageous wealth is ideal, and that success *is* material excess.

But as criminologists Daniel Murphy and Matthew Robinson note, this acceptance leads to a premise that, though not uttered outright, is loud and clear: as long as profit is the goal, it's alright to do whatever it takes. That some laws are broken, ignored—fine. That consumers are misled, harmed—fine. That morality is bent and bracketed—fine.[14] In short, this "maximization," or blurring of illegal unethical practices with legal ones, is accepted as normal not only by the capitalist elite, but also by the public at large.[15]

This is why public outrage is muted in the face of white-collar crimes that cost hundreds of thousands of people their savings and homes, millions and billions of their tax dollars, and their innocent but devalued lives.[16] This is why large corporations—such as automobile, tire, oil, and tobacco companies—can supplant ethics and morality with a cost-benefit analysis or pseudo-science, and after knowingly causing death and destruction, experience no guilt or punishment. *Nada.*

This capitalist logic, with its underlying but unsaid criminal and immoral practices, permeates society. So *getting over, doing what you have to do, doing nothing for free,* the cardinal capitalist premises, creep into impoverished communities. And for the poor, capitalist accumulation and high material consumption are more likely realized through big-time illicit business. Pimping. Numbers running. Drug dealing. Criminal enterprise, then, is not a resistance to dominant society; rather, it is a pledge of allegiance to its logic, material values, and goals.

You Gotta Do What You Gotta Do

And for these Dominican men, capitalist principles formed the foundation of their drug market participation and violence. As long as they were trying to earn money, they spoke as though morally clear. For instance, an entrepreneurial Pablo explained why he dealt drugs: "'Cause I ain't want to get a nine to five [job]. I ain't want nobody tellin' me what to do and I wanted to make money, bro. I wanted to do it myself. It's not like somebody's gonna give me a good job, bro. If you don't got a master's [degree] or something, you ain't gettin' a good job. And I don't want to be no blue-collar worker. They ain't makin' shit."

I then asked what he was trying to achieve through crime. "I want to see the pot at the end of the rainbow, ha-ha," Pablo answered, laughing. "I want to make a million dollars, see a million dollars and then go off into the horizon. 'Cause with a million dollars, bro, you go to another country and you be alright. If you want to be a beach bum, you could be a beach bum, ha-ha. You'll still be makin' money through the interest. It's about capitalism, bro, it's about making that money, even if it don't mean nothing at the end of the day. And basically when you get more, you get what you need—not what you need, what you want. Shit, you don't even think about it, bro. You just buy it. With a million, what can't you buy? Like I could get that house, that car, clothes, all type of shit. I don't have to worry about anything.

"But if you like a regular Joe just workin' for bills, forget it, bro. He gotta pay a mortgage, he gotta pay cable, light, all that shit. If he gets laid off, bro, that's a wrap. The only people that are makin' money, that got it good, are the people in corporate. They lose their job, whatever, they takin' millions with them. But a regular Joe? It's over for him. It's like this guy told me one time, and you gonna laugh when I tell you this shit: *Dios dijo: aquí te dejo; que el ma' vivo viva del pendejo.* (God said: Here I leave you; may the wily live off the fools.)

I laughed loudly at its meaning and rhyme.

"It means that dudes with money got that money by gettin' over on other people. That's the way the world works, bro. The little dude is gonna get stepped on by the big dude. The dude that knows more is gonna step on the dude that doesn't know shit."

David also absorbed the widespread message of becoming rich. And his school failures, lack of resources, and poor upbringing were not stopping him—even if he had to do violence. "You have to look for the riches," David explained, in Spanish. "For instance, there's two ways to look for that money. You can go to school, study, do all that, and get a career, everything's good. Or you can look for it in the street doing a lot of stuff, like selling drugs, or like these guys out here, robbing dealers. There's guys that go to school and they could be professionals. They earn their money and could buy their house, their car, and all that stuff. But there's guys like me that can't with school. We're going to get that money any way possible. Because if I'm not a professional, how am I going to search for that money?"

"But to get what's yours, you hurt people," I stated, in Spanish.

"But if you don't hurt them, the money stays behind. If you have to harm a guy to earn one hundred thousand [dollars], you have to do it. Forget about that. You just have to do it. You're in school and you're getting your money in your way. But I have to get it my way."

Tukee summed it up best by referring to that simple refrain that morally clears rule-breaking capitalists: *You gotta do what you gotta do.* "It's not like I get up in the morning and I want to fuck a nigga up," he explained. "But if you're strugglin', you gotta do it. Because if you do it, then you won't be strugglin', understand? It's the money, man. You gotta do what you gotta do. You don't want it to happen, but it's a high possibility that it's gonna happen. If you gotta fuck somebody up, torture, whatever, then you gotta do it."

But let's return to the topic of state-sanctioned torture. Once locked in place, a morally cleansing societal logic creates the space for torturers to rationalize their face-to-face violence. For instance, in her study of Brazilian police torturers, Martha K. Huggins notes four ways that "violence workers" justify and distance themselves from their inhumane acts.[17] First, the classic: blaming the victim. If victims fail to confess alleged wrongdoings or give up other incriminating information, torturers believe that they deserve the pain. Second, torturers often cite "professionalism," which makes distinctions between good and bad torturers. For instance, the "good torturer" is rational and "correctly" seeks information. The bad torturer seeks pleasure through inflicting pain and loses control. Third, torturers sometimes diffuse responsibility, or attempt to put the onus on fellow perpetrators. In other words, they claim to disagree with the violence and show how they play secondary roles. Fourth, they assert "just causes" for their torture, like portraying themselves as patriots or pointing to urgent situations.[18]

Like state torturers, once drug robbers absorbed a larger morally cleansing logic—for them, the capitalist logic—they could rationalize the one-on-one violence. To be clear, the third and fourth rationalizations—diffusing responsibility and just causes—are not applicable to these drug robbers. They neither blamed other robbers nor cited patriotic causes or doomsday scenarios as justifying their violence. The first two rationalizations, though, are common. The most popular rationale is blaming the victim.

For instance, one day while we were standing by the public stairwell, both Topi and Gus rationalized torture by blaming the dealer. "Listen, if those guys don't want us to touch them," Topi explained, in Spanish, "then they should tell us right away, 'It's right there, take it, leave already, leave me alone.' If they say that, we're alright. We didn't put a hand on them, they're not missing pieces."

"They aren't missing an ear, right, they're intact, there's nothing missing," Gus added, in Spanish.

"Exactly," Topi answered, grinning. "Anyway, those guys know what will happen to them if they don't tell me where it's at. That's why they get hit. If it was up to me, I enter and get the material and leave without putting a hand on them."

"That's how it is," Gus agreed. "Because nobody wants to go through all those problems, right?"

"Exactly," answered Topi. "If we hurt those people, it's because they made us do it. They deserve the knocks [to the head]."

Neno would add a twist to the logic of victim blaming. One afternoon, I was in Maggie's apartment (she was Gus' former girlfriend) speaking with Gus and Neno. After Maggie put away some groceries and retreated to the bedroom, I asked Neno about violence in drug robberies. He argued that resistant dealers delight in the hurt. *Son masochistas.*

"Many times," Neno answered, in a slow, melodic Spanish (he was high), "you have to use violence, split the person open so that they tell you. Because there's people that let themselves be killed to not give it up, see? Those people like that, you have to hit them hard, so that they let go [the information]. You break their big heads. Because, just imagine, you just want to leave with that [the drugs and money] from there."

I asked him to describe an experience.

"The day we put an iron on the guy," Gus helped him recollect.

"Just imagine, I went with him [Gus] on a job and we grabbed this guy. And he didn't want to talk—'Alright, leave me alone! Kill me! There's nothing here!' And we grabbed an iron, real hot—but hot, hot—and put it on his back a couple of times. The guy talked right away and told us where everything was.

"It's that they're masochists," Neno continued. "They like being hit. Because if you know that you're going to give it up, give it up and don't take any beatings."

Another rationale among drug robbers was their version of "professionalism." Disagreements often arose as to torture practices, with the men criticizing each other's efficiency. For instance, in the drug robbery that opened the previous chapter, David argued with Gus, telling him that he was too barbaric. In doing so, David conveyed his own intellectual sophistication, which distanced him from the inhumane act. As he saw it, he was a "good torturer."[19]

"Look, I'm not going to say that you can't hit them, cut off a finger, or even an ear," David explained, in Spanish. "But when you see that with all those bad things, that he still isn't talking, you have to try other ways of getting the information. What happened is that Gus got frustrated. We all got frustrated. But we can't let the moment take us, understand? We all already beat him, we cut off an ear, we did a lot of shit to him, and what happened? The dude did not want to talk. So let him rest and we start all over again. Tell him, 'Look, we don't want to kill you, but we have to kill you if you don't give us what we want, understand?' And you tell him a lot of other stuff to eat his mind. You have to use psychology."

Gus portrayed himself as the good torturer and invoked Jonah as the worst.[20] In the same robbery, he described Jonah's torture tactics as crude, while his own were acceptable and controlled. According to Gus, Jonah had sniffed too much cocaine, which made him repeatedly strike the dealer's head with his gun and fists, and repeatedly stomp the dealer's stomach and chest. For every blow he received, the dealer screamed in pain.

"He was fuckin' him up bad," recalled Gus. "I'm tellin' him, 'You don't have to hit this nigga like that, man. There's a lot of things you could do that don't make no noise.' That nigga would go, 'Ahhh!' every time Jonah hit him with the gun. . . . He's just always coked up so he doesn't have no control over himself. So, if we left it up to him, he would have killed him."

Gus also cited examples of how he developed relationships with his victims. For instance, he sometimes interrupted the torture with breaks to give them food and water, and speak to them about ordinary affairs. Despite his brutality, Gus used these moments to portray himself as a moral human being, as someone doing his job and treating his victim with decency.[21]

"Like after torturin' them for a while," Gus explained, "I sometimes stop and go to the[ir] refrigerator, make them a sandwich or something. Get them some juice. Give them water so they could drink."

"Why?" I asked, surprised.

"Imagine, they been takin' all this torture for hours, for hours, bro. They need some type of food in their system. I know they at least need water, bro. They get real dehydrated after bleedin' and shit."

"What else do you do?"

"I even start talkin' to them, bro. For real, ha-ha. We start talkin' about mad shit. Baseball, D.R. [Dominican Republic], all type of shit, bro."

"Can you give me an example?"

"Like the time with that little nigga that I was torturin' in the basement. We was talkin' about mad shit, bro. We was talkin' about Sammy Sosa [a Dominican major league baseball player at the time], talkin' about all type of shit. Another time I was talkin' to this nigga about food, other shit, ha-ha. Like a lot of times, they don't want to talk. They too fucked up. But sometimes they be talkin' and shit."

"Why would they want to talk to you?" I asked, dumbfounded.

"It's like I tell them that I'm just doin' my job. That shit it isn't personal, bro. I came to get the drugs and I'm torturin' them to get the drugs. And when I'm talkin' to them, they could see that it isn't like personal. I don't have nothing against them. I'm just tryin' to get what I came for."

These men also use a rationale identified by David Matza and Gresham Sykes in their classic "Techniques of Neutralization."[22] As Matza and Sykes argue, neutralizations are ways that wrongdoers justify their wrongdoing. For instance, they sometimes "condemn the condemners," or point to the misconduct of authorities as a way to justify their own misbehavior. Likewise, drug robbers condemn legal institutions and professionals, whom society has historically slapped on the wrist for unethical or immoral behavior. David pointed to lawyers, perhaps the legal professional he encountered most. "For example, like lawyers," David stated in Spanish. "They went to school and got their careers. You think they are good people because they don't live like these guys in the street. But they are disgraceful, those damn dogs. Listen, to earn their money, they would sell their own mother. Even if you didn't have a cent in your pocket, those dogs keep asking for more. And they don't do anything. You both go to court, he says three or four words, and that's it. You lost three thousand, four thousand dollars. And they earn good, those damn disgraces."

Tukee also cited police officers as "crooked" professionals who rob dealers too. "I'm doin' the same thing crooked cops do," Tukee explained. "They be runnin' up into niggas' houses and robbin' those motherfuckas. They take they drugs, money, they take everything, B. You don't be hearin' about that shit on the news. But I know dudes who cops took their shit, bro. They never reported it."

"Who?" I asked. "The dudes?"

"The cops, man. They be findin' shit and don't report it. They know a dude got two kilos, three kilos or twenty thou', they go up to their house, no search warrant, and take that shit. Never report it . . . They doin' the same thing I'm doin'. The difference between me and them is that they got a badge."

And Gus, who watched late-night documentaries and had learned critical ideas in prison, provided a scathing critique of the U.S. government and corporations. It was a response to my comment on how people would not understand his torture. "Let me tell you, Ran, when the government like wants money from some fuckin' dictator, what they do? The CIA, ha-ha. The CIA takes care of that shit. Those motherfuckas will assassinate fuckin' dictators for a fuckin' dollar, bro. Just assassinate the motherfucka. . . . Yo, even fuckin' corporations be doing shady shit, bro. They be sending niggas to assassinate like the people that ain't gonna help them make like profit. All those motherfuckas do it. You gonna tell me that I'm wrong for torturin' somebody? Come on, Bro! Ha-ha-ha!"

Overall, the accounts show how these men internalized the nation's capitalist and material ideology and applied its logic to their crimes. Greed and its immoral underpinnings, with, of course, societal acceptance, creates a space for their drug market violence. For them, this is just how the system works, one where brutality and unfairness are morally justified as long as money is the goal. Then they could rationalize their immediate torture by blaming the victim, showing "professionalism," and citing shady governments and businesses. This, then, is how these men, like state-sponsored torturers, make torture morally bearable.

DRUG ROBBERIES AND EMOTIONS

To analyze the in-the-moment dynamics of South Bronx drug robbery violence, I mostly use Randall Collins' theory of violence, which examines emotions in violent situations.[23] To be clear, this is not the only micro-theory of violence and I will refer to others along the way. I also know that subcultural theories have greatly impacted the study of inner-city violence.[24] But they assume that street violence occurs often and that cultural mandates automatically beckon violence within people.[25] However, with the exception of two street incidents (which I discuss later), I rarely observed street violence.

What I observed was lots of bragging and bluster, lots of talk about doing violence and issuing threats. I heard phrases such as, *Man, I'll beat the shit outta him. I'll fuck that nigga up. He know better than to fuck with me. [Yo] le cargo ensima, [yo] le doy tre' fuetaso a ese mama huevo.* Yet even this bluster was not face to face. Instead, they grumbled from a distance.

Also, these men often joked and acted respectfully, with the occasional vulgar sarcasm found in a Greek fraternity house. They were always high and smiling from smoking weed, and respectful of neighborhood elders, addressing them as *"Doña," "Señora," "Don," "Señor"* (of course, if they had a reason, they would still rob or burglarize the person's home). Mostly, they argued about who had yet to chip in for the next marijuana bag. Thus, my first impression of them: *These men, drug robbers? No way!*

So if a street culture existed, it was a culture of "making claims" to violence, one where most mastered a "bad ass" presentation.[26] For instance, they wore "gangsta" clothes; they made exaggerated gestures; and they sometimes spoke loudly and profanely. Most of them, though, were just not inherently brutal. They depended on emotional and group dynamics for their drug robbery violence. They also depended on an emotional leader, whom I call the Robber Elite.

Emotional Dynamics

In a comprehensive examination of violence, Randall Collins argues that doing *mano-a-mano* violence is hard.[27] For most people, violence contradicts human emotional entrainment, or the human tendency to align in positive solidarity. So while individuals or groups can oppose each other, they mostly do so in bluster, or talk about doing violence *(Don't mess with me)*. Perverse violence only occurs when one side is overpowered (e.g., five British soccer fans trap a lone Italian fan or a child backpedals in a fight). Though both parties experience tension and fear, the advantaged one transforms those emotions into a "forward panic." Thus, most violence—like five police officers beating a handcuffed suspect after a car chase—has little to do with self-preservation. It has to do with the emotional surge after gaining the upper hand in a conflict.[28]

The "forward panic" enables South Bronx drug robbers—like combat soldiers, like sports fans, like private school bullies—to suddenly do violence. First, immediately before a drug robbery, the men experience tension and fear. For instance, on the night of one robbery, this was Gus: he was edgy and anxious, playfully punching David, sometimes shadow boxing with an imaginary opponent, and laughing aloud, by himself. David: he was pensive and quiet, listening to music, trying to remain in the background, acting unlike his talkative and loud self. And Jonah: he was snorting cocaine and drinking liquor, trying to change his mental state. All experienced tension and fear, which they showed and managed differently.

Second, drug robbers got the emotional upper hand by surprising dealers. Through either The Girl's seduction or simply sneaking up on them, drug robbers caught the dealer unawares: There is the dealer having drinks with The Girl, slow dancing, murmuring in her ear . . . There is another dealer who cautiously peeks through a peephole and gladly opens the door to an attractive girl . . . There is one more dealer, who, as he unlocks his apartment door, hears footsteps and turns around . . . When the robbery is announced, they are all shocked and disoriented. The robbers gain situational dominance and emotional momentum.

Third, even before the robbery, the dealers transform the tension and fear into positive emotional energy. Since they have inside information from a treacherous partner, they see the cards stacked favorably. For instance, Pablo saw the robbery as ceremonial, like a ritual before claiming a grand prize. "'Cause when I do something, I do it with someone inside [the dealer's circle]. So I never get like scared or anything like that. I just get a rush. It's like I know I'm gonna get whatever I have to get. It's a rush, that's the only way I could explain it. Because I'm thinkin' about the payday. Imagine, you got somebody inside [giving information], it's like you know it's gonna happen. How's it not gonna happen?"

The perceived advantage gave them an added emotional charge. Katz' insights apply here: the men feel emotionally dominant and powerful.

Gus: "I know for me, it's like a rush . . . like a rush feeling. *[What do you mean, a "rush" feeling?]* Like it's a nervous feeling. It's hard to explain. Like I get nervous right before I do every robbery—every one, bro. *[Does it feel good?]* I mean, I don't know if it feels good . . . It's like I feel nervous and excited, you know what I'm sayin'? So, yeah, I feel excited too. That part feels good. *[Why does it feel good?]* I mean, I guess 'cause you know that you went there [to an apartment] to get drugs and you gonna come out of there with drugs, you know? So that like makes you feel good. Like you know that it's all worth it."

Neno (in Spanish): "It's like you feel a lot of power. Like when you are in there [the apartment] you tell them, 'Be quiet! Don't move, sperm-sucker! If you move, I'm going to kill you!' If they stay still and get scared, you feel a lot of power. *[Why?]* Because they know that if they move you're going to shoot them, you're the one telling them what to do. If they don't do what you say, you kill them. *[How does that power feel?]* It feels like nothing could happen to you because only things are going to happen to them, understand? You are the one controlling what happens. *[Do you like that feeling?]* Of course. *[Why?]* Because when you tell people not to move, not to dare, and they don't do it, because they know that you'll give them a [bullet] shot, it feels good."

And Melissa: "It [the robbery] was exciting. The excitement and the thrill. The thrill was that I had him [the dealer], that he wasn't gonna go nowhere. And I was gonna get paid. That's what the thrill was."

Last, robbery group dynamics increase emotional momentum.[29] Working in groups of four or five, and carrying guns, they bolster their confidence through a common identity and purpose. Like a college football team shouting in unison before a game; like a large number of uniformed Los Angeles police officers jumping out of cars—a team of gun-toting drug robbers get into an emotional zone, get hyped in the presence of others, and produce extraordinary violence. Drug robbers understand the emotional energy of the team, which is why they rarely did major drug robberies alone or in a pair. The emotional energy would be lacking, leading to botched attempts.

For instance, in a rare attempt to do a drug robbery with just one other person, Pablo worked with Willie, who had inside information from the target's partner. The plan was for Pablo to follow the dealer into a building, then upstairs to the drug apartment floor, where Willie, gun in hand, would be waiting to set a trap.

What was the outcome?

Zoom to a cramped elevator: upon reaching the floor, the dealer (and some partners) became suspicious of Pablo, who was wearing a suit that day. Thinking he was law enforcement, they ran down the hallway to their apartment. They knocked and yelled, the door opened, they scrambled in, got away.

Where was Willie?

Zoom to a sunny South Bronx skyline: unable to handle the tension and fear of confronting the dealers with his gun, Willie began hyperventilating in the stairwell. He then climbed to the building's rooftop, where he remained for quite some time, breathing in fresh air.

So doing violence is hard in small numbers, where the emotional energy can get sapped without group support. Getting "hyped" might have been easier for Willie if another drug robber had been waiting with him. Alone, he could not turn the tension and fear into a forward panic, into the thrill and excitement that would carry him through the robbery. Instead, he retreated from the confrontation—even though he had a gun. And Pablo could have put his gun to the dealers' backs—but he didn't.

In short, these factors allow drug robbers to do violence. Drug robbers typically stun the dealer right away and gain emotional momentum. High on the emotional energy of anticipation and the dealer's weakness, drug robbers, as a team, then experience a frenzied move forward, a silent roar, a rise above the confrontational tension and fear. Now, these men can beat, burn, and mutilate a dealer. Now, they can act brutally with only a single rule (*No Lo Maten*) keeping them from a kill.

Yet even among emotionally charged drug robbers, not everyone welcomes violence. In fact, only one or two members stand out: they lead the rush, suddenly striking an unsuspecting victim, pummeling them, choking them, beating them to a pulp. The other robbers "freeze" with gun in hand; or they move only when ordered; or they perform some isolated violence, like dragging victims or occasionally threatening and striking them. For these robbers, the group's forward panic, or state of "hype," is just enough to do sideline violence—they can see it, hear it, and cheer it, and occasionally come off the bench for some play. Torture, though, is too hard for them. Thus, only one or two robbers star in the violent picture event.

Who are the most violent, emotionally charged men?

Randall Collins argues that less than a tenth of the general population is "competently" violent.[30] These individuals are not the biggest (though size helps) or most athletic (though this helps too). Their distinction is that, like star pupils in a math class, they grasp the calculus of violent situations. Through experience, they have learned how to manipulate a target's tension and transform their own tension into an emotional high. So they are not angry hotheads who are genetically wired for violence. Rather, their violence is social, a skill acquired through repetition and practice.[31] This violent elite, Collins observes, can be found across social strata.[32] For instance, they are the enforcers in hockey, hit men in mobs, the cowboys on a police force, the aces among fighter pilots, and the bad asses on the street.

Drug robbers also have an elite. I call them the "robber elite." Gus is one. In drug robberies, he took charge—he was the first to confront the dealer, then beat and torture him. True, others got their kicks and punches in, and a few dabbled in torture. But this violence was supportive. Most listened for neighbors, searched for valuables, and communicated with lookouts on the street. It was Gus, from the stories I heard, who purposely took the violent center stage. After noting this trend, I asked Pablo for his view. "If you askin' me who always took the lead, I would say Gus," Pablo answered. "That nigga was always on some suicidal shit. He just didn't give a fuck. He always was the first one to do everything. No, put it like this, he always wanted to be the first one to do everything. He wanted to be first one inside the apartment, to fuck a nigga up, all that shit. And when he fucked a nigga up, he really fucked them up, bro . . . That nigga loved to torture, ha-ha. He always came up with some crazy shit. Something's really wrong with that nigga."

What made Gus a robber elite was his American-style overachievement within the context of structural constraints.[33] And he took that high ambition and determination into the underground economy's violence. Unlike others, he purchased firearm magazines and catalogues. He created a homemade gun silencer. He discussed the latest weaponry. His diligence and intelligence about violence allowed him to act coolly in a drug robbery.

Both his drug market and incarceration experiences also reinforced his drug robbery dominance. Before his forays into stickups, he beat up "crackheads" and shot several drug market rivals. He also strong-armed weaker inmates while in jail and prison. So Gus knew how to dominate violent situations. And no one else could match him. For instance, David, Neno, and Topi started as teenage burglars, as tiptoe criminals who purposely avoided confrontations. This is why Gus took the lead while they took supporting roles.

Of course, some perceived Gus' violence as chaotic or out of control. So on the street, people referred to him as an "animal," an individual who did a seemingly carnivorous violence. For instance, let's listen in on a conversation where Gus described more of the robbery that started the previous chapter: "The nigga [dealer] was full of voodoo shit, bro! Ha-ha-ha-ha," Gus said, laughing hysterically. "That nigga had a fuckin' horsetail, some shit, braided with some beads and a rosary, bro! Ha-ha-ha-ha!"

"Damn," Pablo said, laughing.

"I was like, 'Yo,'" Gus said, with his eyes wide open. "David was scared. He grabbed that shit with a bag. Ha-ha-ha!"

Everyone laughed.

"Yo, listen," Gus continued, "I asked [the dealer], 'Yo, how many balls do you got?' in Spanish."

"How many what?" Pablo asked.

"How many balls do you got?" Gus repeated. "He told me, 'I got two,' exactly. I remember word for word, he said, 'I got two, just like every other man.' He told me, *'Tengo do' grano', como to' lo' hombre'* [I have two balls, like all men].' I was like, 'Nah, man. *Tu tiene' que tener ma' de do' grano', loco* [You have to have more than two balls].'"

"Ha-ha-ha-ha!" Pablo laughed.

"Tu tiene' que tener ma' de do' grano', loco," Gus continued. *"Deja' ver* [Let me see]."

"Gus want to torture, ha-ha-ha!" Pablo laughed. "You ever seen that Charles Bronson movie?"

"You know what I'm sayin'? Ha-ha-ha-ha!" Gus said, laughing loudly. "Pulled his underwear down, took out his dick. I said, 'Yo, man. You gotta have six balls.' I told him like that, '*Tu tiene que tener sei' bola', loco. De verdad. Y de 'sa sei' bola', una yo me voy llevar.'* [You have to have six balls. For real. And from those six balls, I'm taking one.] I had his dick and his balls in one hand. I had it balled up. I had a butcher knife like this big, bro. I was ready to slice that shit. Ready to take out one of his balls."

"Ha-ha-ha," Pablo laughed, "You an *animal,* bro!"

Stop. Pablo said it: Gus was an "animal." He appeared irrational and inhumane.

One day I asked Pablo what it meant to call someone an animal. "An animal is just somebody who don't give a fuck," answered Pablo. "They just do whatever, whatever. Like a lion in Africa. He rolls. He don't give a fuck. He just goes kill whatever he has to kill. There's no thought behind it. It's just a fuckin' reaction. It's somebody that doesn't think about what they gonna do."

"Who would you call an animal?" I asked.

"There used to be this guy called Bobo. Gus used to hang with him. That nigga used to just shoot people for the hell of it. If he killed them, he killed them, whatever-whatever. That's the type of nigga who just didn't give a fuck. . . . Like Sammy the Bull, he's an animal. That nigga killed like eighteen murders *[sic]*, bodies, bro. He's a snitch and all, but he was an animal, ha-ha. You know, people like that. They just got bodies and to them it's just like breathin' to kill somebody, you know."[34]

Another day, I asked Gus, "What would you consider an 'animal'?"

"Like somebody who didn't have no feelings," Gus answered, "didn't care if he had, you know, to beat people, whatever, as long as we got our money. You know, we just don't have no feelings. Like they take theirs, like when you do a stickup, you know, that's what we do. You just takin' somebody else's money, somebody else's work and stuff. That's what I would consider an animal. I think we don't have no feelings."

Interesting: although I never asked Gus if he considered himself an animal, he used the word "we" throughout his account. Clearly, Gus thought he was an animal, and, as criminologist Lonnie Athens would say, was projecting a "violent image." And he re-created that violent image through the endless retelling of his brutal acts.[35] Here, he showed lots of excitement—to the point of shouting—a resurgence of the emotional high he experienced during the actual drug robbery.[36]

Now Neno. Although no one respected and feared him like they did Gus, he also included himself in the animal category: "An animal," Neno pondered in English. "I mean, people say that to me, you know. The way they see me doin' my job when I go to do that. People say, 'Nigga's a animal. Nigga's crazy.' I abuse those niggas [victims]. I grab those niggas, 'Get on the floor motherfucka!' Niggas be like, 'This nigga's a animal.'"

"Who would you call an animal that you know?" I asked.

"Gus is an animal. I'm an animal. We ain't worryin' about it. We ain't thinkin' about consequences. Nigga don't think nothing. Nigga just do what I gotta do. That's a animal. Nigga don't play no game."

Thus, like Gus, Neno projected a "violent image," one where he tried to show others that he was brutal, chaotic, a heart like stone. But others never called him an animal and hardly deferred to him, as they did to Gus. In fact, in drug robberies, he always passed the ball to Gus, who then scored the most violence for the team. Thus, he had an "incipient violent image," or a status with gray areas about his brutality.[37]

Some perceived the "animal" as a low-status brute. As in the popular media images of the dumb muscle guy in a crime organization, the animal in drug dealing is thought to be a dimwit in need of rational guidance. For instance, Sylvio, Gus' older brother, who had been a successful drug dealer and was now a legitimate businessperson, described the animal in his drug organization as "someone who does things on instinct, who doesn't think about it. An animal is someone who does things without fuckin' any remorse, does dumb shit without givin' it a second thought, you know. That's an animal, someone stupid who you throw out to do dumb shit that you wouldn't do. . . . But there's always someone that could control the so-called animal. You know, someone high in the hierarchy, someone that actually gives the orders. It's always somebody that has a little more control and that has a little more vision. Because the animal, what is he thinkin'? He's only thinkin' about fuckin' food, you know, how's he's gonna get his money . . . He acts on impulse. Your friend tells you, 'Let's do this.' You're like, 'Fuck it. Let's go.' That's basically what the animal does."

Thus, Sylvio regards animals as brutes, as vicious, impulsive, fearless, and remorseless individuals. Jack Katz spins the metaphor further: at any moment, the animal could lose civility, not think, produce social chaos on a whim.[38]

Returning to Pablo and Gus' description of the animal: they surmise that the animal was strong, did not "think," and operated on instinct. But being an animal also involves intelligence: he is the ringleader, the thinker, someone who understands a violent drama. His violence is not irrational, but logical; the animal knows how to dominate targets despite tension and fear. He is also a *man:* strong, dispassionate, and fearless. Gus was that person: the animal, or what I call the robber elite.

SOCIAL STRUCTURE IN VIOLENT SITUATIONS

"Racism," Randall Collins writes, "may contribute to building up some situations of violence, but it is one lead-in condition among others, and neither a necessary nor sufficient condition; the situation of violence itself has a dynamics [sic] that is more pervasive than racism."[39]

With the crux of his argument, I agree. Most violent situations have basic dynamics: tension and fear; emotionally strong or weak opponents; and forward panic. And in some cases, a violent elite emerges—the individual who knows how to do violence. This insight helped me understand a lot about drug robbery experiences. Yet, as Collins himself notes, his theory is micro extreme, purposely omitting social structure: "My preferred strategy is to push as far as possible with a situational approach; eventually we may be in a position to work backward and incorporate some background conditions; but I am not yet convinced that is going to be as important as we have usually believed. Here it may be more useful to reverse the gestalt completely, and concentrate on the foreground to the exclusion of all else."[40]

Problem. If violence were a soup, Collins has only identified the pot, water, and heat that bring it to a boil. Missing are the ingredients that give its flavor or aroma, the ingredients in a violent situation that could urge the violence forward or push it back, shaping its experience and texture.

Compelling me were thoughts on the Reconstruction and Jim Crow eras in the deep South. Frustrated and angry at declining White status, Whites hanged and tortured freed Blacks. White men also raped Black women with impunity.[41] In all, these acts were rooted in race, class, gender, and a historical period. This led me to a specific question: Could race, class, and gender *inform* and sustain the emotions within a forward panic?

I then related that question to my drug robbery accounts. In terms of race, I found no data showing that it informed emotions during drug robberies. The closest example occurred during a street robbery. After about two months of drug robberies gone awry, the desperate crew decided to go on a petty robbery spree. I was shocked at how race played a role in their choice of victims. "Listen," Gus explained to Pablo and me one afternoon, "the plan was, that night, we were gonna straight up rob and shit. We didn' care who it was. We just robbin' Black people, bro. Anybody Black with jewelry on. That's what we was doin'. We were like, '*Vamo' agarrar lo' azulitos*' [Let's go grab the blue people]."

"I went to Post [Avenue], where we buy the weed at," Gus continued. "I saw a Black dude out there. Had a .38 [handgun] on me. It was me, Topi, Topi's girl, and David. Yo, that nigga had some big shit, a medallion. I said, 'That shit is mine.' Pulled [out] the .38. David ain't even get out of the jeep. Me and Topi's girl walked up the block behind the nigga, chillin'. He got to a part, like where you throw the garbage in? Paaah! [smacking his fist into an open hand] Knocked him out. Nigga went right into the garbage. Pulled out the .38. 'My man, I'ma fuckin' kill you. Take off the jewelry.' He threw his chain at me, threw a watch, threw a beeper. Yo, he was throwin' mad shit at me, ha-ha-ha."

"Shit that you didn't even want," Pablo said, laughing. "He even gave you a watch?"

"Yeah, man, he gave me a bullshit watch," answered Gus. "What was that shit? Ay, yo! [Calling Topi in Spanish] The watch? What was the watch? I think it was a bullshit Movado. That shit was even starting to rust on the inside."

"This nigga wears that shit, Neno," Pablo said, with a smirk.

"Yeah, he wears that shit," Gus agreed. "He gonna get gangrene out that shit, ha-ha-ha."

There was more to that account, but the idea is clear. While race did not inform the street robbery's violence, it energized these men to get started. It had to. The Bronx brimmed with ethnic diversity, with many ethnic groups doing better than Blacks. But these Dominican men's hatred of Blacks served as the starting block for the emotional sprint that followed. True, the robbers gained emotional dominance through surprising the victim and were led by Gus, the robber elite. Racial hatred, though, put them in an emotional space that made the violence simpler.

Émasculation Longue Durée

In terms of gender, I found a few disturbing cases where it informed drug robbery violence. Sometimes, if a male drug dealer resisted, drug robbers perceived the act as a manhood challenge. Then their heightened emotions led to emasculating torture. Here, drug robbery violence took a "queered" turn, creating a masculinity crisis among male dealers.[42]

In fact, the torture resembled the workings of a southern White lynch mob.[43] During race-based lynchings, White mobs castrated Black men, a cruel response to their freed status and alleged lust for White women. This masculine concern, then, raised their emotions—added the gender ingredient to their violence. In drug robberies, the social structural reasons differed, yet had the same aim: answering a perceived manhood challenge through brutal emasculation.

I first learned of such torture after reanalyzing a conversation between Gus and Pablo. They were going back and forth about torture tactics, a status competition to show who was the most brutal robber.

"I'ma tell you what they [the crew members] came up with, bro," Gus said. "With the long fuckin' cord, bro, stripped. Plugged that shit in—"

"Yo, Gus," interrupted Pablo, "that shit don't work. That shit can't kill you."

"It does, man!" Gus responded. "I found that shit out, bro!"

"That can't kill you, man," Pablo said.

"It does," Gus insisted. "That shit give you like a hundred volts, bro."

"That shit can't kill you," countered Pablo. "I used all that shit!"

"You know what that shit made?" shouted Gus, ignoring Pablo. "That shit made a lot of noise! *Paahh!* I was like, 'God damn, bro!' *Paahh! Paahh! Paahh!* Every time they shocked him [dealer], it popped! Ha-ha-ha-ha . . ."

"You know what you could've done to him that would've done it?" Pablo asked. "Yo, you could've put a hair dryer in there, Gus. You throw a hair dryer in there, in the water, that shit'll fuck him up."

"Yeah," Gus agreed, "you gotta let it sit for awhile, you gotta leave the voltage on. Yeah. But you know why? Because a hair dryer has the voltage control in it."

"I know a hair dryer would do it," continued Pablo, "'cause it says it, 'Don't put this shit in water!' Ha-ha-ha! . . . Gus, listen to me. Put a wire, you know the hanger, put it in the stove. Put that shit through the nigga's ear. You blowin' up the ear drum. Yo, you ever got a pain in your ear, bro? Imagine something hot in your fuckin' ear, bro. Gus, that shit hurts, kid. [Turning to me] Ran', you know that red shit, when it turns red, that wire, bro, imagine it. *Ay Dio' mio, loco* [Oh my God].

"You could stick it through the ear," Gus agreed. "But imagine the humiliation of gettin' it stuck through your asshole, bro."

"No, fuck the asshole, Gus," Pablo said, exasperated. "Niggas could take that, Gus. Niggas could take it, Gus."

"What you want," explained Gus, "is the humiliation of him just thinkin' about it, 'Damn,' of us havin' to pull his pants down, bend him over and everything. Just the point of bein' raped, the humiliation is enough, bro. Niggas don't want to go through that shit."

"Nah, nah," Pablo disagreed.

A friend then called Gus over, ending the discussion.

By the conversation's end, Gus appeared to be a madman, the ultimate in depravity, a sadist, the ultimate in harming for pleasure, a rapist, the ultimate violator of sexual rights. But his account showed a gendered society, a hierarchical way of seeing heterosexual and gay women and men.

On a larger scale, his emasculating torture is unoriginal. In fact, it resembles U.S. torture on alleged Arab terrorists and insurgents in Abu Ghraib, the infamous Iraqi military prison.[44] In 2004, circulated photographs revealed male detainees simulating oral and anal sex on each other, and their piling into human pyramids. The latter not only forced naked contact, but also posed them on all fours, a position suggesting anal penetration.[45] Official reports also revealed how male captives were forced into women's undergarments; sodomized with chemical light sticks; threatened with rape; and, in a few cases, raped.[46] The photographs? No accident. If detainees failed to become U.S. informants, the U.S. threatened to give those shameful images to family and friends.[47]

This, then, is the larger playbook of torture that Gus operated under. Like U.S. intelligence, he linked torture, masculinity, homosexuality, and shame. And like U.S. intelligence, he not only did situational emasculation, but also emasculation for the long term, or what I call *émasculation longue durée*. He knew that a dealer would experience recurring mental anguish and disgrace.

"Because, think about," Gus later explained, "that shit stays with you for life. For life. No matter what happens to you, that shit'll always be in the back of your mind. That's why niggas don't want to go through that type of torture. It's like they know that shit would traumatize them."

Also, Gus' earlier rationale for emasculating torture eerily resonated with how a former Arab detainee thought about sexual torture:

GUS: *What you want is the humiliation of him just thinkin' about it, 'Damn,' of us havin' to pull his pants down, bend him over and everything. Just the* point of bein' raped, the humiliation is enough, bro. Niggas don't want to go through that shit.

FORMER DETAINEE: "We are men. It's OK if they beat me. Beatings don't hurt us; it's just a blow. But no one would want [his] manhood to be shattered. They want us to feel as though we were women, the way women feel, and this is the worst insult, to feel like a woman."[48]

Similarly, Neno told of sodomizing an obstinate drug dealer. "I remember one day, I got this Colombian motherfucka," Neno recalled, in English. "I put a bottle up that nigga's ass. A Corona bottle up that Colombian nigga.... Nigga was supposed to have eighty G's [eighty grand] and a few bricks [kilos] in there. We don't really find all the money. We found like forty G's and like five bricks. But we thought that nigga was lyin'. They [the informants] told me that nigga had like fifty [kilos]. Nigga only gave me like five. You already know, I burned that nigga like everywhere with the iron. I burned that nigga like a motherfuckin' pork. But that nigga was lyin' to me. So, I was like, 'Oh yeah?' I put a bottle of Corona up that nigga's ass, ha-ha."

"He gave it up there?" I asked.

"Hell yeah. No question. He ain't tryin' to play no game with his little thing [asshole]. I mean, that's his manhood right there, you feel me? Manhood gettin' taken, you feel me? But it was too late for him, fuck it. Too late. And I did it again after he told. Even after he told, I left that the Corona bottle inside his ass, ha-ha."

Like Gus, Neno understood the masculinity crisis of heterosexual men. So when he grew frustrated—rising emotions—he sodomized the dealer. And the power of emasculating torture is that the victim no longer performs his or her own gender within societal practices and norms.[49] Instead, the torturer bluntly and forcibly takes up that role.[50] Neno then "faggotized" the dealer, tyrannically rewriting his gender script.[51] And although the dealer did not perform the act, it had been performed. This is worse than brutal beatings. This is worse than a burning iron. It is an emasculating pain.[52]

But of all the drug robbers, Gus attempted the ultimate undoing of a man. Let us go back to the robbery that Gus described earlier, one that David corroborated.

Gus went into the kitchen and returned with a meat cleaver. "You gotta have more than two balls, *loco*," Gus told the dealer. "Let me see." Gus pulled off the dealer's underwear. "You gotta have six balls, and from those six balls you have, I'ma take one of them with me."

Gus grabbed the dealer's testicles and placed the meat cleaver's edge under them. ("It was a big-ass meat cleaver, bro," Gus recalled. "It looked like it was chipped from choppin' shit in the house.")

But just as Gus was about to cut off the testicle, David stopped him.

"Why do you have to do that?" David asked Gus. "That's too much. Damn, Gus, that's too much."

"But he has to tell us where that shit is at!" Gus argued. "Are we doin' this for no reason? Tell me, are we doin' this for no reason? We can't leave this like that! He has to tell us where it's at!"

"But you don't have to do that to him!"

Here, it was a contest of "balls" that led to Gus' attempted testicle removal, which is more than a "forward panic." As sociologist James Messerschmidt argues, masculinity and crime are both structured social actions and embodied practices.[53] Simply put, this means that social positions—like race, class, ethnicity, and gender—inform how people do crime and gender with their bodies. So if a masculinity challenge arises between males, violence could result.[54] In our case, torture was already under way, so the perceived masculine slight led to an extraordinary violence—the threatened disembodying of a man. Thus, as feminist scholar Dorothy Smith would say, "social relations" mattered in this situation.[55]

The crew's gendered violence was not limited to men. One afternoon when Gus and I were hanging out on the public stairwell, Gus said, *This nigga, Neno, he even raped a bitch that was inside the apartment.*

Word? I asked.

Yeah, he did, bro, Gus responded, matter-of-factly. *He's done that shit before.*

How did it happen? I asked.

While we were torturin', Gus explained, *he just took her to a bedroom and raped her.*

Why did he do that? I asked.

Nah, he just did that shit, Gus said. *That's how that nigga is. He just did that shit.*

But why would he rape her? I asked.

I don't know, man, Gus said, starting to sense my uneasy feelings.

Did you see it happen? I asked.

I ain't really see it happen, Gus explained, carefully wording his response. *'Cause he took her to one room and I was still fuckin' up the dude in the other room. So I ain't see it. But that's how that nigga is.*

I shook my head in disbelief. I knew that these men were brutal robbers, but I never thought of them as "robber-rapists." Troubled, I tried to verify the story. A few days later, I singled out David, who had taken part in that particular robbery. During some small talk, I referred to the rape as nonchalantly as I could.

And Neno raped a woman there? I asked in Spanish. *Because that's what I heard.*

Yes, David answered in Spanish, but with hesitation. *He did that.*

Why did he do that to her? I asked.

Don't know, he responded with caution.

Did you see him? I asked.

No, I didn't see him, he responded. *I didn't even know what he was doing until later, until we left the apartment. I don't know what happened. About that, I can't tell you anything.*

David then pretended to be busy with his betting slip and slid away from our conversation. He confirmed Gus' account, but without detailed information. It was six years before I finally asked Neno about it. We were alone, with me asking him about robberies. I wanted to get his version of the story without implicating Gus or David. So after some questions, I asked him in Spanish:

I heard that sometimes guys rape women during robberies? Have you ever seen that happen?

No, he answered, in Spanish, quickly.

I thought I heard some guys talking about that, I said, with a feigned look of surprise. *Are you sure?*

No, I never saw that happen, he responded, with raised eyebrows. *We always say, if we find women and children, we don't lay a hand on them.*

Oh, this is the first time I hear that, I said.

That's what we always say, Neno said, switching to English. *If we find women and children in the place, we don't touch them. We put them in a room so that they don't see what we do. We don't want them to see burnin' people or nothing. We don't touch them. Hell no.*

Neno was not going to admit that he had sexually assaulted a woman—or any other women—during a robbery.

Overall, the details surrounding this robbery showed how masculinity arose during torture. True: heightened emotions and a forward panic could have led to the rape. True: the thrills of doing rape while on a chaotic robbery could have contributed too. Just as true: masculinity was intertwined with those emotions and thrills. Neno could have raped a male dealer in that apartment, but did not. If he had, his male peers would have rejected his masculinity and consider him "gay." So he only sodomized men with objects, an emasculating act approved by male peers.

A woman, though, he raped, using his body to degrade her in the ultimate violation. And he received no negative sanctions. Thus, as caught up as he was in a forward panic, frenzy, or thrill, gender still shaped his violence. In deeply disturbing ways, then, social structure mattered during violent situations.

In short, I must reemphasize how people do not magically appear in such emotionally and gender-laden "violent situations." Mostly, perpetrators come from marginal social spaces, ones that increase the odds of being swept up in violence. For instance, the perpetrators at Abu Ghraib prison. Though evidence suggests that the U.S. military's upper echelon informally encouraged the sexual atrocities, those who engaged in torture were mostly marginal Whites. That they saw infantry-level military as their best option and joined when the war on terror was peaking and the mistrust of middle easterners was soaring—all increased their chances of appearing in violent situations and then reveling in it.

The same with these Dominican men. Their increasing marginality within both larger society and the drug market raised their chances of being in violent situations. Because not just anyone finds himself castrating a man, or raping a woman, or burning a victim while searching for drugs and cash. Unless, of course, their background and social structural conditions influence them in such directions—unless the intersection of race, class, gender, history, and biography increases their odds.

NINE

Splitting the Profits

ONE LATE SUMMER NIGHT, Gus, Pablo, Dee, Neno, David, Topi, and I hung out by the public stairwell. Some of us drank liquor and others smoked weed. The neighborhood *bodega* had closed for the night, so the weed smokers sent a local "weed head," Joey, to another store for some "munchies." When he returned, Pablo harassed him.

"Damn, bro, where the hell did you go?" Pablo asked Joey, angrily. "Did you go to fuckin' Japan or some shit?"

"I went to 167 [street]," answered Joey, in a low voice.

"Yo, I swear that shit felt like ten hours ago. Where the hell did you go, for real? I know you didn't go to 167 [street] right here, bro."

"I did."

"Tell me you went to 170 [street] and I'll believe you."

"Nah, I went to 167."

"You went to 167? What kind of bike you got? What the fuck is that, bro?"

Pablo inspected Joey's bike. He then snatched the medium-sized grocery bag from Joey, looked in, and retrieved a honey bun.

"You want a honey bun, bro?" Pablo asked Neno, who shook his head. "Who wants a honey bun? Gus wants a honey bun? Nigga's got the munchies?" No one called for the honey bun.

"You want a honey bun, big man?" Pablo asked Joey.

"Nah," Joey answered, nervously.

"You straight?" Pablo asked Joey, who nodded his head. "Yo, who wants a honey bun?"

Gus took the bag from Pablo, looked in, and passed it around. Joey waited on his bike for his tip. Pablo grabbed the bottle of rum, poured a cup, and shoved it in Joey's face.

"*Mira,* drink!" Pablo demanded. Joey turned his head from the cup, shaking his head.

"Yo, finish that cup, for real," Pablo said. "If you fuckin' don't finish that cup, I'ma fuckin' throw this fuckin' bike away."

Reluctantly, Joey took a sip of rum.

"Finish the cup," Pablo demanded. "Finish the fuckin' cup, yo."

"I smoke weed," Joey explained.

"Weed?" Pablo asked, incredulously. "Finish this fuckin' cup. Fuck the weed, nigga." Joey mounted his bike to pedal away. "Yo, you fuckin' break outta here without finishin' that fuckin' cup, you got problems," Pablo warned him.

"You goin' home walkin', ha-ha," Dee said, laughing.

"That bike looks kinda nice," Pablo said, grabbing the handlebars. "Yo, I might just be takin' this home." Everyone laughed.

"Drink it, man," Gus demanded, as he joined Pablo and went to Joey's other side.

"Drink it, bro," Pablo also demanded, placing the cup in Joey's hand.

"I don't drink liquor," pleaded Joey.

"You don't drink liquor?" asked Pablo.

"I don't like it," explained Joey, appearing afraid.

"Oh, man, drink that shit, you gonna love it," Pablo said. Everyone laughed again.

"Yo, drink that shit!" Pablo yelled, as he yanked the handlebars.

"Yo, drink, man," Gus said, joining in.

Joey took a small sip. "Drink another sip."

"Yo, drink it!" Pablo yelled. "Drink that shit, bro."

"Drink it," Gus insisted, a bit more forcefully. "Drink that shit, man." Joey took another sip and then extended the cup toward Pablo.

"Yo, don't come with that shit," Pablo warned. "Don't come with that bullshit."

"That's all it has," Joey said, in a low voice.

Gus tore the wrapper off the honey bun. "Now take a bite out of this," Gus ordered, as he placed the honey bun to Joey's lips.

Joey refused to open his mouth and shook his head. "Take a bite of it," Gus said, forcefully. "Take a bite. Take a bite."

"Aw, man," said Joey, in a melancholy tone. Everyone laughed.

"Yo, take a bite out of this," Gus repeated, angrily. Joey bit a piece of the honey bun.

"Now drink it down with that," Gus ordered as he grabbed the cup from Joey's hand and placed it to his lips.

"He's gonna like it now!" Pablo said, laughing.

"Swallow that shit, bro," Gus ordered.

Joey reluctantly swallowed the rum while still having a piece of the honey bun in his mouth. "Drink that shit, bro!" Pablo yelled. "Yo, I want you to drink that shit before you break out."

"Hurry up!" shouted Gus, angrily. Joey drank slowly from Gus' extended hand, taking small sips at a time.

"Ain't nothing gonna happen to you if you drink that shit," Pablo assured Joey.

"Drink!" Gus shouted, with a menacing look. He placed the cup in Joey's hand. "Ay, yo, drink that shit down!"

"Drink it all, bro!" Pablo yelled. "What the fuck you tastin' it for, bro? You ain't takin' no fuckin' sip."

"Nah, I'm a'ight," Joey said, as he mounted his bike again to leave.

"Hey! Hey!" Pablo shouted, grabbing the handlebars again. "Where the fuck you goin'?"

"Pablo," Gus said, changing his tone. "Pablo, he's alright."

"Drink it," Pablo demanded. "Drink it, bro. I want you to drink it."

"Nah, Pablo," Gus said, now taking a protective stance toward Joey. "Go ahead, go ahead, go ahead," Gus told Joey, making motions with his head.

"I want you to drink it, bro," Pablo repeated, not letting Joey leave. "Why you don't want to drink it? We drink that shit."

"Alright, alright," Gus said, trying get Pablo to release the handlebars.

Pablo, with an arm hanging at his side, made a fist. I immediately went over to him and held his arm. "Let him go, bro," I told Pablo, in a low voice.

"Yo, Randy, yeah," Gus said, seeing that I had a hold of Pablo.

"Let me get it," Gus said, grabbing the drink from Joey's hand.

"Yo, drink that shit," Pablo continued, struggling to get his arm loose.

"Aww, man, chill, bro," Gus said, trying to persuade Pablo to let Joey go.

"Chill, bro," I added, still holding Pablo's arm.

Gus and I pulled Pablo away from the bike. "Go ahead," Gus told Joey, who mounted his bike and pedaled away quickly.

The number 4 train rumbled by on the elevated track; a car drove by slowly playing "White Lines," the chorus-driven classic rap song. Some nodded their heads to the tune; others looked up and down the street. No one said a word.

♪

But white l-i-i-i-n-n-e-s, blow aw-a-a-a-a-y . . . [1]

♪

ESTABLISHING A BRUTAL STREET STATUS

Pablo's bullying of Joey was upsetting. Joey was a neighborhood "weed head" who, for a dollar or two a bike trip, ran errands for the guys. In our limited conversations, I noticed that Joey was a bit dull-witted and rarely strung more than three or four words together. With a belated smile, he simply nodded or shook his head for any social exchange. He was just Joey, the "weed head" who hung out on the neighborhood fringes, away from the action and fray.

Yet the kind of respect Gus and Pablo commanded, I knew, is central to social life. I was reminded of the work of anthropologist Philippe Bourgois and that of sociologist Elijah Anderson on "respect" in the inner city.[2] In poor inner-city neighborhoods, street violence and drug markets define who has a high status and who is a chump. It was the loss of traditional manufacturing and the flight of the middle class that expanded this notion of respect. The rise of crack during the 1980s compounded the problem. Now, respect was linked with violence, a deadly duo with dangerous spins and combinations that led to fear, to iron-barred windows and triple-locked doors. The streets became a world where might makes right, where residents handled "business" on their own.

On this South Bronx summer night, Pablo earned respect through such might over Joey, who had a low status.[3] I saw it coming as soon as Pablo berated Joey for taking too long. And when he ordered Joey, who hated liquor, to drink from a cup of rum, I was not surprised. Pablo sought a violent situation where he could do brutality to raise his status among the men. And Gus, who thrived in such moments, inserted himself in the drama. Like Pablo, he ordered Joey to gulp down the rum and then added a honey bun to the humiliation.

Initially, I thought it senseless to bully a nonthreatening person. Later, though, I saw how it made sense to Pablo and Gus. Especially Pablo. Other than with Tukee and Gus, he had not gone on drug robberies with the neighborhood guys. So he needed to clear doubts about his capacity for violence. And he responded brutally to a minor "injustice" so that others could only imagine his reaction to a major one. He also unconsciously displayed his drug robbery skills. He angered quickly, threatened force, (almost) brutalized, and scared someone into acting against his will. Pablo simulated robbery dynamics right there on the street.

Pablo's behavior was tied to an incident occurring two weeks earlier, when we were all hanging out near the public stairwell. Topi, who had just walked out of the store with a Philly Blunt cigar (to smoke the weed in), said aloud: *"Los tigueres de verdad—pero de verdad, de verdad—'tan muerto o 'tan en la carce. Todo lo' tiguere' que tan aquí afuera son todo' palomo'."* (The real thugs—but real, real—are dead or are in prison. All of the thugs that are here outside are all punks.)

Topi was aiming the putdown at David and Neno, who had refused to chip in for a bag of weed. Only Gus had contributed, yet they expected to smoke. Pablo, who had not been present but arrived just in time for the denunciation, thought Topi was implying that he was a punk too.

"Yo, Gus, what the fuck did this nigga just say?" Pablo asked. "Does that nigga know me?"

"No, chill, Pablo," Gus answered, sensing a misunderstanding. "He doesn't mean it like that."

Topi, who was several yards away, repeated his claim in Spanish: "The real thugs are dead or are in prison. All the thugs that are here outside are punks."

"Yo, what the fuck did he just say?" asked Pablo again. "Yo, I'ma fuck this nigga up. He don't know me from fuckin' Adam."

"Chill, Pablo," Gus repeated. "He don't mean you, man. He ain't say it like that."

Topi again: "The real thugs are dead or are in prison. All the thugs that are here outside are punks."

"Yo, ten cuida'o con lo que tu dice', yo, porque tu no me conoce'," Pablo called out to Topi. (Yo, be careful with what you say, yo, because you don't know me.)

"But it's that the real thugs are dead or in prison," answered Topi in Spanish, appearing unaware that he had offended Pablo.

"Listen," Pablo said, "I don't say that I'm a thug and I don't want to go to prison, but be careful with what you say."

"Chill, Pablo," Gus said, trying to calm him. "He don't mean you, man. He don't mean it like that."

"Just don't fuck around," Pablo warned Topi, "because I will fuck you up. You don't know me."

"Yo, chill, Pablo," Gus repeated. "Man, you takin' it the wrong way. He don't mean you." Topi looked confused and then drifted toward some guys hanging out on the other side of the *bodega.*

"Yo, you listenin' to that nigga?" Pablo asked me. "He better watch what the fuck he sayin'. He don't even fuckin' know me like that."

"Come on, man, chill," Gus repeated. He then slapped Neno playfully on the back and said, "*Ven, vamo' fumar, ha-ha-ha*" [Come on, let's smoke]. Neno laughed.

Gus then explained to Pablo what had just happened between Neno, David, and Topi, and why Topi continued making the declaration. Pablo listened, but remained silent and upset.

Later that day, Pablo and I were sitting on a car, and I explained how Topi had targeted David and Neno, not him. "Nah, I know," Pablo said. "What he meant was these niggas around here. But I just took it like he was talkin' about me too. That's why I told Gus, 'Yo, I'm about to fuck this nigga up.' But he's cool with Gus, you know. For real, for real, I didn't fuck him up and made an example out of that nigga because Gus was like, 'Yo, chill, Pablo. It's not like that. He didn't mean you.'"

"You were gonna make an example out of him?" I asked.

"Yeah, bro, because I guess these niggas don't know that I'll fuck somebody up quick. And like he's supposed to be their little leader or whatever, of the stickup guys . . . I was gonna make a example of his fuckin' skinny little ass. But you seen, Gus was like, 'Yo, chill Pablo.' I guess Gus is tryin' to stay in that group or whatever, so he's tellin' me to chill. 'Cause he be goin' on a lot of stickups with those niggas. He don't want to fuck that shit up." So Pablo wanted to make a public example of Topi to instill fear in the neighborhood guys. But since he could not brutalize Topi, he tried to make Joey the "example" instead.

And it was violence and its threat that dictated street status. For instance, Neno described a street hierarchy where brutality earned respect. "I mean, the streets is crazy," Neno told me one day in English. "'Cause people won't respect you for who you are, but for what you do. It doesn't matter, [you] always gonna have people who are more scared and gonna feel more, how you say, more fear to a person than to another person. And that's what happens."

"How do people get other people to have fear of them?" I asked.

"I mean, like me," Neno answered slowly, "my reputation is crazy. People know what I do. They see me around and they have seen me do what I have to do."

What Neno did was threaten violence. For instance, on one occasion, which I did not observe, but heard much about afterward, he played dice with another drug robber, Rolando, who sometimes appeared on the block. After losing his money, Rolando continued to play, trying to win it back by rolling on "credit." Soon, he lost even more money and owed Neno four hundred dollars. But Rolando could not pay. Neno then retrieved a gun to settle the dispute. A couple weeks later, I asked Neno about why he retrieved a gun.

"That nigga had to give me my money. What's mine is mine. Then all these niggas gonna take what's mine. I ain't gonna let that happen. You can't let that happen. Then these niggas will abuse you. They'll just take your shit."

Later, I found Gus and asked him about Neno's reaction. He would evoke a street code that required violence to correct a perceived wrong. "'Cause it's about reputation," Gus explained, "especially with us and shit. If he wouldn't have done that, the dude would've thought he was soft and later on down the line, it could've escalated into something bigger. People would've talked about it. It's not good just to let people get off and shit. Eventually it sticks with you, like you let somebody get over on you one time."

"Why do people get guns if they feel they got offended?"

"I guess that's just how it is on the streets. You get a gun or a knife. Like I'm not into knife shit, ha-ha. These motherfuckas, they'll get whatever they can. I guess it's just that they don't want people to cross the line. What they gonna do? They gonna talk him into givin' up the money?"

"So you're sayin' it's hard to talk things out?"

"Of course. It's not like you could go to the cops and tell 'em, 'Look, this guy owes me money over this dice game, can you go and get it for me?' It has a lot to do with face, just with your reputation. Nobody wants people to think that they're soft."

The root of this ethos was utter marginality, which, under the right conditions, created the potential for deadly status-seeking violence on the street. I was reminded of this one summer night while some of us were hanging out. There we were, drinking, joking, and laughing, having a good time—then: *Boom!* Like an abrupt, ugly scratch on a spinning vinyl record, our merriness was disrupted.

"Yo, who the fuck did that shit?" Tukee asked angrily. There had been a gunshot.

"Damn, yo, what the hell is wrong with that dude?" I asked, inebriated, yet surprised. "He shot himself?"

"Nah, he shot up in the air," answered Tukee.

"Yo, I know you drinkin' some more, man," Dee interrupted, pointing at my empty plastic cup.

"Nah, bro," I answered, patting my stomach, "That shit makes my stomach hot. I need a beer to cool that shit down."

"You saw that shit [the gunshot]?" Tukee asked, keeping the focus on the young guys walking across the street, outside the public park.

"You see the guy?" asked Pablo. "Who did that, Tukee?"

"The guy in the green shirt," Tukee replied, staring contemptuously at the young men.

"What's that supposed to mean?" Pablo directed at the young men.

"Those are probably used bullets," joked Tukee, loudly. Everyone laughed. [To Dee] "Yo, go get the nine [millimeter handgun]."

"Go to the roof!" Pablo yelled to the young men, who, as they walked closer, appeared to be teenagers. "Niggas is goin' to the fuckin' park. They should go to the fuckin' roof to do that shit."

"It's crazy, right?" Dee asked, agreeing with Pablo.

"Go to the fuckin' roof!" Pablo yelled again.

"And then he has the two niggas behind him like, 'Yeah, that's my man,'" Dee added, mocking them.

"Yo, go get the nine, kid," Tukee repeated to Dee. "Let's start shit out here."

"Nah, relax, bro," Pablo said, trying to calm him. "I feel nice right now."

"That nigga got me mad, B, fuckin' doin' that shit." Tukee argued. "We could start shit right now. Yo, go get the nine, B. Who the fuck they think they is?"

"Nah, relax, man," I said, taking Pablo's lead. "You gonna fuck up my buzz."

"Let that nigga do that bullshit with that .25, whatever the fuck he got," Pablo added, diminishing them again.

Still looking at the young men as they disappeared into the park's darkness, Tukee let it go. He had demonstrated enough brutality, enough for Pablo and me to dissuade him from retrieving a gun. Yet the question remained: What if Dee had retrieved a gun? Perhaps I would not be here writing up my observations. It was that close of a call.

But in that moment, I saw more than Tukee's status-seeking behavior. Ten years ago, those youths were us. Though they looked different—they wore large baseball caps and baggy clothes; we had sported flattops or Jerry curls, and tighter shorts—the marginality was the same. As teens, we walked proudly with Gus, the boy-man who would suddenly shoot a gun at the night sky. The bullet would shatter the midnight silence, ripping our status desires through the hot and heavy air. Attention and respect. That's what we sought.

And I can only imagine that back then, some older, street-wise men admonished us from a distance. And I can only imagine that ten years from now, those same youths will be grown up, still marginal, but wiser, and just as critical of their status-seeking juniors. But my imagination becomes reality when I think about the unending cycle of such status-seeking behavior. As long as social inequality exists, what is old becomes new again. The marginal will find creative, and sometimes deadly, ways to earn respect.

To be somebody.

BRUTALITY AND BETRAYAL VIOLENCE

These street status competitions amount to more than creating a street hierarchy between the most brutal and the most punk. A brutal status shapes how drug robbers split the profits, how everyone decides who gets what. The danger lies in greed, which made these robbers individualists. Thus, *betrayal violence*—which I define as violence that results from an offender physically harming a co-offender for higher criminal gain—is widespread. A brutal status, though, dissuades others against such violence and allows its owner to wield it instead.

Long gone are the days of Chic Conwell, the early twentieth-century professional thief studied by criminologist Edwin Sutherland.[4] Though not robbers, thieves apparently had a strict code of honor; out of ten basic rules, two stand out (I paraphrase here):

1. The division of all gains is to be even, with no one getting more or less than anyone in the group.
2. Members must deal honestly with each other and not report less than what was actually found. Lying is considered more unethical by thieves than by the law-abiding.[5]

Nearly a hundred years later, though, honor is almost nonexistent among these drug robbers. Rather, as Timothy Black found among Springfield

[Massachusetts] street dealers, they would, if possible, cheat everyone, operating under the force of "greed is good."[6] Still, they understand that greed can be bad, especially as to their profits and lives. For instance, in drug robberies, many roles are involved, like drivers, informants, The Girl, lookouts, torturers, and so forth. And after a drug robbery, each role is evaluated and assigned a monetary worth. But like the old adage goes, *Money does funny things to people.* So some earn way more, some way less—and some are even considered better off dead. Betrayal—that's the name of the game.

Admittedly, their betrayal stories made me question my trust in them. At first, our longtime bonds made me feel secure as I hung out on the block. However, as I learned about dealers betraying partners and drug robbers betraying each other, I saw that friendships and camaraderie meant nothing. Double-crossing was the norm.

I was also stunned over their debates about whether to kill a robbery partner rather than pay the person fairly. Even more stunned at how the potential victim was someone they greeted warmly and embraced. These moments felt surreal, as though I played a character in an Italian mafia film where greedy mobsters thought little of killing childhood buddies for individual gain. And like some of the film characters, I became paranoid and overanalyzed their every move and every word. *If they could harm and kill friends, what wouldn't they do to me?*

I was the most devastated at Pablo, Gus, and Tukee's terrible transformation. As teens or young adults, I never heard them plan to ruthlessly hurt or kill longtime friends just for money. I began to see them as immoral and treacherous human beings. They no longer had hearts. They no longer were human men.

But as a sociologist, I saw that they were marginal men pushed to marginality's most dangerous end. As the crack market plunged and legal opportunities shrank (they had criminal records, little formal education, and were aging), they sank deeper into underground capitalism and became its worst predators. They were also enmeshed in a capitalist dog-eat-dog world where "compassion" is the kryptonite of the self-interested superwoman or man. This forced them to confront a victim intimately—face to face, close to home, in the family. Betrayal violence became the norm.

And they knew this. So they relied on their street reputations to escape victimization. For instance, one day I asked Pablo about whether he trusted the other crew members. He revealed that status or "reputation" trumped trust in terms of betrayal violence.

"Reputation," Pablo explained. "It's none of that about trust. For example, if he knows that I smoked [shot] a couple of people before, he ain't gonna try and fuck around, because if he does, he knows he's gonna get smoked. In the back of his mind, yeah, he wants to get down with us and do it, but he sayin', 'Shit, I might get smoked too. So I better do shit right.' It always lurks in the back of your mind when you go do a job with someone that you really don't know and you really don't trust. [Because] when you talk about a lot of money, people start gettin' funny ideas."

Later, Pablo provided a chilling account of how the lure of profit maximization could lead to betrayal violence, especially to a killing. "Like for example, we one time had a job. It was me and like three other people. This job was a job of one hundred ten thousand dollars. My plans were to smoke [kill] the guy who gave me the job, and smoke the other one who helped me, and split two ways instead four ways. Because, practically, me and the person I could trust with my life, we were gonna do it. The others were just gonna get paid. One [guy], because he knew the information, and the other one because he gave us the job. So for informin' us about it, they wanted to get half. And I don't think that's right if I'm doin' the dirty work."

But it does not end there: "Even once you got your money, [or] drugs," explained Tukee, "you gotta worry about niggas' breakin' into your crib [apartment or house]. Believe me, if niggas know you just did a stickup and you got a hundred thou' in your house, you better believe they gonna come try and get that shit. And if you're there when they come, B, you gonna get blasted. Niggas will put you out [kill you]."

"Why?" I asked.

"They got to or else they givin' you a chance for payback."

"So how do you make sure that people don't come take the drugs that you just took?"

"Niggas have to fear you, B, for that to happen. Like if they know you got a gun and you blasted some niggas before, they might think it's not a good idea. But you never know, a hundred thou' is a hundred thou'. That might give some niggas the heart to go get that shit."

Again, what stops others from betrayal violence is a brutal street status. This is why Gus never worried about his safety or being shortchanged. Added to his violent reputation, legend has it that he once turned the tables on a drive-by shooter: as the passenger in a car shot at him, Gus ducked and dodged the bullets as if he could see them. Then, after the gun emptied, he ran up to the car, snatched the gun, and hammered the shooter's face with it.

The driver put his foot to the pedal and screeched away. Whether the event happened like this is debatable—I did not witness the drive-by shooting. However, that the story existed and no one disputed it solidified Gus' brutal status. Moral: even with a gun pointed at him, Gus won't back down.

I asked Gus if he thought people would cheat him out of his share. "I think it's that with me," Gus responded, "people know that I always have a gun. So they don't know if I have one on me or if I don't. And like most nig-gas know how I am, that if I got a gun on me, it could be in my waist or whatever, if you got one on me, I'ma try get my mines [mine] out. If I get shot, everybody's gonna be shootin'! And people know that's how I am so they probably really think about that shit like, 'Damn, yo, it's probably not even worth tryin' to rob this nigga.' They don't know how it's gonna turn out."

But how do members with weak or unknown statuses avoid betrayal vio-lence and keep their fair share? Most do so by being crafty, like pretending to be a potential resource for future robberies. For instance, Pablo described having once joined an unfamiliar robbery crew. Since he was new, the others were unaware of his brutal reputation. And one member projected an ex-tremely violent image. "There was this guy I didn't trust, right," Pablo recol-lected. "I thought he was gonna bag [kill] me. I really didn't know this guy at all, but he sounded like he really can't be trusted a hundred percent. Not even fifty. Not even forty."

Surprised to hear Pablo admit fear, I asked him about what the guy said to make him concerned. "Well, he gave me a little story," Pablo said, "of what he did in the past to someone he went after for like six months. And you know, that made me think about it. He's been after this person for six months. He knew him. He doesn't know me. Shit, fuck he'll do to me? So you know what I came up with? I came up with, 'Okay, we're gonna go do this job, right, but then you know what? I got this other job set up that we're gonna do.' I stood alive for that moment that we were gonna do our job. You know why? 'Cause he's thinkin', 'Damn, this nigga got another job after this job, so I'll probably keep him around to the next job.' So you see, I 'psyched him out,' in other words. Then when the time came that we had to do my job, I just came up with a bullshit excuse, 'Damn, man. It fucked up.' "

Smaller scale deception is quite common. Everyone expects others to stash for personal gain. So if a robber rips jewelry off a dealer's neck and stashes it in his sock or searches through a dealer's pocket and takes his cash, nothing really happens to him. He'll be recruited for future robberies. Gus explained: "I'm sayin', like there's no feelin' in this. We be tellin' each other, 'Yo, empty your pockets.' I've caught Neno with money and shit, stashed!"

"Yeah?" I asked, surprised.

"Yeah, bro! He had like five hundred dollars that he took out of a nigga's wallet, the one that we had tied up. And when we was countin' money . . . he was like, 'I got this five hundred dollars. I had 'em before the job.' So one of the girls that was there with us, she looked at the money and she said, 'These shits is fake.' The nigga that Neno took it out of his pocket, he had counterfeit money in his pockets. So he was tryin' to tell us that those five hundred dollars was his."

"So how do you feel now that you caught him doin' that?"

"It's that I know people tell you that shit. Like when somebody gives us a job, and we about to do it, and that nigga [informant] is not there, that's all niggas talk about—'Try to stash whatever you can. If you find a little jewelry, try to stash the shit.' That's what niggas do."

A BRUTAL STATUS IN ACTION

To illustrate a brutal status during a robbery, let us return to the robbery that I have been using as a guiding narrative. (Again, this is how Gus and David recounted the event to me.)

After the dealer refused to disclose the whereabouts of the drugs and cash, Gus took the dealer's apartment keys and drove alone to Washington Heights. In the dealer's rented room, Gus did not find the expected forty-eight thousand dollars. However, he found over 250 grams of heroin and 460 grams of cocaine. On the return trip, Gus stashed about 200 grams of heroin in a side panel in the jeep. When he arrived at the apartment, he confronted the dealer.

"Oh, I thought you don't sell drugs," Gus told the dealer, holding the drugs in his face. "What the hell is this?"

"I don't know what that is," replied the dealer.

"Look, we got it out of your apartment and we took the keys from you. And you still sayin' you don't know what it is? Come on, man!"

Gus put the drugs on the table. David weighed everything: the heroin, 66 grams; the cocaine, 460 grams. "This is it?" asked Jonah.

"Yeah."

"Where's the money?

"There was no money."

"There was no money?"

"Nope. I swear to my kid. That's all that was there."

"That can't be. There had to be more than that."

"You don't believe me? I don't give a fuck. That was all the stuff that was there."

Listening to the exchange between Gus and Jonah, the dealer finally spoke: there was much more heroin in the room, he said—about three hundred grams.

"Yeah, but all we found was sixty-six grams," Jonah told the dealer.

"*Imposible*," responded the dealer, "there had to be more than that. At least three hundred grams. There's no way that it could only be sixty-six. There has to be more than that."

"What's going on?" David asked Gus.

"I don't know what the fuck he's talkin' about," Gus answered. "That's what's there. I don't give a fuck. You could believe that nigga or you could believe me. I didn't find no money. I didn't find nothing else."

The argument continued. No one believed that Gus found so little. To settle doubts, Jonah and Gus drove back to the dealer's room for a re-inspection. They found nothing. The next afternoon, they released the dealer on a Bronx highway and then went back to the apartment to split the profits. They each earned roughly $2,500. If Gus had brought back the total score (the stashed heroin), each member would have earned roughly $4,000 more. Furthermore, if Gus had found the money—the $48,000—and delivered it without stashing, each would have added between $9,000 and $10,000 to their share. Then everyone would have earned between $16,000 and $19,000.

Angry, Jonah threatened to get to the bottom of the missing drugs and cash. Gus replied: "Check it. I live on 165th Street. I'm there everyday. I'm not gonna move from there and I'm there tomorrow, the day after, and after that. You got a gun and your man got a gun. If you feel that I stashed something, you do whatever you want."

Serious challenge. Jonah had a reputation for brutal violence too. In fact, Gus had to restrain Jonah during the robbery. And even if Jonah's violence depended on cocaine, there was a problem: Jonah was always on cocaine. I then thought that a showdown between them would soon erupt—a shoot-out, a knifing, something bloody. And I waited: Gus and Jonah are walking by each other (any second now); Gus and Jonah are shaking hands (any moment now); Gus and Jonah are in conversation (here it comes now); they're talking louder now, they're raising voices now, they're excited now . . .

Nothing. Nothing ever happened. They shook hands, talked, and joked. Everything was fine.

A couple of months after the robbery, I asked Gus if he felt that Jonah still wanted to get him back. "Nah," Gus answered. "'Cause we went to do more jobs together after that. You know, he's come around to get me [for jobs]." Then Gus paused. He suddenly scowled, as though angry at the thought of having someone come after him.

"'Cause these people think that by intimidation," Gus continued, "that he could talk hard, that he could try to intimidate people into doin' what he wants and shit. So he probably thought that if he kept insisting, this and that, and you know, try to talk like he was gonna do something, that I was gonna be like, 'Alright, I did take something.' Fuck that nigga."

"He always looks upset, for real," I said, laughing. Gus was still serious. Then he said: "He's always tryin' to act intimidating. Like he's a killer. He ain't no fuckin' killer, man."

In the end, Gus' challenge went unanswered. Against a strong opponent like him, one-on-one violence is too hard. This is why Gus could short-change everyone even when his intention was obvious.

He is a brutal man.

TEN

Living the Dream

LIFE AFTER A DRUG ROBBERY

AFTER GETTING HIS SHARE, Gus drove back to his uncle's apartment, where he was staying. He weighed the stashed drugs on his scale. Two hundred grams. Sixteen thousand dollars. *Yo!* But not so·fast. Gus needed to find buyers, which wasn't so easy. For help, he told Julio about the hidden drugs and offered him half the earnings for whatever he sold. Julio agreed. Now both searched for dealers willing to buy large amounts of drugs.

The cocaine found a quick buyer, a small-time dealer agreeing to buy it at twenty dollars a gram. However, the dealer did not pay cash up front. It was a consignment arrangement where Gus and Julio had to wait for its sale in Massachusetts before seeing profit.

"I gave it to this kid to sell so that he could sell it to somebody else," Gus explained. "But I don't see no profit until he sells that shit. Like the nigga has to sell it, get his profit, and then after all of that, I see my money."

Their other option involved higher risk and more time: cutting the cocaine into single-gram packets, then selling them on the street for several months. But Gus and Julio wanted their cash fast, within the week. Fortunately, the dealer returned three days later, with thirty-eight hundred dollars.

Now the heroin. Gus and Julio contacted several dope dealers and gave them free samples. However, the trial users said it was "no good." Gus was deflated. After seeing him sulk for several weeks, I asked him about the dope. "I thought I was gonna see some real money off this shit," Gus explained. "Now nobody wants it. Yo, I can't even give this shit away to people. I gotta trick somebody into buyin' this shit. But then they might see that the dope is no good and then they come back. And I gotta be like, 'Fuck it, you bought it, that's it.'"

I asked Gus about what he was going to do with the heroin if he couldn't sell it. "I'ma sell it," Gus insisted. "I just gotta wait to trick somebody to buy that shit. I'm givin' it at fifty-five dollars a gram. It cost eighty."

At $80 a gram, Gus' heroin was worth $21,280; at $55 dollars a gram it was worth $14,630. So, Gus was willing to concede over $6,000 just to get rid of the bad heroin. With a price reduction, the dope—even bad dope—would sell itself.

Two months later, Gus still had the dope.

THE MIDDLEMAN

Thus, middlemen (I only saw men) are key for turning drugs into cash. They purchased already-packaged drugs from wholesalers and then sold them to drug entrepreneurs. So the middleman eased drug dealing: drug robbers avoided risky street dealing and street dealers got drugs without upper-level drug connections.

One afternoon, Tukee explained the role to me. Earlier, a guy had pulled him aside to speak. When he came back, Tukee explained that the guy was a drug robber who had just robbed some bundles of heroin off a dealer. He offered each bundle to Tukee at sixty dollars apiece. Each bundle contained ten packets of heroin, and each packet was worth ten dollars on the street. So a bundle had a street value of one hundred dollars. For Tukee, this presented two dealing options.

Option 1. If Tukee bought a bundle at sixty dollars and sold each packet, he would earn a forty-dollar profit. So if he sold one hundred bundles, he would earn four thousand dollars—all without a wholesale connection and without wasting time and money to package the drug. However, street selling required that Tukee have an established drug operation—which he did not.

Option 2. If Tukee bought the heroin at sixty dollars a bundle and then became a middleman, he could sell each bundle to another street dealer at eighty dollars. Here, Tukee would earn twenty dollars a bundle. So if he sold a hundred bundles, he would make a two-thousand-dollar profit.

Tukee preferred option 2, the middleman role. "Look, I don't care if these niggas [dealers] take it at eighty [dollars a bundle]," Tukee explained. "I'll take a twenty [dollar profit]. If I sell a hundred [bundles], I'll make two thousand. I'm not a greedy nigga, bro. You hear me, nigga? I'm not a greedy nigga, bro. I don't need to get the whole four thousand. Nah, I just need to get rid of that shit quick. No fuckin' problems and no fuckin' headaches. Just get quick cash."

For robbers, then, getting a middleman is the quickest and safest method for getting cash. As Gus argued, it made no sense to sell robbed drugs on the street for maximum profits. "After you gone through all this shit," Gus explained, "torturin' a nigga, gettin' the drugs, carryin' guns, carryin' the drugs, worryin' about if people saw you and shit, if people heard you, if when you drivin' back, Five-O [police] gonna stop you—riskin' a lotta shit, man—after you go through all that shit, you want to get rid of all the dope and coke real fast. Think about it, that shit don't make no sense, that you gonna waste all that time to sell the drugs. Then what the fuck you robbin' niggas for?"

What made dealing cocaine difficult was that the lucrative crack era was over. Dealing dope was equally hard since established heroin dealers either blocked entrée or made dealers pay a huge price to get in. So Pablo agreed with Gus, adding that setting up a drug operation was time-consuming and dangerous. "Because to set up a drug operation takes time," Pablo explained. "It takes a couple of months before you start seeing some real serious money. It's gonna take the users, the junkies, to get familiar with you bein' there, that you gonna be reliable, that you gonna be there every day . . . You gotta find the right spot and dedicate time like anything else, and then you'll make money. That's if you don't get bagged [arrested] before you make that shit, ha-ha. Because when you do drug dealin', you gotta worry about everybody. You gotta worry about fuckin' police. You gotta worry about fuckin' stickup kids. You gotta worry about your own girlfriend. Yo, you really can trust nobody. You fuck her [girlfriend] up, she tells the cops you a drug dealer. That's it, ha-ha. Now what you gonna do?"

SPENDING THE PROFIT: HIGH LIFERS
AND VENTURERS

After selling the drugs, robbers experienced that magical moment: they were rich. In fact, some of their accounts support the insightful robbery research of criminologists Neal Shover and David Honaker, Richard T. Wright and Scott Decker, and Bruce Jacobs.[1] After a score, the Bronx men lived "life as a party," an all-out burst of hedonism and pleasure. With their pockets full, they stepped on the accelerator, reached an exhilarating speed, and the pleasurable images became a blur . . . nude women . . . champagne bottles, nightclubs . . .

drugs and laughs . . . food . . . get up, go . . . a life on full-throttle, or as they called it, a life *a todo lo que da*. In the end, the splurge left them penniless again, in search of a jackpot to re-create that magnificent moment.

Still, the splurge is not typical of all drug robbers. Like conventional folks (and this may surprise many criminologists), some robbers actually planned for the future. They created economic umbrellas for bitter, rainy drug market days; they nurtured economic nest eggs for life after the drug game; and they hopped on a legal vehicle, chancing an unfamiliar road out of crime. So not all robbers lived on the verge of a biblical Armageddon. Some wanted legal prosperity now, financial security ahead.

I call these two contrasting types the "high lifers" and the "venturers." After a successful drug robbery, the high lifers live a roller-coaster ride of material and drug consumption, spending money as though it had no end. The venturers, on the other hand, invest robbery earnings in legal pursuits. Here, I use the word "venturer" because it connotes an investor who gambles on upstart businesses and expects a high return. In this study, these men had no formal business education, but had high expectations for investments worked through acquaintances, family, or friends.

Clearly, these two types are not mutually exclusive. Some high lifers dabble in legal investments, while some venturers spend money on expensive material items, women, alcohol, and drugs. The difference lies in the intensity of activities, leaning some in one direction and some in the other. And this distinction is crucial. I suspect that most previous street crime research has focused on high lifers, who are likely to attract attention with their spending. Venturers do not flaunt their wealth. Moreover, they generally conceal their legal pursuits. If not for our deep friendship, the venturers on this block could have easily gone under the research radar, giving high lifers the spotlight. Hopefully, then, this distinction complicates and corrects popular assumptions on criminal "self-control."

The High Lifers

Topi and Neno spent their robbery profits in splurges, or excess gratification. They went all out drinking, dancing, and drugging in nightclubs, having all-night orgies in hotel rooms, all-out feasting in restaurants, all-out high life in Miami or in the Dominican Republic. This was their moment, the moment when they could participate, as closely as possible, in our nation's ideal of the material high life. The financial worries, gone. The daily danger and struggles, gone. Their masculinity rating, sky-high. Then, after their money ran out, they were back on the street, searching for more drug dealers to rob. They had to live a *todo lo que da* one more time.

In the beginning, I struggled for descriptive accounts of those high-powered masculine adventures. First, while I had observed them spend their small drug robbery earnings in rapid bursts, I had never observed them splurge on a mighty jackpot. Second, although some had hit mighty jackpots in the past, they remained vague about the subsequent spending. For instance, the word on the street was that Topi once scored four hundred thousand dollars in a robbery and then blew it in several months.

"So what did you do with the four hundred thousand dollars?" I asked him, in Spanish.

"I went to Santo Domingo [in the Dominican Republic]," answered Topi, in Spanish. "*Muchacho,* I had fun. Women, *a todo lo que da.* Drinking with all of the guys from the barrio, dancing in the club, eating every day . . ."

"What about your friends? Did you hang out with them?"

"Every night. We were smoking [weed], drinking with women, wearing ourselves out. Imagine."

"Did they pay for anything?"

"No, I had all the money. I spent all of the money."

"Why?"

"You know, because those guys didn't have money, they're from my barrio. If I have money, we're all going to have fun, forget it."

"How long did it take for you to spend the four hundred thousand?"

"Like three, four months."

"How did you spend all that money in three or four months?"

"It was drinking *a todo lo que da.* It was getting high *a todo lo que da,* [and] women. It was all of that."

Obviously, Topi's spending was about partying. However, he showed how it also gained him a paternalistic status among his barrio peers. He took them out to dance clubs and paid for their food, drinks, and drugs. But in another sense, he played Robin Hood; he stole from the rich and spread wealth among the barrio poor. Through this criminal role, he secured a heroic status, one that temporarily lifted peers out of their misery and despair.

Later, I asked Topi if he planned to set aside money for retirement. He argued that even large sums of money did not guarantee the material and hedonistic pleasures of the super elite. In fact, he directly challenged the popular U.S. myth of how any hardworking poor boy can strike it rich.

"But why didn't you save your money, invest it in a business? Why did you spend it all?" I asked.

"Listen, one lives like an unfortunate," Topi answered, in Spanish, "doing this and doing the other, never enjoys life. So that you know, before I got into this [robberies], I was working in a supermarket . . . a poor unfortunate. I earned a dollar, two dollars, to carry bags for people. I was working to not enjoy my life. Nobody that worked there enjoyed their life. Not even the owners [of the supermarket]. They were unfortunates too, working every day, for money they were not going to enjoy. They were going to bury themselves with that money. Me, now, doing what I'm doing, I'm enjoying my money. I find a hundred thousand, two hundred thousand, I'll go to Santo Domingo, enjoy it."

"But now you don't have money and the 'unfortunates' do—someone could tell you that."

"Yes, but I'll look for some more and I'll find it."

"How about if you don't find it?"

"*Que se joda,* I'm fine with that. I've already had fun. But I keep looking because it's out there. I can find it."

Neno spent his profit similarly. After earning seventy thousand dollars in one drug robbery, he flew to Miami with some friends and did the heavy drinking, dancing, and drugs, including orgies with women. The seventy grand? Gone in two weeks.

With a smile and groggy eyes, Neno reminisced about this splurge, that splendid moment when he spent money as though it had no end. "When we were in Miami," Neno explained, in Spanish, "forget it, it was drinking, women—it was new ass every night . . . I went to the clubs with the guys, we danced with women, with tables and drinks, drinking the entire night, imagine. We spent three hundred, four hundred dollars eating every day. Sometimes we spent four, five hundred dollars just for dinner . . . We met women in the strip clubs, where you have all those whores naked. We used to take them to the hotel. Forget it, we made them do everything. We were sticking it in them [having sex with them], everyone, all the guys at the same time. They were sucking me in front of everyone. They were drinking, sniffing [cocaine]—they were doing everything. We had them doing *tortillas,* all of that craziness."

"What's a *tortilla?*"

"You know, when they get together and they get pussy to pussy, and they do it to each other, we had them doing that. We had them sucking each other's pussy, sucking their asses, we were sticking it in their asses—we had them doing everything."

"Did you pay them?"

"Of course it was paid. You know we had to pay them, ha-ha."

"How much did you pay them?"

"A thousand, two thousand dollars. Sometimes three or four thousand for four or five women. . . ."

"And you got back with nothing?"

"With nothing. Imagine, the money left us, ha-ha."

For Neno, then, the splurge involved a hypersexual manhood, showing a clear link to how he treated female drug robbery victims. With the money, he exerted power over women, forcing them to live out his sadistic male fantasies. A splurge amplified his male privilege—*a todo lo que da.*

I asked him how it felt to spend all that money. "Like a king, you understand? Everything I wanted to do, I did it . . . There was no problem."

The Venturers

An example is Tukee. He once earned one hundred and ten thousand dollars in a drug robbery and, with the encouragement of Juanito, a neighborhood friend, he invested some of it in a pet store. Though Tukee knew nothing about animals, Juanito had once been a pet store manager and would take legal ownership. The profits were split evenly, which, according to Tukee, ranged from six hundred to fourteen hundred per week. He explained how the pet store served as a security blanket and a potential exit from crime.

"What made you put all that money down in a pet store?" I asked.

"Just need security, B," Tukee answered.

"Security?"

"Yeah, security, B. This drug shit don't last forever, you hear me? Believe me, that day will come, 'Time to hang shit up. Time to get the fuck out. Wastin' my time out here.' You wanna be a fuckface and stay out here? A'ight, stay out here on the streets, you fuckface. Let's see what happens to you, when you old and shit. You ain't gonna have shit, B. Yeah, you gonna have the streets, but the streets ain't gonna have shit for you. Me, I'm gonna have security, B. To tell you the truth, if I could open up one, two more pet stores, I'll be al-l-r-i-i-ght. I'll just be collectin' money. Don't wanna hear about no drugs. [Pretending someone asked him about drugs] 'Drugs? Don't know what you talkin' about, B. Get the fuck outta my face with that shit, B.'"

Pablo also earned a hundred and ten thousand dollars in that big robbery. Like Tukee, he was guarded about his legal activities. For instance, it took over a year for him to tell me about his "security" in the Dominican Republic. Even then, he gave no details and quickly changed the subject. As an ethnographer, I was surprised by his caution. During the fieldwork, I learned that with time people volunteered private information. So I remained patient, biding my time with touchy subjects. Often, it worked, with people eventually confiding secrets. But after a couple of years, Pablo was still silent on his "security." My curiosity continued gnawing at me, and one afternoon when we were alone on the public stairwell, I asked him about the money.

"What money?" Pablo answered, hesitant.

"The one you got in that robbery where you made a hundred and ten thousand dollars."

"Oh, that money," Pablo responded, pretending to just remember. "Yeah, I got it in [the] D.R. I got it workin' out there."

"How you got it workin' out there?"

"I bought some houses, you know, like four or five houses. I got a lawyer out there, who's lendin' some money to people, to make money like off the interest."

"You're rentin' the houses?"

"Yeah, I got those shits built and I'm rentin' them out."

"But you're over here, bro. How do you keep tabs on that shit from here?"

"Naw, I gave the money to my mother out there. She's the one doin' all of that for me. She's like the one buildin' all those houses. Like she rents them out to people, makin' money like that for me."

"You gave her all the money?"

"Yeah, I gave her all the money 'cause she's a penny pincher, bro. She likes to save money. So she's out there makin' and savin' money for me. But it's like her money too. She doesn't have to work, so she's livin' off of it too. I didn't want her to work any more."

"Why didn't you invest the money here, in New York?"

"Nah, I sent the money out there because I just didn't want to go crazy and blow it here. I just didn't want to do that because that's what happens if you don't invest it. You just blow it. So I don't touch it at all, at all. The only time I touched it was when I went to [the] D.R. I spent like sixty thousand pesos like in three weeks. The peso was like at twelve to one [dollar], so I spent like four to five thousand dollars in three weeks."

"Yeah, you spent money."

"You understand? I just spent that shit like nothing, bro. That's why I don't want to touch that money, bro."

But Pablo's marginality made him vulnerable in his legal investments. He lacked the education or cultural capital to keep tabs on what others did with his money.

"You got a lawyer lendin' your money out there too?" I asked Pablo.

"Yeah, I got this dude out there lendin' my money. But I don't know, man. I think he's usin' that shit for himself. Like he makin' it look like he lendin' money, but in reality I think he usin' it for himself. I just don't want to go out there and have to straighten that nigga out, you feel me? But yeah, I'm supposed to be makin' money off the interest. Like he lends the money to people and then I make the money back plus the interest. He makes a little percentage off of that shit too."

Pablo described his legal business activities as "security" for himself and his daughters, who were under the age of five. "If everything doesn't work out here [in New York], I got that security workin' for me out there. Like I said, that's why I don't touch it. Even if I'm not doin' good here, I don't touch it. It's like it's not even there, bro.

"But to be honest with you, bro, that money ain't for me," Pablo revealed. "I'm savin' that money for my daughters. That's why I'm not touchin' it all. So when they get older, they could use it like however they want. I got a big house out there that my mother built—in fact, she just added two more rooms to that shit—that house is for them. If things don't work out for them, they could sell it and make money. They could do whatever they want with it. Like if something happens to me, that's their security, bro. I'm gonna die knowing that I just ain't leave them out there with nothin'. I could die in peace, bro."

And in the next chapter, we will see that Pablo remained true to this promise. Even under financial hardship, he never touched his daughters' money. He would rather die.

Several months after the robbery, Gus was doing poorly. Although he had gone on more than a dozen robberies since then, most yielded little. On one afternoon, I found Gus quietly standing by the public stairwell. Our ensuing conversation revealed how a high lifer like Gus, who spent drug robbery earnings *a todo lo que da,* perceived the venturer.

"You alright?" I asked.

"I'm just chillin' here and thinkin'," he said, looking into the park. "Niggas is doin' grimey shit to make money nowadays. Yo, I never paid a lot of mind to money, man. If we all together, we all make money together. I don't give a fuck if it's a thousand dollars and there's seven of us. We break the thousand dollars up, you know what I mean? But I found out a lot of shit, man, that money uses people. We could be together, bro, and—I just never knew it was like that."

I was surprised to hear Gus complain about how money used people. I always felt that money "used" him—money made him shortchange partners or conspire to "smoke" them. Yet underneath it all, I sensed his anger at someone and a danger loomed. But I said nothing. Just listened.

"You know," Gus continued, "I talk to them discreetly, like to Pablo and Tukee. Those niggas came off—they got a hundred and ten thousand [dollars] each for the hit that they did. Yo, I know I was in jail for that shit. [But] I didn't ask nobody for nothing, you know what I'm sayin'? This kid was tellin' me that Tukee and Pablo was talkin' about that they was gonna put five thousand dollars each aside for me . . . They was gonna buy me a car. Came home, I settled, bro, by myself. I ain' care.

"You seen my chain—the chain that I got? I pawned that shit for eight hundred dollars. I [also] robbed this kid, with the nine millimeter I had, with the silencer. We got a little ten thousand dollars for that shit. I sold that shit [gun] for four hundred dollars 'cause I ain't want it no more . . . So, in a discreet way, I showed them, you know, this is all I got. I have two or three more guns, but that ain't shit. I'm strugglin' 'cause I got a struggle, know what I'm sayin'?"

Gus, it turned out, was broke. I could see it too: his hair was unkempt and his clothes were worn. And lately, he seemed homeless, often sleeping on people's couches and visiting his older brother Sylvio's bar for free food. Overall, his image was changing; he no longer appeared like a high lifer, someone spending *a todo lo que da*. And his high lifer image was crucial to his identity, which added masculine consumption to his brutality.[2] It was an image he could not give up.

Unfortunately, he had saved no money since getting out of prison. Because when he did successful robberies—which earned him between twelve and twenty-five thousand dollars—he immediately high-lifed it, often flying to the Dominican Republic and spending it within weeks. Lately, the robberies were inconsistent; broke, he desperately evoked a criminal code.

"So, after awhile, I thought about that shit," Gus explained. "If it would've been me, and I would've came off with a hundred ten thousand dollars—if Pablo would've been in jail—I would've said, 'Yo Pablo, this shit is yours when you come out. Tuke? You fucked up? This is yours when you come out.'"

Although I never saw it practiced, Gus called up that particular criminal code: criminals must set aside profits for imprisoned partners.[3] In doing so, he shifted the blame for his financial distress onto Pablo and Tukee.

However, Gus' account only partially held true. True: both Tukee and Pablo did not share robbery profits with him. *Untrue:* Pablo refused to give him financial support. Instead, I observed Pablo give him small sums of money, from ten to forty dollars, for daily survival. This is why Pablo later complained about Gus.

"That nigga, I don't know, bro," Pablo confided in me. "He gives his money away, that's what I'm thinkin', to these hookers or whatever. Blows it. I mean, that nigga cannot have cash in hand, bro. The minute it comes in, the minute it's gone. But damn, he knows I'm kinda fucked up, you know what I'm sayin'? That's the part I don't get, man."

"What, he owes you money?" I asked, confused.

"Nah, he don't owe me, Randy," Pablo responded. "But, yo, I looked out for that nigga. The time that he was [living] here like for nine months straight. I looked out for that nigga. He ain't do nothing. You know, I ain't gonna lie. I wasn't givin' him a hundred fuckin' dollars because I know he'll blow it. But you know, in a week it'll add up to a hundred. [Pretending to talk to Gus] 'Here's ten [dollars]. Here's twenty. Here's fifteen. You know, so you won't be broke.' Yo, and I'm not askin' for nothing back, bro. And I been lookin' out for Gus for a long time, kid. It ain't from now. I mean, I love that nigga and everything, but damn, yo."

My observations generally supported Pablo's view. Of all the drug robbers, Pablo was alone in helping others financially. In fact, he sometimes stuffed fifty to a hundred dollars in a struggling friend's shirt or back pocket as they exited his apartment. He then closed the door quickly, avoiding any protest to his generosity. And during most of my fieldwork, he supported Gus with money, food, and shelter.

Pablo was also right about how Gus could not hold on to money. When he ordered food from a nearby restaurant, the rice, beans, and meat were for everyone; when he smoked weed two or three times a day, everyone shared the high; and when hamburgers, hot dogs, and beer were needed for a barbeque, he footed the bill. Yes, Gus rarely paid mind to money—until, of course, he had none. Then he desperately clung to a charitable criminal code.

Yet, again, I never observed that code in action. In fact, generosity meant including a released partner on a drug deal or robbery, something to help "you get back on your feet." For instance, when Gus was released from Rikers Island, Pablo and Alex made him a drug-dealing partner on their trips to Ohio; when Manolo was released from a New York State prison, Pablo, Gus, and Freddy[4] recruited him for a drug robbery. None of this was money put aside. It was work and risk, a matter that could land them in prison again.

For friends to expect a share of drug robbery profits was pointless. The high lifer's drug robbery earnings, no matter how large, disappeared within a matter of weeks. Venturers looked ahead, hiding their money and making it legal. They kept silent about these legal investments. Otherwise, partners would be asking for large handouts or loans. Gus called on Pablo and Tukee to do just that, to pull some of their money out for him. However, investment earnings were sluggish, taking time and patience to accrue.

Money for Gus? No way.

PART THREE

Todo Tiene Su Final

I swear to God,
I just want to slit my wrists,
And end this bullshit
Throw the magnum,
To my head,
Threaten to pull shit,
And squeeze,
Until the bed's,
Completely red,
I'm glad I'm dead,
I'm a worthless fuckin' buddah head,
The stress is building up,
I can't . . . I can't believe,
Suicide's on my fuckin' mind,
I want to leave,
I swear to God,
I feel like death is fuckin' calling me,
But, naw,
you wouldn't understand . . .

The Notorious B.I.G. "Suicidal Thoughts"

ELEVEN

Fallen Stars

GUS WAS IN THE DOMINICAN REPUBLIC when he received the call. He had gone back to the island to clear his head. Now Pablo urged him to get on a plane and come back to the Bronx. *I need you for a job that's easy,* Pablo told him.

When Gus arrived, Pablo informed him about how Willie had "fucked up" an earlier robbery. Now they targeted the same drug dealer; they planned to confront him on the street and snatch his briefcase, which carried one hundred and forty-seven thousand dollars. The informant, who had set up his business partner—his own nephew—wanted it done immediately. *Just grab the suitcase on the street,* he said.

On the appointed day, Pablo, Gus, and Freddy waited for both the uncle and nephew in a parked car, with the engine running. After watching the pair leave the building, all three got out, jumped on the nephew, punched him, knocked him to the ground, grabbed the suitcase, and drove off.

Later, at Pablo's apartment, everyone sat at the dining room table, waiting. Pablo then placed the briefcase on it and opened it. Empty. Not a penny inside.

"By chance," Gus explained, "the guy [nephew] had collected thirty thousand dollars more. It didn't fit in the briefcase that he had. So he took all of the money and put it in a duffel bag. He gave the duffel bag to his uncle and he came out with the briefcase. But we don't know that. I'm still thinkin' that the money is in the briefcase. So when he came downstairs, I'm not really payin' attention to his uncle's duffel bag. We grabbed the briefcase. We get to Pablo's house, we all sittin' at a table. He opens that shit. The briefcase is empty. Yo, Pablo almost cried, man. The nigga almost cried. I saw it in his eyes, bro, that he almost cried."

Everything was falling apart.

This failure, which Pablo and Gus recounted to me, reflected the overall drug robbery picture. The robbery profits had gotten so bad that Gus would periodically visit the Dominican Republic, where his mother helped support him.

And Pablo. He was barely surviving. There were no more dance clubs and restaurants, only stays at home; no more women, only the mothers of his two daughters; no more muscles, only his weight ballooning out of control. Pablo had become a hermit in the South Bronx.

"Let's go get a drink," I suggested once. "Just one drink, bro, so you could get outta here, at least for awhile."

"Nah, I don't got no money to be goin' out like that, Ran," Pablo answered. "When I go out, you know I like to carry real money—five, six, seven hundred dollars. How am I gonna talk to a bitch with just thirty dollars in my pocket? Shit ain't the same, Ran. Before, forget it, bro, I used to do all that shit, bro . . . Now, shit ain't the same. For that, bro, I don't go out. Fuck for? *Por eso me quedo tranquilo, loco* [For that I stay put]."

Although I am no psychiatrist, I could only describe Pablo as *depressed*. The Pablo I remembered had it all—the women, the cars, the clothes, the muscles, the swagger, the loot. Now nothing. *Ni un centavo.*

Clearly, he could have gotten a legal minimum-wage job or perhaps opened up a *bodega,* with his mother's know-how. But his previous drug-dealing and robbery success had made him think big, in the six-figure-income sense. Minimum wage would be a ludicrous way to reach that lofty goal. Owning a *bodega* would be too much work and time just to recuperate his initial investment (a twelve- to sixteen-hour work day, and six- or seven-day work week, for about five or six years). So Pablo pursued legal work that could replicate his previous drug market earnings.

However, Pablo would encounter four main barriers: a prison record, the wrong cultural capital, limited legal social networks, and crack-market-like income expectations. As a "venturer" he had several legal investments—in a gimmicky home key finder, in an inexperienced truck driver who transported oranges from Florida to New York, and in a pseudo-mathematician who searched for a math formula that could predict lottery numbers. However, I will focus on the scheme that he put all his hopes and dreams into, his heart and soul.

One winter morning at around 11:00 A.M., Pablo called me, saying that I had to get to his house fast. I was tired, I told him, because I had hung out until about 6:30 A.M. with Gus and Freddy at Sylvio's club. However, he kept insisting that it was important, that I had to see him. Okay, I said, I'll be there in an hour or so.

When I arrived, I saw about a dozen booklets and folders lying on his dining room table. Many had huge dollars signs imprinted on their covers. Then a tired, red-eyed Pablo spoke. *I finally got my money-making system.* His face grew solemn, his eyes wide. *Yo, Randy, wait till you read this and I'll tell you my ideas. I'm gonna make you rich. Trust me, this is it. This is my way out of this fuckin' ghetto. I couldn't fuckin' sleep. I was up all night thinkin' about it.*

I sat down, picked up several booklets, and thumbed through the "money-making system." It was a popular get-rich-quick scheme sold on a late-night infomercial by an enthusiastic, wide-eyed entrepreneur. Each booklet had a different method for making money, such as Internet marketing strategies, product sales through newspapers ads, and "900" number services. They were about twenty pages each, with huge print and spacing, and with many illustrations, mostly wacky cartoon figures and large dollars signs.

After reading the material and discussing some of its strategies, Pablo explained how he wanted to translate these booklets into Spanish to sell in the "Hispanic" market. In fact, he wanted to make Hispanic "infomercials" based on the material. *I could put on a dope suit and look all dapper,* Pablo explained, *and say [now acting serious and professional], 'Señores y señoras, esto es un systema que usted puede utilizar . . . [Ladies and gentlemen, this is system that you can utilize . . .]' I could say all that. I could go in a room full of people and act. Yo, it's a fuckin' actin' job! I know I could do it! Trust me, Ran, it's gonna work! There's a big Hispanic market out there and I know they're gonna want to buy this and make money! I know this is gonna work!*

Although Pablo planned to break copyright laws, I agreed—for the sake of agreeing—that it was a good idea. The Hispanic market was large, I told him, especially the Dominican market.

Sensing my hesitance, Pablo then said, *Look, Ran, if you wanna make money, someone has to feel it. Someone has to lose. No matter what type of business you go into, someone has to be exploited. I know how you feel about that shit, but someone—someone—has to pay. Someone has to get stepped on. In every business someone wins and someone gets stepped on. Then no business in this world would work.*

I nodded my head slowly. Pablo sounded as though he had prepared the short speech to counter my feelings against the capitalist exploitation of poor communities. Not wanting to discourage him, I went along with his Spanish translation scheme. Later, though, I would worry about his expectations. It seemed like his plans were riding on me.[1]

The Mark of a Criminal

After some more talk, I questioned him about my role in his get-rich-quick scheme. *Look, Pablo,* I said, *I'm looking at all of this and listening to these ideas. And they're good ideas. But to me, I see it like you could do all this by yourself. I don't see how you can't do it all by yourself. What I want to know is, why do you want me to get in on this?*

Why do I want you to get in on this? Pablo said. *Okay, listen. Look, I can't trust nobody but you. I just don't trust nobody else. Look, I know you and I know you ain't a shysty nigga. I know that ain't your style. Like me, I fly straight and I know you fly straight. And I have a bad record, so I can't put all of this under my name. Then people might look me up and see my record and not be too happy, you know what I'm sayin'? I could put everything in your name and everything would be better.*

I was not surprised. Pablo knew he carried the mark of a criminal record.[2] Like most ex-offenders, Pablo faced limited legal income opportunities. For instance, many U.S. states would bar him from certain jobs or professional licenses.[3] Clearly, some state denials are understandable—like barring a convicted child molester from working as a child-care provider. However, even if Pablo applied for an occupational license that was unrelated to his previous offenses, his prison record would be enough to prove his "lack of good moral character." So licensing in real estate, plumbing, medicine, education, law, and nursing—even hair cutting!—would be denied because of his two drug convictions.[4] His age would not matter, his time served would not matter, his attempt at legal pursuits would not matter at all.

These brutal state denials steered Pablo to legal jobs that paid much less than those available to non-offenders, giving him an automatic "wage penalty" on his legal earnings.[5] Even at low-level jobs, employers would be reluctant to hire him, especially in money-related and customer-service work.

Pablo's brown skin color would also worsen his chances. In her illuminating study, Devah Pager found that employers were generally willing to hire White ex-offenders over Black *non*-offenders![6]

Sensing this, Pablo once confessed: "I wish I didn't have a [criminal] record. Then I could practically be whatever I want. I could'a been a police officer or in the FBI doing all type of shit. I would know where all the criminals be at and what they do, how they think. You know what, too? I always wanted to work in a job like where you wear a suit to go to work, you know, look proper. Nice clothes, you know, you look a'ight, legit'. But I fucked up, ha-ha. I sure fucked up. Man, you lucky. If I was like you, I could do all type of legit' shit. I wish I could do it all over again." But Pablo knew that ex-offenders got no do-overs, no second chances. Employers would not trust him. Potential clients and customers would fear him. The state would punish him for life.

More troubling was how his criminal record impacted him psychologically. For instance, he feared giving his real name for car or movie rentals and always had girlfriends purchase services or products. He always paid—never skipped town. He just worried that someone might check his background and criminalize him because of his record.

Just as troubling were the limited social identities open to Pablo. For instance, at one point I suggested that the host at Sylvio's social club could be a great Hispanic infomercial star. Pablo, however, thought the guy was *shystee* and *if he fucked up 'cause of some sneaky shit, I'll beat the hell out him*. In fact, he would bring *some ol' thug attitude* to anyone in his company.

You could be easily sued and put in jail, I argued. But as a counter, he brought up Suge Knight, the former head of the hip-hop label Death Row. According to Pablo, when rap artist Vanilla Ice refused to sign another Death Row record deal, Suge Knight and his crew held him over a hotel balcony ledge by the leg until he agreed to sign. *Trust me, Ran,* Pablo said, *when niggas see where you comin' from, and see that you'll put a serious hurtin' on them, they won't fuck with you. Fear is stronger than respect.*

Pablo's "thug attitude" originated from jail and prison experiences. As Timothy Black observes, former inmates struggle as they transition from a brutal prison world to a legal one, with nonviolent rules of confrontation.[7] It also originated from his criminal stigma, which created legal and social barriers that pushed him toward a criminal self-concept.[8] The "thug attitude" benefited him in just one social space: crime. The drug market did not shun him or forever stigmatize him for acts he had committed as a young man.

The Wrong Cultural Capital

Look, Ran, Pablo explained at one point, *I want you to do it in English. I know you could do it. I can't fuck with that. You speak better English than me. I would get stuck real easy and not know what to say and fuck up.*

Now here, I was surprised. I never, ever wanted to be an infomercial star. True, in my late teens, I too stayed up to the early hours watching infomercials. Worse, I even spent my hard earned minimum-wage pay to buy some get-rich-quick real estate programs. Though the programs promised instant wealth without a need for capital or financial backers, I found that I needed capital or financial backers to succeed. But I had none and failed, again. Later, I became appalled at infomercials, figuring out that they shrewdly played on the desperation of poor folks, people the nation framed as failures if they did not attain the American Dream. So I had to tell Pablo that he could do this alone, that he did not need me. He disagreed. *Nah,* Pablo replied, *when it comes to English, I know you could do it. I know you're in school and you're used to talkin' in front of people and doin' shit like that. Aren't you always talkin' in front of people? You got more experience.*

I don't know, I said, uncomfortable.

Yo, trust me, Ran, you could do it. You got that shit down packed. You could travel everywhere and act like [the infomercial star]. I mean not the same exact material. We're gonna have to change it. Don't worry, Ran, you could do it easy.

No one had to tell him. Pablo knew that he held the wrong cultural capital. And opportunities for acquiring the proper cultural capital were as limited as job opportunities. In 1994, Congress barred prison inmates from receiving the Pell Grant, a noncompetitive, government-sponsored financial fund granted to disadvantaged college students. They could not reward criminals, Congress reasoned, while noncriminals struggled to pay for college tuition.[9] Congress knew that the higher someone's education, the lower their chances for arrest and imprisonment, or for re-arrest and re-imprisonment. But it based its logic on politically motivated moral panics. So, ex-offenders like Pablo would have to borrow cultural capital from people like me.

Still, I could not commit to Pablo's project. Not only was it against my morals, but I was also aspiring to become a sociologist. Like a mind reader, Pablo would say: *Look, I know you in school and that's your thing. Don't worry about it. You're smart and you could do this too. All that counts is money. Money and only money, is what counts.*

I then tried to explain how money is not, for some people, the most important criterion for choosing careers—how, for instance, most professors went into their fields because of research or to write books on subjects they loved. In fact, the books often sold poorly because the general public found them boring.

So, you just want to write a book and not have it sell? Pablo asked, confused.

It depends on what you want to do with a book, I answered. *Like you could write a book that helps others understand a group of people, a step toward helping them.*

Blank look. He wasn't buying it. But I could not fault him for his all-embracing capitalistic framework. The problem was that he needed me to make up for his educational deficits. And my reluctance made me feel horrible. This is it, he had said, his chance to finally leave crime.

Super Capitalist to the Core

After more talk, he suddenly asked: *Randy, do you always remember your girl's birthday? Your mother's birthday? Your brother's or your sister's?*

Most of the time, I answered.

You gonna tell me that you remember their birthdays exactly every single time? he asked me loudly, appearing annoyed.

To be honest, I answered, *I really don't care much for birthdays and holidays.*

Come on! he said, bothered. *You always remember Valentine's? Now you can't tell me you always remember Valentine's, 'cause I know every year you ask me to go with you the day before to buy something, even the same day, because you forgot!*

He had me there. I nodded.

Look at this, he said, handing me a letter that had come with the package. *Now Randy, this is going to be the money maker.*

The letter stated that anyone could become partners with the infomercial star in a reminder service program. They just had to sell the reminder service, which reminded customers of important holidays and events. It wasn't a bad idea, I told him, but how would he sell the service to people? He didn't have that fully covered, Pablo answered, but he planned to create his *own* reminder service company. He then showed me a notebook page with a bunch of scribbled numbers indicating the costs of everything involved—the bulk postage, printing, postcards, membership costs, and employee wages. From me, he just needed a list of computer software programs to establish the service.

As for sales, he planned to have three salespeople standing on corners in downtown Manhattan and offering the service to people walking by. I shifted in my seat. Noticing this, Pablo said in a dramatic, intimidating tone, *Look, this idea sells itself. You gonna tell me that people really remember every single holiday and birthday in time?* He then pointed to a column on the scribbled page that listed all the holidays and events an average person could celebrate.

An average man, argued Pablo, *has three kids . . .*

Actually, 1.5, I interrupted.

Just listen, Pablo said, annoyed. *This is just an example to see how many cards we have to mail out in a year.*

Pablo resumed. The average man had three kids; two sets of parents (in-laws included); two sets of grandparents; three grandkids; two sets of one niece and nephew; and one brother and sister. Then he tallied the special dates and the amount of cards he needed to mail out; then he estimated the amount of sold memberships in a year; then he added a monthly fee; and then he subtracted worker commissions. First-year profits: two hundred and seventy-three thousand dollars.

I said nothing. His capitalistic drive was driving him mad, I thought as I later left his apartment.

A couple of days later, I went back to Pablo's apartment. When I arrived, his first daughter's mother, Lydia, was sitting at the dining room table. She was dressed in a sweatshirt and jeans, had on no makeup, and her hair was tied in a ponytail. She looked tired, sad; after we greeted, she walked to the bedroom and closed the door. A few moments later, she reappeared with their three-year-old daughter. Both had coats on and marched slowly and silently. As Pablo led them out, I heard him say, softly, *Don't worry, baby. Things are gonna get better.* Dramatic scene. I felt so bad.

After sitting down, Pablo explained that he hadn't slept for two nights straight. He was rereading the booklets, hatching up more plans to make money. *I'm tellin' you, Randy,* he reassured me, *this is it. Everything keeps fallin' into place. It's like God is finally givin' me this chance to get the fuck out of here.*

Since he expressed concern with "what to say" on brochures and leaflets, I suggested that we go on the Internet to get ideas from existing reminder services. The search turned sour. We found over three thousand reminder services with their own websites. And most companies offered more services than Pablo and at lower membership costs. Pablo's spirits sank. But he resisted defeat. *Don't worry,* he repeated to himself. *Gotta think positive. Can't let it get you down. Think positive, baby. I'm not gonna let it bring me down.*

After about an hour, I suggested we stop. *Damn, man,* Pablo admitted, *that shit kind'a brought me down.* To cheer him up, I told him that, unlike the Internet companies, he should focus on the Latino community. *Nah,* Pablo said, psyching himself up again, *I'm not gonna let it get me down. I'm gonna go with my plan. I'm not changin' anything.*

Pablo and I then discussed sales commissions and profits. Each reminder membership would cost about forty dollars, and if salespeople received ten dollars for each sold application, we would profit about thirty dollars.[10] So, if one hundred applications were sold, profits would be about three thousand dollars. Unsatisfied, Pablo insisted that workers should only receive five or eight dollars for each sale. If the commission were too small, I countered, they would be unhappy with their pay. I suggested that they receive fifteen dollars for each sale to keep them motivated on slow days. And since Pablo included me in the business (and I wanted out), I offered up my profits to improve their pay.

No! Pablo shouted, angrily. *How you gonna give them so much money?*

The extra money, I explained, would come from my share. He would not have to worry about losing money. Pablo looked confused.

Why you gonna give them so much? Pablo asked again. *You say you don't care about givin' up that money? Give that money to me!*

Pablo. A capitalist to his core. With no concrete reason, he demanded outrageous wage differentials between owners and workers. For him, just thinking about improving a worker's pay was illogical . . . unnatural . . . infuriating. Without knowing it, he mimicked the exploitative practices of American CEOs. For instance, in 1965, U.S. CEOs earned about 24 times more than average workers. By 2000, they earned *298* times more![11] This wage disparity reflected a drop in the real wages for average workers—along with lowered health benefits and pensions—and a pay raise of the average CEO (who retired themselves with more too). Pablo thought no different. He used his power to evaluate the worth of his potential workers. His conclusion: *Don't give it to them! Give me some more!*

Then the tragic irony. As we strategized on recruiting salespeople, we found that our ideas sounded similar to one that a catalogue company had used on us as teens. While looking for summer employment, Pablo, myself, and some others were once lured by a newspaper ad searching for "sales managers." Arriving at a Manhattan location, we entered a room with about twenty-five others like ourselves, young minorities eager for work. Three charismatic upper-level sales managers, all minorities, with expensive suits and jewelry, then took charge, boasting about their extravagant lifestyles and sales success. By the session's end, about half the room was convinced that they could become filthy rich through catalogue sales.

Pablo and I were two of those unfortunates. In the subway on the way home, we were pumped up, ready to make some real money. However, after about a month of knocking door-to-door—*Sorry, not interested*—we had only sold a couple of catalogue memberships. We quit. We were *had*.

The company preyed upon young minorities who had little chance of striking it rich. Through rehearsed tales of earning and spending big money, they conned us, knowing that we wanted someone to tell us that we could drive expensive cars, own luxurious homes, and travel around the world. And we gulped down those concoctions telling of people who started like us and made it big through hard work alone. *Sell, Sell, Sell,* we were told, *and you can realize your hopes and dreams. Look at me, look at me.* Sadly, we were unaware of the equation's other side: that along with hard work, education counted a lot, and being in the right circle of important people counted even more.

Freddy, whom Pablo had let crash and was napping, got up and listened to our story. He then recounted a similar experience in a sales job operated by a Jamaican businessman. The company, according to Freddy, was a multi-million-dollar enterprise that employed hundreds of inner-city young people. The youths spent hours on the street, selling and lugging boxed products all over the city. The owner had "gassed" Freddy's head up, making him think that he would become rich as a sales manager. *They put me in a room with two other guys,* Freddy recalled. *Then they looked at our applications and picked me. They picked the dumb nigga. I was dumb and they picked me. They gassed me and pumped me, tellin' me that I was gonna be a manager. I was only nineteen and never really worked and I hear somebody say I could be a manager. But they picked me, a dumb nigga. They not gonna pick somebody who was a manager of a supermarket or who had a lotta good jobs. They can't gas [fool] them. So they picked me and I was like, "Word?" I fell for it.*

Pablo and I laughed. Still, I knew that Pablo's company would take advantage of young people, just as similar companies had taken advantage of us. I wanted out for good.

A week later, I sat uneasily in Pablo's house. By now, he had calculated our potential earnings at seven hundred thousand dollars a year. But the venture was getting complicated. He needed a respectable business address, but a business owner that he knew would not return his calls. Also, he needed more capital, but potential backers avoided him, also not returning his calls. At one point, Pablo turned serious and in a low voice said: *Yo, and if this doesn't work, I'll just get me apartments and divide them into a lot of rooms. Just get a bunch of Mexicans to live in them. Trust me, the apartments would go. They always lookin' for places. Like this apartment, I could divide the living room into two parts, split it straight down the middle. The other two bedrooms, I could do the same thing. And then with that little room [pointing in its direction] I could make a lot of money. I could just charge each person in each room like a hundred a week. My man, that's five hundred dollars a week. And then I would just keep gettin' more apartments. I could live off of that.*

The backup plan meant that Pablo realized that no one really shared his vision of the reminder service. Surely, he sensed my reluctance and perhaps realized that other people felt the same. The day before, I had spoken to Gus, who mentioned Pablo's ambitions. "Yo, that nigga Pablo is way over his head," Gus told me. "I have to leave his house because all that nigga talks about is his idea. I'm tellin' you, he expects to make too much too soon. He told me to drop everything I was doin' [the drug robberies] to work with him. I can't do that, you know what I'm sayin'? That nigga said that I was stupid for waitin' for a 'big hit' to make it. But he's doin' the same thing with this business thing. He expects it to be a 'big hit.' That nigga is goin' crazy over this."

So no one took Pablo's side. And he watched his legal dream crumble, slowly. After about three weeks, Pablo never mentioned the reminder service again. Back to crime. *Sorry, Pablo. I know you tried.*

GUS GETS DESPERATE

Because of drug robbery struggles, Gus secured clean, nondrug work. It was in his older brother's social club, which catered to the neighborhood drug dealers. Sylvio hired him as a bouncer from 9:00 P.M. till closing (which was between 5:30 A.M. and 6:30 A.M.). Mostly, Gus scanned the room with a glower, ensuring that no fights broke out and no one smoked. He also stationed himself next to the men's room, which barely fit two people. If someone stayed in there too long, he swung the door open to surprise potential smokers. *No Smoking!*

Overall, I observed that Gus was punctual, exuded seriousness, and enjoyed his job: he interacted with customers and flirted with waitresses; he received free food and drinks; and he watched female strippers on Tuesday and Thursday nights. More important, he confronted and fought rule-breaking, drunk customers, with his background giving him a violent edge.

For instance, on one work night, Gus, Freddy, and I stood by the restroom. Gus suddenly swung the restroom door open, revealing a middle-aged man smoking. He rushed in and told him that he either had to put the cigarette out or go to the bar. Then the door closed and I could not see inside. The door swung open again as a customer walked out. I caught a glimpse of an angry Gus and the smoker, who seemed just as angry. The door closed again.

Freddy, who had been watching, said, laughing, *I know how Gus is. He's gonna start swingin'.* And I expected the same: earlier, Gus had playfully punched me in the arms and ribs with a dull pair of brass knuckles. If he had them, he would use them.

The door opened again as another guy walked in and tried to make peace between Gus and the smoker. The offender finally put out his cigarette. The door closed. A few seconds later, Gus stormed out. The peacemaker followed, trying to calm him down. The smoker then left the bathroom and as he walked past, he said something in Gus' direction.

Gus' head snapped. *Que!?!* He rushed toward the smoker and confronted him. The smoker then immediately changed his angry face into a scared one and *calmly* questioned the rules. Gus then walked the smoker to Sylvio for confirmation. Close call. But that was Gus' job, to watch for rule breakers and potentially beat them up when they got out of line. He was on cloud nine.

After a couple months, though, he quit.

When he first started working, Sylvio paid Gus five hundred dollars a week for nine-hour shifts, six days a week. But as the weeks wore on, Sylvio gave him less. For instance, by the third week, Sylvio paid Gus only three hundred dollars. By the fourth week, two hundred dollars. By the sixth week, nothing at all. Sylvio kept making excuses for the nonpayment, saying that he would pay Gus after some bills were cleared.

But Gus could not wait. He had no stable home, no spending money, and no new shoes or clothes. His special skill was violence, which he had perfected in jail and prison. However, his criminal record barred him from the most lucrative legal violence work, like law enforcement. He was lost.

Eventually, he started spending more time with David, Topi, and Neno. Soon he focused on drug robberies full-time again. Apart from a two-week stint, where he worked on rehabilitating an abandoned restaurant Sylvio had purchased, Gus would not labor outside crime again.

Times, as the street saying went, were hard on the Boulevard. No one, it seemed, could escape the no-money-making plague. It spread through the neighborhood, overcoming each drug market player, one by one. Pablo was confined to his home, almost bedridden. Gus was robbing people for chump change. Most of them were desperately trying their hand outside crime to reverse the decomposition of their minds, bodies, and money-loving, capitalist souls.

Some contemplated death.

SUICIDAL THOUGHTS AND SELF-DESTRUCTION

To echo C. Wright Mills, these South Bronx men would start experiencing their lives as a sequence of traps.[12] In fact, suicide would be on their minds. During their glory days, they had acted confident, bold, and socially and financially under control. And peers treated them like the neighborhood's all-Americans, the great drug market players excelling on the financial gridiron.

Yet their status and glamour had taken a sudden dive. And they then agonized under that dreadful curse—the curse of the all-American hometown superstar. Because after the cheers, accolades, and money disappeared, they suffered as they tried to readjust to their new lowly ground. Now, suicide and self-destruction entered their bodies and minds. Now, they became crime's version of those *triste* fallen stars: the individuals who experience a meteoric rise and then an equally meteoric fall.[13] Because just like those meteors that zoom across the midnight sky, they were heading rapidly into a tremendous crash—and Boom—these men indeed dropped violently, producing an emotional collision that disoriented them, or as early turn-of-the-century sociologist Emile Durkheim would say, put them in a state of anomie.[14]

Anomie, according to Durkheim, is an anguished human condition caused by a sudden social or personal crisis that weakens society's moral grip.[15]

With little moral order, some people feel lost as to their proper desires and needs. Then their passions run amok, uncontrolled, leading to dangerous outbursts of living or bouts of despair. At the extreme, a few commit anomic suicide—they kill themselves because of no moral guidance.[16]

For instance, if someone suddenly won the lottery, the abrupt change could disrupt their moral base.[17] Now they wield unfamiliar financial power and live unfamiliar lives—now they could catapult into anomie, the anguished state of not knowing what to do. If they fail to morally readjust, then, worst-case scenario, they commit anomic suicide. And the reverse is true. If society experiences an economic depression, people are quickly forced into unfamiliar lifestyles and restraints.[18] A general failure to readjust to fewer resources lets loose an anomic mood, which then raises the anomic suicide rate.

I would observe this side of the anomic coin within the drug market. Because when crack market and drug robbery opportunities shrank, some participants experienced dramatic shifts in daily work routines, earnings, and status. Anomie would set in as they tried to cope with their new position. They then became anomic, acting recklessly and suicidal, rejecting their status as the drug market's fallen stars.

For example, Pablo. For over a year, he barely survived, living off some stashed money from his last drug robbery. So he no longer ate in restaurants, drank or danced in clubs, took girlfriends on dates, or wore expensive jewelry or fashionable clothes. Also, for the first time, he looked to lenders to finance his enterprises. In the past, borrowers always came to him, all humble, all smiles, showering him with compliments about his sex life before hitting him up for some cash. Not anymore. People now avoided him, afraid he would ask *them* for money. Pablo was no longer Pablo. He was a fallen star.

Also, Pablo could no longer splurge on his children, something that had always made him proud. The thousand-dollar birthday parties and bi-monthly shopping sprees for his daughters—no more. And his children's mothers, who had gotten used to receiving an allowance, complained often. They could not understand how Pablo no longer "had it like that," and Pablo was at a loss. In fact, he disappeared for a period, when he no longer hung out or returned my calls. Sensing that something was wrong, I showed up unannounced at his home one evening.

I knocked. He opened. We greeted each other. I sat on a living room couch. He sat opposite me. Silence.

"Yo, wassup?" I asked, after turning on my tape recorder. "I been callin' and you never pick up."

"Yo, bro, I know, man," he answered, looking away. "It's just—I don't know, man. It's just shit ain't right. Shit just ain't right."

"Like what?"

"Look, man, to tell you the truth, I just don't feel right. I feel real low, man. I feel sometimes just like takin' a gun and blowin' my fuckin' head off, bro. I don't tell nobody, bro. You the first person that knows this, bro. I'm tired of this shit, man. I never saw myself like this, kid, for real. I feel like just endin' it, man. That's how deep it is, man."

"Yo, but you're alright, bro."

"Bullshit, bro. I got problems with this one, got problems with that one, bro. But nobody knows, bro. Everybody thinks that Pablo is havin' this wonderful fuckin' life. Financially, bro, it's not the same. Yo, man, before I could go to any fuckin' store and buy whatever I fuckin' felt like. You know, I can't do those things."

"Yeah, man. But sometimes, bro, you just can't, bro."

"I can't do those things."

"I can't do that, bro, and I'm alright, bro," I lied.

"I know, Randy. But when you used to a certain lifestyle, you understand? And I been used to it for awhile, you know. I heard about the lows and shit. But I never felt that . . . I never thought I would be in that category, bro."

"I mean, it's for awhile, man," I said, trying to comfort him. "Then you get yourself on your feet, bro."

"Fuckin' depressed, bro."

"I know you don't have the money and shit, but don't you have that shit in Dominican Republic?"

"Yeah, man," Pablo answered. "but that shit is for my kids, man, you know what I'm sayin'? I got too much, I don't know, I guess pride, whatever you want to call it. I don't want to take that shit from my kids. Like if something happens to me, at least I know I gave something to my kids. To tell you the truth, Ran', there's times that I've walked from here to Kingdom Come, just to save money. I never walked in my life like that, yo. Whenever I had to go anywhere, I just used to drive or take a cab. I can't even do that shit no more."

Pablo stopped. Tears formed in his eyes. I felt uncomfortable, not knowing what to say. I stayed silent.

"And nobody knows, bro." Pablo finally said, with a trembling voice. "You the first person I'm tellin' this to, Randy, bro. For real, I'm at a point, bro, you don't know, bro. I feel like takin' that fuckin' shotgun I got here and just sometimes just blowin' my fuckin' head away, man. Just fuckin' end this shit already. I'm not used to this, bro. For real, man. I'm not used to this at all, kid."

Pablo's tears slid down his face. Yet, again, I did not know what to say. I felt my own eyes well up. To prevent the tears, I finally said: "Yo, times can't be that hard, bro." I said.

"Yo, to me it is, Ran," Pablo said, wiping his face and trying to regain his composure. "For me it is, bro. You know what's that I can't even buy my daughters anything. [Taking a deep breath] Kid, yo, it's hard, bro. All I used to do, bro, go shoppin' and I used to shop for my daughters. Can't even do nothing for them, you know? It's crazy, for real."

"Go to D.R. [Dominican Republic], bro," I suggested, weakly.

"Nah, I don't want to go to fuckin' D.R.," Pablo answered. "D.R. ain't for me, Ran."

"I mean, for a little while, man, just for a minute, like for like six months."

"That shit's not for me, man. Gus likes that shit—loves that shit. That shit ain't for me, man. I want to stay here, man."

"Just to change the setting."

"Yo, Ran, I haven't shopped like in two years," Pablo continued, returning to his financial problems. "Luckily, I got the clothes that I have, kid. I got two years without shoppin' at all, bro. I'm depressed, bro. Depressed about everything. Look, my daughter's birthday is coming, bro, and I don't even got shit, yo. You saw the way I went all out for the older one's birthday, bro. I spent mad money, man. You know, I got all of that shit in one day, bro. Everything on me."

Pablo then revealed a main source of his anomie: his inability to be paternalistic to his girlfriend, Lydia. Because of his work struggles, Pablo could no longer play sole breadwinner and provider. Worse, he had made Lydia dependent on him by giving her money, jewelry, and clothes while restricting her forays outside the home. Thus, she also had trouble readjusting to their fallen lifestyle.

Pablo then shifted the blame to her. "It's not like I could say that I got a girl[friend] that could help, Pablo explained. "Like Lydia . . . it was like a hundred percent Pablo, a hundred and ten percent Pablo, you know. Lydia don't want to do shit with her fuckin' self, bro. I'm like, 'Yo, you could do anything. You don't got no fuckin' criminal record, man. Go to school. Do something, man!' She always fuckin' saying, 'Oh, I'm sick of this life.' I be tellin' her,

'Yeah, now you sick of this life 'cause I don't got it the way I used to, right?'
Nah, forget it, bro. Talkin' to that bitch is like talkin' to a fuckin' wall."

And as Pablo struggled, he desperately searched for a moral order, a way
to understand and reverse his downward spiral. Thus, he turned to a karma-
like interpretation of his life in which he rationalized that his good deeds
would eventually outweigh the bad, returning him to a state of economic
grace.

"Ran, man," Pablo continued, "I'm not a bad person, you know, even
though I've done bad things and stuff. But I still look out for everybody. I
don't know, man, my day, I guess, will come, when things will be alright
again. That's the way I feel, man. Everything's gonna be alright, bro. That's
what I gotta keep sayin' to myself, man. 'Cause, man, Randy, I'ma tell you
the truth, bro, I came real close to puttin' an end to this shit [his life]."

"Nah, bro, things are gonna get better," I said. "But it might not happen
as soon as you think."

"Yeah, that's what I gotta keep sayin' to myself. Everything's gonna be
alright, Pablo. The old Pablo's gonna be back soon."

Pablo. He once could get almost anything he wanted. *Pablo.* He once had
lots of jewelry, women, cars, and clothes. *Pablo.* He once had power and respect among his peers. *Pablo.* Everyone once wanted to be around him when
he flicked his gold. *Pablo.* Money once made him popular, once made him
loved. *Pablo.* The end of crack was the end of Pablo. *Pablo? Who him?* Now,
he wanted *muerte.* He was a fallen star.

I was sad for him. Yes, he had dealt drugs, caring little for the community
and putting profits above all. Yes, he had robbed dealers, beating and burning and maiming them to get their drugs and cash. Yes, in sum, Pablo had
persecuted others in his pursuit of money, power, and respect. Still, I knew
that he saw his behavior as no ideal.

"You think I like that I have to do all this shit to make money?" Pablo
asked me once. "I ain't proud of all the shit I did. That shit don't make me
feel good, bro. I wish I never done this shit in my life. I only do it 'cause I
have to. This is the only way I have to survive, you understand? You think I
don't wish that I could say that I'm like a lawyer or something, or like some
professional or some shit? Bro, I wish I could say that. I wish I could make
my money clean. 'Cause I'm not proud of the way I make my money. It's
dirty money."

And these words were not all *talk,* as some would think. Pablo assured
better opportunities for his four-year-old daughter. On several occasions, I

dropped by Pablo's apartment while he cared for her. Every time I visited, he was helping her learn to read, mainly through a popular reading program he'd purchased. The activity books and flash cards would be spread on either the dining room table or the bed in his room. And although I was visiting, Pablo continued the lesson. So I observed his praises when she got a word right (*That's great! You're so smart! I'm so proud of you!*); his encouragement as she tried to sound out unfamiliar words (*You can do it, Don't give up, You almost got it*)—his voice soft and tender, thickly coated with the enthusiasm of a kindergarten teacher. He also smiled at her, kissed her, and hugged her. Pablo expressed warmth and caring, traits no one saw on the street.

One day, I asked Pablo about why he purchased the reading program for his daughter.

"Believe me," Pablo explained, "I spent a lot more money in things that didn't benefit me or my daughter that much. So I was like, 'Why not invest in her? This would benefit her for life.' I want her to be smarter than me, you know what I mean?"

"What do you mean, 'smarter' than you?" I asked.

"I mean, I wasn't the smartest kid when I was little in school. I couldn't read that good, like I had a lot of trouble readin' in kindergarten, first grade . . . My mother didn't help me when I was small. But she couldn't because she didn't know English at all. All I had was just channel 13 [PBS] and school, and that's it. You know, they [school and PBS] try to teach you, but it's not the same as 'one on one.' Like in school, they have like thirty kids in one class. That can't help kids the same way like if it's 'one on one.' So that made me think that I wanted my daughter to be beyond that level when she goes to school. I want her to be at a advantage, not a disadvantage. And when you think about it, without a good education, man, she's just gonna be a statistic. And a life on welfare is hard, man. But education is something you could never take away, you understand?"

Pablo also prepared his ten-year-old half-brother (whose father lived in the Dominican Republic) for a baseball career. On weekends, Pablo traveled around the Bronx, taking him to various baseball leagues. On weekdays, Pablo spent early afternoons practicing with him, honing his baseball skills and prospects. One evening, I asked Pablo about his devotion to his little brother. "One day he told me he wanted to play baseball," Pablo explained, "that he wanted to be a baseball player. I told him that in order to be a baseball player, you gotta play baseball. So I wanted to see if he was for real. So I put him like in three teams in his first year. And he's still like in three teams now. He goes from one game, to another game, to another game . . . We put in hours, so we spend a lot of quality time together, practicing on everything—on his hitting, on his catching, on his throwing, you know. I mean, he told me that he wanted to be a baseball player. In order for you to be a baseball player, you have to practice. So I make sure that he practices. 'Cause I want him to be the best out of everybody."

Then Pablo rationalized in what most would consider a middle-class framework. The quality time he spent with his little brother, he reasoned, not only steered his little brother toward athletic success, but also into over-all positive growth. Because in the end, Pablo realized that marginal children need investment in them, especially to reduce their chances of doing crime.

"So why are you doing all of this?" I asked.

"Why? Because nobody did it with me. 'Cause I want his dream to come true. I don't know, like, I always felt like I'm his brother, but I'm like a father to him too. I just want to make this dream come true the way a father would. I didn't have the same support, you know what I mean? If I had the support, I would've gone further. Maybe not in football, but maybe I woulda never hit the streets. . . . I don't want him to go through the same stuff that I been through. I tell him, 'I don't want you to be like me. I want you to be better than me.' And when you love someone, you want the best for them, you don't want the worst. . . . So I don't think, so far, that he's gonna catch the streets. He's not gonna do what I did. That's what counts."

This is why I was sad for Pablo. Unlike most, I knew that he cared for his daughter, for his little brother, that he spent countless hours preparing them for success. I also knew that he now saw his criminal life as undesirable, un-glamorous; that when he championed the "thug life," it was because society gave him little alternative. Last, I knew that he struggled to reconcile his desire to be both law-abiding and economically successful, that the turmoil had him investing in others, one of those being me. He told me once:

"I'ma try to help you out so you could write this book. Any information you need, just let me know. I know I can't do much, you know, like I can't get you a gig like at a big school, a USC, or a Nebraska, or some Division I school like that. I just don't got it like that. If I did, like if I knew somebody that worked in those colleges, believe me, bro, I would try to hook you up. But, you know, I just do what I can. I'll try to help you as much as I can. I want you to be successful, bro. I want you to get outta this fuckin' ghetto. You know, my life is all fucked up, but that don't mean that I can't try to help you, you understand? Just let me know what you need and I'll help you, bro."

Yes, Pablo was a drug dealer and drug robber, but in some moments, Pablo was well meaning and had a heart. Under different social circumstances, I always imagined, Pablo could have been a different man. Perhaps he would have never done crime.

GUS: HEADED FOR SELF-DESTRUCTION

I doubt that Durkheim would have seen an illegal drug market as a moral regulator. In his time, he warned about the dangers of booming industries that were based on unrestrained capitalism and greed.[19] So for him, capitalist-based drug markets would be worse—shooting nouveau riche dealers into an anomic spiral of hedonism and disorientation. However, Robert Merton later theorized that the disadvantaged relieved anomie through economic crime.[20] Later still, Philippe Bourgois showed how drug markets could provide moral regulation: a crack market's work shifts, work identities, and mentor support often regulated a dealer's drug use and raised self-esteem.[21]

For Gus, I extend these observations: the penitentiary and drug market structured, or regulated, his behavior. In prison, he followed prison rules, which told him when to wake up and sleep, when to engage in leisure and when to eat. Though Gus sometimes resisted those rules, his opposition was in keeping with the moral order of inmate deviance, which, as Durkheim argued, was relative, dependent on social circumstances and situations.[22]

And in the drug market, Gus followed a schedule as he purchased, packaged, and sold drugs, and rounded up, fired, and paid workers. He also spent most of his time trying to increase profit and production. In other words, he filled his days with work. Not that women, partying, and material consumption were minor. He lived an extravagant lifestyle by South Bronx standards. Yet once the crack market shrank, he lost it all. Anomie then crept in. Gus became a *fallen star*.

Becoming a drug robber worsened his anguish. Now he spent his days waiting for tipsters to provide robbery information, with large spans of time, like three or four days, or sometimes a week, in between each hit. Also, the expanded leisure raised his drug use and spending; he no longer performed daily tasks that limited pleasure-seeking.[23] Worse, the leisure gave him more time to dwell on past crack glories and everything that had gone wrong since then. Thus, Gus lost order in his life and sped down a self-destructive path.

I first noticed his fall when I saw that his Timberland boots had worn out and the colors of his T-shirts had lost luster. Also, he rarely had money for a haircut and started asking me to trim his hair. But he wanted to keep his fall a secret. After learning that his older brother, Sylvio, owned and rented out a taxi cab, I asked Gus about why he didn't drive it for money.

"I ain't gonna drive no cab, man," Gus answered, laughing. "How I'ma look pickin' up passengers after I made so much money sellin' drugs and doin' stickups? What niggas gonna say about me, like the people that knew me before? They gonna be like, 'Damn, look at Gus drivin' a fuckin' cab. That nigga's doin' real b-a-a-a-d. Nah, man, I can't let niggas think that I fuckin' dropped so low and shit that I have to drive a fuckin' cab."

And Gus saw salvation in stickups. For some time, Gus informed everyone about a *big palo*—the mother of all drug hits—that was going to set him up for life. He and two other drug robbers, Sergio and Alberto, planned to rob two hundred kilos of cocaine off a boat that transported drugs from a Caribbean island to a New York City harbor. After the robbery, the cocaine was to be divided in three: sixty-five kilos for Gus; sixty-five kilos for Sergio; and seventy kilos for Alberto (the mastermind). In all, Gus could earn over a million dollars.

However, one fall afternoon, I found Gus standing quietly by the public stairwell. He appeared high; his eyes were red and he was unusually relaxed. After some small talk, I asked him about the boat robbery. It was canceled, he told me, because Alberto got cold feet and feared taking the risk. "But that's bullshit," Gus said, suddenly rising from his *tranquilidad*. "Those motherfuckas probably did that shit on their own. They just ain't tell me."

About a month later, Sergio drove up in his new, late model Ford Expedition, with music blasting from a booming system. His wife (he called her his wife) sat in the passenger seat, and his son sat in the back. After getting out of his car, he called Gus over and spoke furtively with him. Later, they came over to the group, with Sergio inhaling a few hits off a blunt that was being passed around. Then he drove off.

Immediately, Gus pulled me aside: According to Sergio, Alberto did the robbery alone, but only stole ten kilos. So not even he, Sergio, who was Alberto's brother-in-law, got a share.

"That motherfucka's lyin'," Gus said, angrily. "How the fuck you think he bought that Expedition? These motherfuckas think I'm fuckin' stupid or something, like I'm a fuckin' kid. Yo, I found out that that motherfucka Sergio even bought two fuckin' Lincolns, bro. . . . He's rentin' those shits out [to cabdrivers]. Man, both those niggas did that shit. They ain't tell me shit. They ain't even hit me off, you know what I'm sayin'? Those niggas makin' more than a million off that shit and they can't even give me something."

Gus then broke into disappointment and in a low voice said: "Yo, Ran, this was gonna be the robbery that set us up for life, you understand? Everybody was gonna get rich off this shit. Nobody was gonna have to do these robbery shits anymore. Me, Pablo—nobody was gonna have to rob niggas again. Not even you, bro, was gonna have to worry about money. Everybody was gonna get rich. Like for me, I saw it like, this was it."

Over the next several months, Gus struggled financially, and his violence erupted in irrational outbursts. Aware of his new tendency, he retreated into drugs, mainly by self-medicating on weed. "Sometimes I spend like a whole day smokin' weed, bro, just trying to fuckin' relax," Gus explained. " 'Cause all the problems I got, I got 'cause I'm fuckin' broke, man, broke, broke. That shit just makes me upset over shit I never woulda got upset about. Any little thing right now—yo, shit that like a month ago, I woulda not thought twice about, bro—now, you don't know. I just feel like gettin' violent, man. That's why I don't drink liquor, 'cause, not for nothing, that shit makes me violent. That's why I just be smokin' weed, bro. It's like when I smoke weed, I don't be thinkin' about none of my problems. That shit just like gets me mellow and shit."

Tragically, his growing depression created an anomic cocktail that he tried to water down with weed. It was just as tragic, if the rumors were true, that he started smoking angel dust (PCP), while also using cocaine and heroin. The structural problems that caused his legal and illegal marginality were too deep; his drug use spiraled out of control.

And his unregulated violence included lashing out at those closest to him. For instance, on a New Year's Day at around 11:00 A.M., I received a phone call. Pablo. *Yo, Ran, that nigga tried to come in strong on me, man,* Pablo said, in a shaky voice. (I heard the traffic, so I knew he was calling me from an outdoor public phone.)

Yo, who? I asked, immediately concerned.

That nigga, Gus, man, Pablo answered, as his voice cracked and then broke into a sob. *Yo, man, he fuckin' charged me, to set it off on me, kid. I don't know what the fuck is up with him, man. He changed, man. He ain't the same no more. I ain't fuckin' with him no more. I don't know what the fuck is wrong with him. He changed, man. He changed.*

What happened? I asked, surprised.

Nah, just know that he's dead to me, Pablo said, crying. *I don't know that nigga anymore [he started sobbing heavily; I could hear his chest heaving]. Just know, kid, that I would never do something like that to you, kid. I got a lotta love for you, man. I would never turn on you the way that nigga just did to me. I got a lotta of love for you, man. I love you, man. A'ight?*

I know, man, but what happened?

Nah, kid, I gotta go, Pablo said, his voice cracking. *Just know I got a lotta love for you, man.*

Pablo then hung up.

Before this incident, Lydia had moved in with Pablo. She did not break the lease on her apartment because she wanted to keep her Section 8 voucher. Pablo persuaded her to let Gus stay in the now-empty apartment until he found a stable home. She agreed—as long as Gus did not jeopardize her Section 8 status.

But Gus began using Lydia's apartment as a marijuana haven, a sanctuary where he and Melissa spent their days in weed-induced bliss. Every time I visited them from then on, both were meditative, mellow, with small-eyed grins, and the apartment had the sweet, funky aroma of weed. During those moments, Gus appeared content. Melissa and his bong made him forget about his financial worries.

The problems started on New Year's Eve when Lydia visited the apartment to pick up some clothes. She later claimed that some designer jeans were missing, as well as some shoes. She also found marijuana paraphernalia all over the dining table and in the bathroom. Last, she discovered a phone plugged in despite her stipulation, *No Phone Allowed.* (She kept her phone line connected, but did not want Gus to run up the bill.) Afterward, she complained to Pablo, who went to the apartment the next morning, on New Year's Day, to find empty weed bags and paraphernalia—everywhere. Pablo proceeded to scold Gus and Melissa, who had just gotten in from a New Year's bash.

"I told him that I was fuckin' doin' him a favor," Pablo later recalled. "Fuck, the least he could'a done was maintain shit the same way like when he got there. Then I told him that there was clothes missin'. That nigga was like, 'Yeah, yeah, whatever.' Yo, then he put a phone in the apartment after Lydia had took her shit out. I told him about the phone. I told him about leavin' all that weed shit lyin' around. Imagine [that] Lydia loses her Section 8 over that weed bullshit."

Having had enough of this lecture, Gus suddenly charged Pablo and tried to wrestle him to the ground. Pablo was stunned. "Like he rushed me," Pablo said, "like wrestling, bro, to knock me back. We was like wrestlin' for a minute, bro. I can't even talk about that shit, man. What hurt, kid, was that he would even think about doin' some shit like that to me. We like family, you know what I'm sayin'? I looked out a lot for that nigga, man, a lot. I always treated that nigga like he was my own brother, man. Better than my own real brother, in fact. . . . After that shit, I just fuckin' bounced, man. I just walked and walked, bro, just thinkin' about that shit. That nigga changed a lot, man. He ain't the same Gus."

Afterward, Gus disappeared and stopped returning everyone's calls. Sylvio and I worried. *Gus, where you at, man?*

Two months after his disappearance, I got a call. Gus. He heard that I was looking for him and told me to come over to Sylvio's apartment, where he was now staying. When I arrived, we greeted each other and sat in the living room. I looked at him. He appeared humble, changed.

"Yo, everything, Randy, has gone wrong for me, kid," Gus started. "No bullshit, bro. I sold my gun. I sold my jewelry. I sold all that, bro. Everything, bro. I don't know what's been goin' on. I buy drugs [and] by the time I sell it, I just make back the money to just buy again. Sometimes barely, man. The stickups? Those shits never come through, bro. Everything, man, is just goin' wrong for me."

I then asked him about the incident between him and Pablo. The night before, Gus explained, he and Melissa had attended a New Year's Eve party. Throughout the celebration, he had been in low spirits because of his terrible financial situation. He fell back to the thing he did best. Violence. "I was just stressed out that night," Gus recalled. "New Year's day, bro. *Stressed out.* Just thinking about all my problems, bro, all those shits. Then Julio's cousin kept asking Melissa to dance and shit, man. And like she told me, 'Yo, this nigga is botherin' me.' And I didn't even think, bro. I just started fuckin' him up. Knocked him out. Started stompin' him."

When they got back to Lydia's, Melissa and Gus smoked some weed to relax. Several moments later, there was a knock on the door. Pablo. "So I had weed on top of the table," Gus recalled. "And I had a bong and shit that I had bought. And you know how that nigga is and the way he talks. He was like, 'Yo, man, what's all this paraphernalia and shit up here. Clean this shit up!'

Then he told me something about the phone. Lydia had took her phone and I had bought one and had it connected. So he told me, 'Yo, Lydia had took the phone so you won't run up her bill.'

"So, I'm thinkin', damn, man, fuckin' Pablo, bro. To tell you the truth, it was all the shit that I had on my mind, bro. So I start screamin' at him. I was like, 'Yo, man, fuck that! If it's money that you want for this, for all the shit that I been usin', here, I'll pay you. That ain't shit.' So he said something else like, that it wasn't the money, that he was doin' me a favor. And then . . . I don't know, man. It was just me, bro. Just all the stress that I had on my mind, man. And, yo, I cried all day that day, bro, on New Year's Day, bro. Bro, all day I was stressed out. And I just didn't know . . ." Gus paused. His eyes watered.

"I ain't know how to approach him after that shit," Gus continued, as his voice and mouth quivered. "Then I had seen him like a month later and shit, like walkin' to Kingsbridge. And he looked at me, bro. And I didn't know what to say to him. I just kept walkin'. I acted like I ain't even know him and shit, bro. Damn, man."

Gus paused again. Tears fell from his eyes. He fought his emotions, trying not to break into a full cry. I felt my own eyes well up and held my composure the best I could. After a long pause, he said slowly: "Honestly, bro. I don't even know, man. That job on the boat was like my last chance—it was like my last chance to get some money and just try to take care of all the problems I got, man. That shit didn't even go through, bro."

I then asked him about his whereabouts since the incident with Pablo.

Gus explained how he and Melissa had traveled to New Bedford, Massachusetts, to sell heroin. However, his customers stopped paying him and he began owing money to his suppliers. So he switched to weed dealing, but failed there too. Then he moved to Providence, Rhode Island, to sell more weed—but failed again. So then with Willie (who was still desperately trying to strike it rich), Gus purchased cocaine in New York to sell in Providence. Coke sales, slow. Gus became more distressed and reckless.

"Like I was desperate," Gus said. "I was just stoppin' people in the street, like crackheads and people that we seen sellin' drugs and shit, and tellin' them that we got coke, that we sell coke, and give them our number. I was doin' like shit real reckless. Crackheads were coming to my house to buy crack and shit, man."

However, the business never took off. Everything just went wrong. Willie could no longer take it and left Gus alone. "Even when we sold the drugs,"

Willie explained later, "they didn't pay us the money. They paid us late. Everything was lost. We lasted about two or three weeks like that. It was a waste of time—a waste of my gasoline. And my car was sufferin'. I used to drive there [from New York to Providence] almost every day. Hardly sleepin', hardly eatin' over there. Strange people, strange places. I said, 'I'm leavin' this.'"

Willie also noted how Gus became reckless with his violence, which could have brought unwanted attention. "He's a little crazy, *muy* hyper," Willie explained. "Once he took a wheelchair from the mall, like he couldn't walk too good [he had hurt his ankle]. They asked him for a license, an ID. He didn't want to give a license or anything. He created a disaster in the mall. He got arrested. *Le dieron una golpeza de madre* [They gave him a mother of a beating]."

"Why did the cops beat him up?" I asked.

"They beat him up 'cause he got stupid over there. He started punchin' people, hittin' people. He's crazy. He's hopeless, hopeless. And when he did drugs, forget it. That's why I separated from him because imagine, he gets into trouble, I get in trouble too. For nonsense. I would tell him, 'We're here to make money, not to get into problems.'"

Between the violent outbursts, Gus' days dragged. After switching to weed sales again, he did little except wait for payments on drugs he gave on credit. The slow pace provided no structure or regulation, giving him too much time to dwell on his misfortunes and sink deeper into gloom.

"Every day," Gus said, "I just lay there, bro. I just fuckin' lay in bed and think about all the problems, man, that I'm having. Yo, man, I lost my appetite, bro. I eat sometimes just because I know I gotta eat . . . Just stress, bro. Stress, stress, stress. I wake up, I think about problems. I think about what I'm gonna do that day. Yo, sometimes I don't do shit. Sometimes I go like two, three days without doin' nothing, bro. Nothing, nothing. . . . Just be in my house, man."

Soon Gus experienced the psychological symptoms associated with depression and hopelessness. Like Pablo, he avoided family and friends. "It's like I went through a depression, bro," Gus explained. "Yo, depression and anxiety, all that shit's for real, man. I always thought that shit was bullshit. But all that shit's for real, bro. I just want to black out, just avoid everybody, bro. I just avoided everybody, bro. Imagine, for New Year's I didn't call my mother. Nobody. For Christmas, nothing, bro."

Then he described his anxiety and panic, something I never thought I'd hear. His body and mind started to act alone, to the point where he could no longer breathe. "One day," Gus said, "I got a headache so bad, bro. Yo, then this shit just came outta nowhere, man. I couldn't breathe or nothing, like I was short of breath. I felt like I was passin' out, bro. I was just buggin' out, man. Like I had lost control of my body, bro. I was shakin,' I was like, 'Damn, what the fuck is wrong with me?' . . . I felt like I was goin' crazy, Randy. I felt like—it's something like that I can't even explain, bro. Like I've been tryin' to read up on that shit [on the Internet]. Like I think they call that shit anxiety attacks and shit, or like panic attacks or something."

A major cause of his distress was Melissa's pregnancy: he already had two sons (he rarely saw them) with two different mothers, and had a girlfriend in the Dominican Republic who was ready to deliver his third child. Melissa's child would be his fourth, and Melissa, mother number four. Gus agonized over the situation and wanted to walk out on Melissa, for good.

"I don't want to go back [to Providence, where Melissa waited]," Gus continued. "In about two more months, I could say, Melissa's gonna have that kid, bro. What I'ma do then? Yo, honestly, man, sometimes I like used to wake up and go to the store like to buy something, and I used to just think that I should just disappear. I should just leave and just leave her stranded, bro. I could honestly say how I could understand how people do that shit, just abandon their family and just walk away from all that shit . . .'cause I been feelin' that shit."

Then he said: "Lately, I ain't even gonna lie to you, man. The only way out that I saw was goin' back to jail, bro. I was like, 'Fuck it,' I'm in jail, I do six months, a year. In jail, my life would get simpler, bro. All my problems would be taken away from me. I'm not responsible for nothing no more 'cause I'm in jail. 'I can't be with you [Melissa]; I can't be with nobody—I'm in jail. I can't do nothing—I'm in jail.' Fuck that."

"But wouldn't your life be harder in jail, bro?" I asked, shocked.

"Jail is not as hard as people think it is," Gus answered. "You adapt, you know what I'm sayin'? There's nothing you couldn't do. You in jail, you gotta accept it. And I guess jail is hard for people that are scared to be in jail. But jail for me was never hard, man. I think jail was harder for the people that cared about me. I think it was harder for my mother, for Sylvio, for everybody than it was for me."

"But wouldn't you be fuckin' fightin' every day in jail, man?" I asked, still digesting the information.

"But that's what I'm sayin', man," Gus explained. "That doesn't bother me. It doesn't bother me to fight . . . I'm not gonna say that it felt like home.

Honestly, shit has been so hard, bro, to me, jail was easier than bein' with all these fuckin' problems that I had lately. I think that's why there's people that have done shit to go back to prison, man. That they just couldn't take it in the street no more—"

"What would you have done like to go back to jail?" I asked.

"I was gonna . . ." Gus then paused, seeming embarrassed. "Yo, bro, I was just gonna have some weed on me, just like let that shit fall in front of the cops or something. Like do some funny shit to make the cops search me. 'Oh, you caught me with weed. Goin' to jail now.' For real, man. I was like on some real self-destructive shit."[24]

Then Gus turned to religion to understand his moral crisis. I was surprised because Gus was the most critical out of all the study participants. Also, he always challenged God's existence. But now he evoked biblical interpretations of his sufferings; now, God punished him for his sins. "Yo, I'm not religious," Gus said, "but I told you how I believe in God, but that God doesn't really have like a real hold in our life. Like God doesn't really make shit happen in our life. I always thought that shit happens to us because the way we live, you know, our actions, whatever. But I'm tellin' you, man, lately I been fuckin' scared. I really been thinkin' about shit, man."

"Scared of what?" I asked, in disbelief.

"Like all the bad shit that I've done, bro," Gus explained, in a low voice. "God is really like punishin' me for shit that I've done, bro. Put it like this: everything that I've done, all those robberies that I've done, it's led up to this point. I'm to the point right now that everything is goin' as worse as it can get. Now I started fuckin' with Melissa knowin' that I got a girl out there pregnant in Dominican Republic. Now Melissa's pregnant. Now that's another headache. I'm lookin' at that as like my punishment for just being with her knowin' that I left my wife [girlfriend] pregnant in Dominican Republic to come over here to get money and to go back and to take care of her, like to take care of my mother. . . . Honestly, man, it's like I'm being punished for just the shit that I've been doin'."

On a deeper level, Gus used religion for more than understanding his chaotic, depressing turn. It was his torch as he searched for a moral order, one the drug market no longer provided. In doing so, he placed himself within a mainstream "God-fearing" society, calling himself out as a wrongdoer, a deviant, a sinner who brushed against the moral grain.[25] Thus, his wade into the religious stream represented more than his belief in a fiery higher power. It showed how he frantically turned to conventional society to readjust his expectations, wants, and needs.

Yet it was an uncritical search for moral order. Rather than see how larger race, ethnic, and class inequalities had set the context for his wrongs; how a larger material and capitalist culture had driven him to achieve success, no matter what; how his poor community, the crack market, the prison, and his gung-hò capitalist family had shaped his criminal path, Gus blamed himself, depicting society as the perfect Eden, the paradise where he alone had eaten of the forbidden apple and was now eternally damned. His fallen state had disoriented him; he was convinced that he burned in a hell-on-earth for his crimes.

Later, Gus revealed how he had recently seen Pablo and that both had spoken about changing their lives. Pablo had also embraced religion to cope with his fallen status. And he embraced the righteous path with characteristic zeal. In fact, he even called me sometimes and urged me to change my nonreligious ways. But since I always pointed out contradictions (though not too harshly), he eventually stopped calling me. I was not offended. I knew that religion provided him with moral order and kept him from a suicidal state.

Eventually, he reached out to Gus, who then experienced great shame. "Like when I got here [Sylvio's apartment]," Gus said, "out of all the people I woulda expected to see, I see Pablo. He was here when I got here and he was tellin' me that he wanted me to change my life and he didn't want me gettin' killed or shot, or gettin' locked up. He told me that he wanted me to take care of myself and shit, like do the right thing, like by God. I was surprised to hear him say that, man. I ain't even know what to say, man. Look, I want to talk to my uncle . . . [his voice starts trembling] but I don't even know how to tell him, you know, how to explain how I didn't come around for New Year's, bro."

He paused, fighting to stay composed. Then with a trembling voice: "All I could say is that I'm sorry, bro, to everyone, man. That's it. That's all I been tellin' everybody, bro, 'Sorry, man.'"

Tears ran down his face. With a weak, shaky voice, he then explained how chasing the American Dream, with its almost unattainable fantasy of wealth and riches, had led to his current crisis. And for the first time, he spoke of pursuing a quiet, humble life, one that settled for less material achievement and crawled rather than sprinted toward a comfortable end.

"The attitude that I have now," Gus explained, "is not the attitude that I had three months ago, four months ago. I feel like there's just nothing left for me to do. Like I tried everything I could in my life and I might as well be content with the way I am now and just go to D.R. and live a humble life. And there's nothing wrong with that, man. You know, just work the rest of my life and just live to just pay the bills and that's my life. All the dreams that I had of havin' a fuckin' beautiful house, a beautiful pool, you know, if I get it, I would have to wait ten or fifteen, twenty more years to get it working honestly, whatever. Because I feel as though, this is what I've done all my life and it hasn't given me shit. Nothing but fuckin' headaches, bro. A fucked up life, bro.

"Yo, man, I feel like my life is really fucked up. Fucked up. This is like the final chapter of the book, bro, ha-ha-ha. I was telling Pablo that if Randy was really writin' a book, man, this is where the book would end, man. This is where everybody would be like, 'Well, this is how our life just stayed. Gus ended up doin' this. Pablo ended up doin' that.' This is the end, man."

Conclusion

THE CRACK ERA WAS (to paraphrase Charles Dickens) indeed the best of times, the worst of times—the age of power and respect, the age of violence and self-destruction. It was the hour of instant bliss and riches; it was the hour of panic, confusion, and doom. We had the world right before us, the world was no longer before us, we reveled in the season of hope, we anguished in the season of despair. It was the most crucial point of our lives.

And more than a decade later, members of the crack era generation are still recuperating from the devastating impact. Some may never recuperate at all. For instance, the once-committed crack users must always monitor their daily cravings, peers, and behavior. The suffering parents still anguish over their dead, imprisoned, or drug-committed children. The convicted drug offenders must bear the heavy burden of a criminal mark.

For the main study participants, though, the crack era's impact was about more than drug use, or personal losses, or prison experiences, or criminal stigmas. It was about accepting their status as fallen stars. Even though they entered the market right after its peak, the crack era had lifted them to unimaginable heights, providing them a world of power, money, and consumption that they could not have achieved legally. However, the crack era's end would be the end of them. Because as they fell from grace, they would become drug robbers whose brutality rivaled that of state-sanctioned torturers around the globe. Then, after failing as drug robbers, they self-destructed as they fought against their new identity as fallen stars. As C. Wright Mills would say, they could not grasp their place within a rapidly changing drug market. They could only focus on their immediate sense of feeling "trapped."[1] Thus, a structural shift within the drug market would reduce opportunities and lead to more innovation, more violence, and more self-destruction.

Yet their lives showed the complexities of the American Dream as it played out in the South Bronx. As these Dominican men—and one woman (we cannot forget Melissa)—chased our nation's sacred material and monetary goals, they sought a simultaneous rise in masculinity and femininity, while dealing with their racial anguish, or *angustia racial,* too. Thus, they would dehumanize and emasculate both robbery victims and Black men while dehumanizing and objectifying Black women. Melissa would reframe her robbery role as empowering—as a way to overcome gender oppression through using her body to deceive men. In the end, their overall social project was not to obliterate, but to prevail within the oppressive race, class, and gender hierarchies that they faced as marginal women and men.

GENERALIZING FROM SOUTH BRONX VIOLENCE

In generalizing my approach to other social contexts, I immediately think of the ongoing Mexican drug wars. In 2001, they would yield a little over 1,000 drug-related killings; by 2006, just over 2,000; by 2008, over 5,000; and by 2009, an astronomical 6,587![2] To understand these drug-related killings, we must go beyond analyzing each killing alone, or as isolated violent encounters, or as reflective of individual emotional dynamics or drug culture. Something else is going on. Something structural.

Consider the following. During the early 1980s, Mexican traffickers were mostly go-betweens for Colombian cocaine cartels that supplied U.S. cocaine demand. Both the Mexicans and the Colombians received protection from Mexico's top political party, the Partido Revolucionario Institucional, and they had coordinated a loose alliance of drug organizations. However, in the late 1980s, the PRI would lose its political foothold, and a top Mexican trafficker, Miguel Angel Félix Gallardo, would be arrested for the kidnapping and murder of a U.S. drug enforcement agent.[3] As a result, the Mexican drug world would begin a phase of restructuring, with different drug cartels competing for the best market shares and regional spots. Unsurprisingly, violence would increase.[4]

The bloodshed would worsen after the September 11, 2001, terrorist attack that destroyed the World Trade Center.[5] As a show of force, the United States intensified its security along the Mexican border. This move slowed Mexican drug trafficking into the U.S., which reduced profits in heroin, marijuana, and cocaine distribution. Once again, violence would increase as traffickers gun-battled, kidnapped, and killed each other to protect their earnings in a disrupted market.[6]

The greatest surge in violence came after 2006, when newly elected Mexican president Felipe Calderón launched forty-five thousand soldiers and government police to combat the drug cartels.[7] The U.S. would also join in the fight, providing its own resources and federal agents. In the end, the dual effort succeeded. Drug flows into the United States were reduced, and high-level Mexican cartel leaders were arrested.[8]

These efforts, however, failed to curb U.S. drug demand. Drug-related violence then rose to unprecedented heights. Traffickers kidnapped, shot, and murdered more competitors, along with police, politicians, and their relatives. They even killed folk musicians whose only offense was immortalizing opposing traffickers through song.[9]

In short, when drug markets reach a crisis point, whether the crisis is induced by political policies (as in Mexico) or by community empowerment (as in the South Bronx), violence increases. Structural shifts can set the conditions for rising violence, whether it be shooting a meddling Mexican police officer or torturing a resistant South Bronx drug dealer.

DOING SOMETHING: REDUCING DRUG MARKET VIOLENCE

The tragedy of ethnographic research is that policy makers rarely use it to shape their work. The problem is that policy makers are politically embedded, often matching their proposals with the current political and public mood. And more often than not, political or public opinion is not based on empirical research, but on anger, fear, and frustration that have been stirred up for political ends. For criminal justice policy, this is dangerous. Policy makers can easily ignore or dismiss criminological research that counters the prevailing politics. Or they can easily use research that fits the political script, even though it may have serious flaws.

As a sociologist wanting to uplift marginal communities, I am deeply concerned about this. I am especially concerned with the policy implications of the current robbery research.[10] For instance, these researchers mostly conclude that street criminals would not take legal jobs, even stable, well-paying ones. Criminal culture, they argue, is just too empowering and alluring: "What policy makers are up against," Bruce A. Jacobs concludes, for instance, "is a lifestyle as entrenched as it is intractable, forged from a noxious combination of low self-control, desperation, and [criminal] cultural imperative."[11] So, for them, focusing on crime victims is the best option—for example, reducing their vulnerability and moving toward a cashless world.

True, Jacobs goes on to say that if society refuses to address the root causes of street crime, then it will "perpetuate the conditions that produce generations of *intractable* criminals" (emphasis added).[12] Yet he fails to address how society can stop perpetuating inequality, simply reinforcing how, for street criminals (whom he also calls "incorrigible"),[13] there is nothing we can do. His use of words like "intractable" and "incorrigible" makes me uneasy. Because when I think of my study participants, like Pablo and Tukee, I know that those descriptors are hasty and deficient. Both men are trying desperately to succeed through legitimate enterprises, but struggle because of their lack of educational, social, and cultural capital. If anything, their persistence demonstrates their commitment to the legal world, to mainstream values and goals.

Overall, I wonder why Jacobs and like-minded researchers have failed to ask the following questions: Did the so-called robust 1990s economy actually create stable and well-paying jobs for the working class and poor, or those prone to street crime? What can society do to assure that the next generation of poor, inner-city children see crime as less viable than in the past? I conclude that a strictly emotional and cultural analysis does not invite such questions.

Such policy recommendations, I fear, just reinforce the "prisonfare" side of what social scientist Loic Wacquant calls the "carceral-assistential continuum."[14] This social manifestation has deep historical roots: U.S. society has consistently stigmatized minorities, then segregated them to harsh social conditions. And when crime increased among them, U.S. society built more prisons rather than dealing with the social and economic injustices that initially caused their plight.

I also fear that such policy ideas might inadvertently bolster the kind of conservative, genocidal public sentiment that has been articulated by William Bennett, who served as secretary of education under President Reagan. Upon learning that an economist had linked higher rates of minority abortions with a reduction in the number of crime-prone individuals,[15] Bennett would say the following on his nationally broadcast radio program: "But I do know that it's true that if you wanted to reduce crime, you could—if that were your sole purpose—you could abort every black baby in this country, and your crime rate would go down. That would be an impossible, ridiculous, and morally reprehensible thing to do, but your crime rate would go down."[16]

Certainly, Bennett would stop short of solving white-collar crime in the same way. But he *innocently* suggested this about African Americans, a minority group that our country has historically portrayed as morally and culturally inferior to Whites. This is a bad sign. Hardly a discussion of changing economic conditions that hurt the working class and poor; of new social policies that favor the nation's wealthy and rich; or of underhanded political strategies that justify inequality by portraying Black and Brown citizens as dangerous.

Clearly, the criminologists I have just critiqued have never suggested the massive lockups or annihilation of poor minorities. In fact, Neal Shover, Richard T. Wright, and Scott H. Decker have all expressed strong doubts about long-term incarceration as a crime solution. Nevertheless, their research approach points to no other way. For them, the problem is both crime's attractions and a criminal culture that pervades poor, inner-city neighborhoods. That is why their best solution is to protect crime victims. Nothing else is possible, nothing else would work.

In contrast, my own policy suggestions are hopeful. Though not novel or painstakingly detailed (I am not a policy planner), my recommendations come from my methodological approach, which looks at larger structural transformations, especially ones that affect the drug market. First, at a larger level, we obviously need to increase the wages of the least educated and skilled laborers in fair proportion to the wages of the top income earners. For the last forty years, the former have suffered as the gap between the super-rich and everyone else has deepened.[17] And our current economic recession, where unemployment has sometimes matched levels of the Great Depression, can only worsen the gap.[18] Yet no matter how difficult, we must lessen this enormous inequality through both creating stable and well-paying employment and *redistributing* wages and income. This would socially and financially empower disadvantaged communities to ward off social problems such as drug use.

As drug scholars Craig Reinarman and Harry Levine argue, suburban communities were protected from the crack epidemic by their social, structural, and economic stability; some suburban drug users might experiment with crack, but they had solid defenses against committed crack use.[19] When crack emerged in places like the South Bronx, though, it would lure a larger proportion of its residents. In fact, some of them would welcome this drug because of its economic potential. This is why a generation of Bronx minorities, like Pablo, Gus, Tukee, and others, would get caught in the crack market's web.

Second, since South Bronx–like communities are vulnerable to hardcore drug markets, we need more drug treatment programs, which would help to reduce demand.[20] The challenge lies in our nation's love affair with harsh, military-type drug reduction strategies, like drug interdiction, crop eradication, drug task forces, high arrest rates, and long prison sentences. As I discussed in an earlier chapter, this approach ignores how the public generally regulates itself, first falling in love with an obscure hardcore drug and then later rejecting it altogether.[21] Poor drug users are ill-equipped to financially afford drug treatment. So, compared to high-income users, they have more trouble stopping drug use.

The law-and-order approach ignores important lessons from history. For instance, during the early twentieth century, well-meaning moralists attempted to curb our nation's appetite for alcohol. They succeeded in having lawmakers enact Prohibition, which banned its production and sale. Prohibition, however, did not decrease demand. The net result was an increase in organized crime groups; they not only made fortunes selling alcohol in underground markets but also engaged in more violence. Eventually, lawmakers realized that banning alcohol did not decrease demand, but increased mayhem; in the end, they repealed Prohibition.[22] The lesson: as long as demand for a suppressed drug is high, robust markets and violence will follow.

Our more recent history, though, shows directly how drug treatment can greatly reduce hardcore drug crime, markets, and demand. Surprisingly, it would be a conservative politician during the early 1970s that would pave the way for that realization: President Richard M. Nixon.[23] To reduce the period's rising crime rate, Nixon allotted about two-thirds of the federal drug budget to a national drug treatment program. The main ingredient was methadone, which was used to combat heroin withdrawal. After some testing, the 1972 crime numbers were astounding. In one year, ninety-four of the nation's largest cities experienced crime drops. Among them were New York City, with an 18 percent drop, and Washington, D.C., with a drop of 26 percent.[24]

Yet Nixon would later revert to law-and-order policies. Why? A Republican New York governor, Nelson Rockefeller, was making a run at him in the next presidential primary. Despite New York's treatment success and related crime drop (and Rockefeller's acknowledgment of it), the governor proposed a set of draconian drug laws that would punish low-level drug offenders with life sentences. Worse, a political poll showed that two-thirds of New Yorkers agreed with his harsh proposal. Nixon would respond by increasing the federal punishment of drug offenders and reallocating drug treatment funds to create the DEA, or Drug Enforcement Agency.[25]

In the end, the obvious promise of drug treatment would not matter to politicians or the public. Only political factors—such as fear-mongering and gamesmanship—would shape the course of our nation's problem solving. As a historically informed public, we must admit to how politics can set the stage for hardcore drug epidemics and violence. The politically driven law-and-order model developed during the 1970s would later contribute to the unfettered growth of crack markets and its demand. As the examples of Prohibition and the Mexican drug wars have shown, supply will follow—whatever the cost in human misery.

Third, and perhaps most impossible to reach, we need to reduce the allure of both our nation's capitalist greed and its single-minded focus on material consumption as the greatest good. It might seem odd that I should touch on such an abstract issue; but a capitalist ideology is the bedrock underlying my study participants' motives for and justifications of crime. As noted earlier, entrepreneurial crime is not resistance to or deviance from dominant society; instead, it is a pledge of allegiance to its logic, material values, and goals.

But I cannot provide concrete suggestions; the sophistication needed to undo centuries of capitalist indoctrination, to undo the glorification of the robber barons, to undo the exaggerated success stories of the poor man who became rich, to undo the black-and-white film reels that glorify the sprawling mansions, the polo fields, the safari and fox hunts—to undo the recent appeal of cable television programs like *MTV Cribs*, which rubs in our faces exaggerated homes and material consumption, or *My Super Sweet Sixteen*, which deifies obnoxious rich kids who get parents to spend hundreds of thousands of dollars on birthday extravaganzas (that feature grand halls, music pop stars, luxury cars, and hundreds of teenagers who roar and scream and shout as the little King or Queen makes their entrance)—the sophistication needed to undo all of this is expansive and beyond me to recommend.

Yet these hollow messages continue to be repeated relentlessly. It makes the young dream of impossible financial accumulations, of what the odds say almost no one can reach; it makes them measure people based on their earning power and purchases; worse, it makes them measure themselves by those same standards, which in turn can pressure them to pursue alternative paths to succeed; in the end, it disappoints them as youth fades and they realize that they will fail at reaching the ultimate goal: *riquezas,* which, for most, is an unreachable dream.

For the Dominican participants in my study, the capitalist ethos motivated them to enter the drug market. There they would play out, with the little they had, our nation's cultural messages of material success. And in the end, they would not only brutally hurt others but also hurt themselves. So for the sake of not creating more human misery, we must let the word out that the pursuit of material gain is not the only road to travel, that a good life is not defined solely by exaggerated power and riches. There are alternative ways to live that define a life as having "made it," as being "someone" who matters to family, community, and friends.

I wish that such a message had reached the child beings of Pablo, Gus, Tukee, and the rest of the men and women who used the drug market to chase the impossible Dream. Perhaps they might have found less harmful ways of overcoming barriers, like organizing to challenge their marginal status or pursuing work that had less to with achieving wealth and more to do with pursuing passionate interests. But, again, changing our national cultural orientation is complicated. I cannot even imagine where to begin.

I can predict, though, the vicious political backlash against this kind of thinking. The current public mood—"We Want Our America Back"[26]— would frame it as undoing what the nation's founders had in mind, or as the seeds of a socialist revolt. However, I am not pessimistic. I have faith in my readers. Readers can use this ethnography to understand the marginalized urban men and women who begin from the furthest starting blocks and run the race despite little chance of gaining ground. Readers can understand how frustration can lead the marginal into crime, the nonviolent into violence, the violent into using brutality as a status symbol, and the fallen into suicidal despair. Readers can listen critically to political rhetoric and recognize the ideological sleights of hand used to polarize well-meaning people. Readers can pay attention to recent and past history, and reverse regressive policies based on distorted research or pure ideology alone. Most of all, they can discuss all of this with intimates, colleagues, and friends, the real sources of social progress in this country. We must cut the pain, suffering, and brutality that this South Bronx ethnography has revealed, an anguish that for some will never subside.

NOTES

PREFACE

1. Ansley Hamid, "The Developmental Cycle of a Drug Epidemic: The Cocaine Smoking Epidemic of 1981–1991," *Journal of Psychoactive Drugs* 24, no. 4 (1992).

2. Joseph B. Treaster, "New York State Reports a Drop in Crack Traffick," *New York Times,* December 27, 1990.

INTRODUCTION

1. Andrew Karmen, *New York Murder Mystery: The True Story behind the Crime Crash of the 1990s* (New York: New York University Press, 2000).

2. For an overview of the 1990s debate on the crime drop, see Alfred Blumstein and Joel Wallman, *The Crime Drop in America* (New York: Cambridge University Press, 2000); Karmen, *New York Murder Mystery;* Loic Wacquant, "The 'Scholarly Myths' of the New Law and Order Doxa," in *The Socialist Register 2006: Telling the Truth,* ed. Leo Panitch and Colin Leys (New York: Monthly Review Press, 2005).

3. Jack Katz, *Seductions of Crime: Moral and Sensual Attractions of Doing Evil* (New York: Basic Books, 1988).

4. Neal Shover and David Honaker, "The Socially Bounded Decision Making of Persistent Property Offenders," *Howard Journal of Criminal Justice* 31, no. 4 (1992); Richard Wright and Scott H. Decker, *Burglars on the Job: Streetlife and Residential Break-Ins* (Boston: Northeastern University Press, 1994).

5. Bruce A. Jacobs, *Dealing Crack: The Social World of Streetcorner Selling* (Boston: Northeastern University Press, 1999); Bruce A. Jacobs, *Robbing Drug Dealers: Violence beyond the Law* (New York: Aldine de Gruyter, 2000); Bruce A. Jacobs, Volkan Topalli, and Richard Wright, "Carjacking, Streetlife, and Offender Motivation," *British Journal of Criminology* 43, no. 4 (2003); Bruce A. Jacobs and Richard

T. Wright, "Stick-up, Street Culture, and Offender Motivation," *Criminology* 37, no. 1 (1999); Richard T. Wright and Scott H. Decker, *Armed Robbers in Action: Stickups and Street Culture* (Boston: Northeastern University Press, 1997). In his description of Black Philadelphia, Elijah Anderson does the same by opposing middle-class ideals to those of the working class and poor. See, for instance, Elijah Anderson, *Streetwise: Race, Class, and Change in an Urban Community* (Chicago: University of Chicago Press, 1990).

6. I cannot similarly criticize Jack Katz since he argues that the emotional allure of crime is equally strong across race and class groups; it just looks different.

7. It seems as if people forget how early sociologists and journalists described the urban social ills and crimes of the immigrant poor, who were of European origins. For instance, Frederic Thrasher's classic study of Chicago gangs in the early twentieth century found that most gangs were comprised of European ethnics. "Negro" gangs, as they were called back then, made up only about 7 percent of the gang population. Frederick Thrasher, *The Gang: A Study of 1,313 Gangs in Chicago,* 2nd ed. (Chicago: University of Chicago Press, 1936).

8. C. Wright Mills, *The Sociological Imagination* (New York: Oxford University Press, 1959). For an excellent ethnography using a C. Wright Mills approach, see Timothy Black, *When a Heart Turns Rock Solid: The Lives of Three Puerto Rican Brothers on and off the Streets* (New York: Pantheon Books, 2009).

9. Since I am little inclined to categorize myself as a certain "type" of ethnographer, I hesitate to call myself a cultural criminologist. Yet I am certainly tuned in to cultural criminology, which theoretically aims to link emotions, resistance, culture, and social context. See Jeff Ferrell, Keith Hayward, and Jock Young, *Cultural Criminology: An Invitation* (Los Angeles: Sage, 2008). My approach also lines up with Patricia Adler's outstanding 1970s ethnography of upper-level drug dealers, which captures many of these elements. Patricia Adler, *Wheeling and Dealing: An Ethnography of an Upper-Level Dealing and Smuggling Community* (New York: Columbia University Press, 1985).

10. Robert K. Merton, "Social Structure and Anomie," *American Sociological Review* 3, no. 5 (1938). Merton has been highly criticized for a later version of this strain, or anomie, theory, where he makes it seem as if only low-income groups feel a pressure to do economic crime. Robert K. Merton, *Social Theory and Social Structure* (New York: Free Press, 1968). While I wholeheartedly agree with the criticisms, I believe that his later failure does not diminish the value of his first formulation. For an expanded and highly nuanced version of strain theory, see Robert Agnew, "An Overview of General Strain Theory," in *Explaining Criminals and Crime,* ed. Raymond Paternoster and Ronet Bachman (Los Angeles: Roxbury, 2001). For a version that focuses on how our economic institutions dominate all other social institutions, which eases economic crimes, see Messner and Rosenfield, *Crime and the American Dream.*

11. Richard A. Cloward, "Illegitimate Means, Anomie, and Deviant Behavior," *American Sociological Review* 24, no. 2 (1959); Richard A. Cloward and Lloyd E.

Ohlin, *Delinquency and Opportunity: A Theory of Delinquent Gangs* (New York: Free Press, 1960).

12. See for instance, Eloise Dunlap and Bruce D. Johnson, "The Setting for the Crack Era: Macro Forces, Micro Consequences," *Journal of Psychoactive Drugs* 24, no. 4 (1992).

13. They were like the few New Jacks that criminologist John Hagedorn found in a Milwaukee gang, and like the Puerto Rican robber that anthropologist Philippe Bourgois found in East Harlem. See Philippe Bourgois, "Overachievement in the Underground Economy: The Life Story of a Puerto Rican Stick-up Artist in East Harlem," *Free inquiry* 25, no. 1 (1997); John Hagedorn, "Homeboys, Dopefiends, Legits, and New Jacks," *Criminology* 32, no. 2 (1994).

14. For a general representation of young people in New York City, including second-generation Dominicans, see Philip Kasinitz et al., *Inheriting the City: The Children of Immigrants Come of Age* (New York and Cambridge: Russell Sage Foundation and Harvard University Press, 2008); Nancy Lopez, *Hopeful Girls, Troubled Boys: Race and Gender Disparity in Urban Education* (New York: Routledge, 2003); Katherine S. Newman, *No Shame in My Game: The Working Poor in the Inner City* (New York: Knopf/Russell Sage Foundation, 1999).

15. The astronomical number of minority lockups during the 1980s and 1990s resulted from drug policies that politicians created to gain popularity among White, working-class voters (see especially Katherine Beckett, *Making Crime Pay: Law and Order in Contemporary American Politics* (New York: Oxford University Press, 1997); Michael Tonry, *Malign Neglect: Race, Crime, and Punishment in America* (New York: Oxford University Press, 1995).

16. Loic Wacquant, "From Slavery to Mass Incarceration," *New Left Review* 13 (2002).

17. This is a description of the old Yankee Stadium. A new stadium has since been built.

18. Big Punisher and featuring Fat Joe, "100%," in *Yeeeah Baby* (Sony Records, 2000).

19. Fernandito Villalona, "Tabaco Y Ron," in *El Mayimbe* (Kubaney Records, 1982).

20. See Mitchell Duneier, *Sidewalk* (New York: Farrar, Straus, and Giroux, 1999).

21. For a similar account, see Sudhir Venkatesh, *Gang Leader for a Day: A Rogue Sociologist Takes to the Street* (New York: Penguin Books, 2008).

22. Duneier, *Sidewalk;* Elliot Leibow, *Tally's Corner: A Study of Negro Street-corner Men* (Boston: Little, Brown, 1967).

23. Sandra Harding, *The Science Question in Feminism* (Ithaca, N.Y.: Cornell University Press, 1986); Dorothy E. Smith, *Institutional Ethnography: A Sociology for People* (Toronto: AltaMira Press, 2005).

24. Patricia Hill Collins, *Black Feminist Thought: Knowledge, Consciousness, and the Politics of Empowerment,* 2nd ed. (New York: Routledge, 2000).

25. For the record, they were not my dissertation committee members.

26. Patricia Hill Collins, *Fight Words: Black Women and the Search for Justice* (Minneapolis: University of Minnesota Press, 1998).

27. Sudhir Venkatesh, *American Project: The Rise and Fall of a Modern Ghetto* (Cambridge, Mass: Harvard University Press, 2000); Sudhir Venkatesh, *Off the Books: The Underground Economy of the Urban Poor* (Cambridge, Mass.: Harvard University Press, 2006); Venkatesh, *Gang Leader for a Day*. For an example of how being French created opportunities for mutual explanations by study participants and researcher, see Loïc Wacquant, *Body and Soul: Notebooks of an Apprentice Boxer* (New York: Oxford University Press, 2004); Loïc Wacquant, "Carnal Connections: On Embodiment, Apprenticeship, and Membership," *Qualitative Sociology* 28, no. 4 (2005).

28. For an ethnographic example of how larger U.S. materialistic messages play out among young minority boys in the inner city, see Scott N. Brooks, *Black Men Can't Shoot* (Chicago: University of Chicago Press, 2009).

29. See Mary E. Pattillo-McCoy, *Black Picket Fences: Privilege and Peril among the Black Middle Class* (Chicago: University of Chicago Press, 1999).

30. Phillippe Bourgois, *In Search of Respect: Selling Crack in El Barrio,* 2nd ed. (New York: Cambridge University Press, 2003); Katz, *Seductions;* Randall Collins, *Violence: A Micro-Sociological Theory* (Princeton, N.J.: Princeton University Press, 2008).

31. Although around earlier, the reflexive move among ethnographers took a serious turn after the publication of James Clifford and George E. Marcus, eds., *Writing Culture: The Poetics and Politics of Writing Ethnography* (Berkeley: University of California Press, 1986). For a recent overview of scholarly trends of the "self" in research, see Norman K. Denzin and Yvonee S. Lincoln, eds., *Handbook of Qualitative Research,* 3rd ed. (Thousand Oaks, CA: Sage, 2005). For a discussion of more complicated reflexivity—a combination of positional, textual, and epistemic reflexivity—see Pierre Bourdieu and Loïc Wacquant, *An Invitation to Reflexive Sociology* (Chicago: University of Chicago Press, 1992).

32. Just to name a recent few, see Bourgois, *In Search of Respect;* Duneier, *Sidewalk;* Wacquant, *Body and Soul.*

33. I am not referring to autoethnographers, who see exploring themselves as the central method in understanding their research. For an interesting experimental text that explains autoethnography, see Carolyn Ellis, *The Ethnographic I: A Methodological Novel about Autoethnography* (New York: AltaMira Press, 2004).

34. For a moving commentary on research as "pimping," see Mark S. Fleisher, "Ethnographers, Pimps, and the Company Store," in *Ethnography at the Edge: Crime, Deviance, and Field Research,* ed. Jeff Ferrell and Mark S. Hamm (Boston: Northeastern University Press, 1998). For an interesting commentary on research as a "hustle," see Sudhir Venkatesh, "Doin' the Hustle: Constructing the Ethnographer in the American Ghetto," *Ethnography* 3, no. 1 (2002).

35. For an example of paying book royalties to study participants, see Duneier, *Sidewalk.*

1. U.S. Census Bureau, "Table 1: Annual Estimates of the Population for Incorporated Places over 100,000" (Washington, D.C.: U.S. Census Bureau, 2008); U.S. Census Bureau, "Table B-1: Area and Population" (Washington, D.C.: U.S. Census Bureau, 2007).

2. Mayor's Press Office, "Mayor Guiliani Announces Amount of Parkland in New York City Has Passed 28,000 Acre Mark" (New York: Archives of the Mayor's Press Office, 1999).

3. New York City Department of City Planning (NYCDP), "Newest New Yorkers 2000" (New York: New York City Department of City Planning, 2004).

4. U.S. Census Bureau, "S1501, Educational Attainment" (Washington, D.C.: U.S. Census Bureau, 2006); U.S. Census Bureau, "Small Area Income and Poverty Estimates" (Washington, D.C.: U.S. Census Bureau, 2008); New York City Police Department (NYPD), "Compstat" 15 (9) (NYPD Compstat Unit, 2008).

5. Katz, *Seductions,* 247.

6. William J. Wilson, *The Truly Disadvantaged: The Inner City, the Underclass, and Public Policy* (Chicago: University of Chicago Press, 1987).

7. To be fair, Jack Katz has recently called attention to how historical forces have to play a larger role in urban ethnographies. See Jack Katz, "Time for New Urban Ethnographies," *Ethnography* 10, no. 2–3 (2009).

8. Michael Burawoy, *Ethnography Unbound: Power and Resistance in the Modern Metropolis* (Berkeley: University of California Press, 1991).

9. Although few ethnographers take pains to frame their research within a historical context, three outstanding examples exist: Patricia Adler, *Wheeling and Dealing: An Ethnography of an Upper-Level Dealing and Smuggling Community* (New York: Columbia University Press, 1985); Timothy Black, *When a Heart Turns Rock Solid: The Lives of Three Puerto Rican Brothers on and off the Streets* (New York: Pantheon Books, 2009); Bourgois, *In Search of Respect.*

10. Jill Jones, *South Bronx Rising: The Rise, Fall, and Resurrection of an American City* (New York: Fordham University Press, 2002).

11. Ibid.

12. Evelyn Gonzalez, *The Bronx* (New York: Columbia University Press, 2004); Jones, *South Bronx Rising.*

13. Jones, *South Bronx Rising;* Lloyd Ultan and Gary D. Hermalyn, eds., *The Bronx in the Innocent Years, 1890–1925* (New York: Harper Row, 1985).

14. Gonzalez, *Bronx.*

15. James L. Dietz, *Economic History of Puerto Rico: Institutional Change and Capitalist Development* (Princeton, N.J.: Princeton University Press, 1986).

16. Robert Caro, *The Power Broker: Robert Moses and the Fall of New York* (New York: Vintage Books, 1975); Jones, *South Bronx Rising.*

17. Caro, *Power Broker;* Jones, *South Bronx Rising.*

18. Caro, *Power Broker;* Jones, *South Bronx Rising.*

19. Gonzalez, *Bronx;* Jones, *South Bronx Rising.*

20. Gonzalez, *Bronx.*

21. The rest of this section is based on the fascinating research of Robert Fitch, *The Assassination of New York* (New York: Verso, 1993).

22. Ibid.

23. Ibid., vii.

24. Jones, *South Bronx Rising.*

25. *"Tecatos"* is a label Latino residents used to identify committed heroin users. Research on Mexican gang and drug culture has many references to this label, an early example being Joan Moore, *Homeboys: Gangs, Drugs, and Prisons in the Barrios of Los Angeles* (Philadelphia: Temple University Press, 1978).

26. Jones, *South Bronx Rising.*

27. Gonzalez, *Bronx.*

28. Ibid.

29. Michael Jacobson and Philip Kasinitz, "Burning the Bronx for Profit," *The Nation,* November 15, 1986.

30. Jones, *South Bronx Rising.*

31. Ibid.

32. Jonathan Mahler, *Ladies and Gentlemen, the Bronx Is Burning: 1977, Baseball, Politics, and the Battle for the Soul of the City* (New York: Picador, 2006).

33. Eric Lichten, *Class, Power, and Austerity: The New York City Fiscal Crisis* (New York: Bergin and Garvey, 1986).

34. Ibid.

35. Raquel Z. Rivera, *New York Ricans from the Hip-Hop Zone* (New York: Palgrave Macmillan, 2003).

36. On the role of the South Bronx in the development of salsa music and dance, see Roberta L. Singer and Elena Martinez, "A South Bronx Latin Music Tale," *Centro Journal* 16, no. 1 (2004).

37. Jim Rooney, *Organizing the South Bronx* (Albany: State University of New York Press, 1995).

38. Jones, *South Bronx Rising;* Rooney, *Organizing the South Bronx.*

39. For global ethnographies, see Michael Burawoy et al., *Global Ethnography: Forces, Connections, and Imaginations in a Post-Modern World* (Berkeley: University of California Press, 2000); Zsuzsa Gille and Seán Ó Riain, "Global Ethnography," *Annual Review of Sociology* 28, no. 1 (2002).

40. David F. Musto, "Opium, Cocaine, Marijuana in American History," in *Drugs, Crime, and Justice: Contemporary Perspectives,* ed. Larry K. Gaines and Peter B. Kraska (Prospect Heights, Ill.: Waveland Press, 1997).

41. Craig Reinarman and Harry G. Levine, "Crack in Context: America's Latest Demon Drug," in *Crack in America: Demon Drugs and Social Justice,* ed. Craig Reinarman and Harry G. Levine (Berkeley: University of California Press, 1997).

42. James A. Inciardi, *The War on Drugs IV: The Continuing Saga of the Mysteries and Miseries of Intoxication, Addiction, Crime, and Public Policy* (New York: Pearson, 2008).

43. Ibid.

44. Robert Sabbag, *Snowblind: A Brief Career in the Cocaine Trade* (New York: Grove Press, 1998).

45. Inciardi, *War on Drugs IV.*

46. William Adler, *Land of Opportunity: One Family's Quest for the American Dream in the Age of Crack* (New York: Penguin Books, 1996); Inciardi, *War on Drugs IV.*

47. Adler, *Land of Opportunity.*

48. Michael Agar, "The Story of Crack: Towards a Theory of Illict Drug Trends," *Addiction Research and Theory* 11, no. 1 (2003).

49. Adler, *Land of Opportunity,* 65.

50. Agar, "Story of Crack"; Inciardi, *War on Drugs IV.*

51. Agar, "Story of Crack."

52. Michael Massing, *The Fix* (New York: Simon and Schuster, 1998).

53. Adler, *Land of Opportunity.*

54. Agar, "Story of Crack."

55. Adler, *Wheeling and Dealing.*

56. Ansley Hamid, "The Political Economy of Crack-Related Violence," *Contemporary Drug Problems* 17, no. 1 (1990); Ansley Hamid, "The Developmental Cycle of a Drug Epidemic: The Cocaine Smoking Epidemic of 1981–1991," *Journal of Psychoactive Drugs* 24, no. 4 (1992).

57. Massing, *The Fix,* 166.

58. Ibid.

59. Agar, "Story of Crack."

60. Ibid; Richard D. Lyons, "Cocaine Survey Points to Widespread Anguish," *New York Times,* January 3, 1984; Massing, *The Fix.*

61. Margaret Engel, "Cocaine: Pleasure Fades Fast, Problems Linger," *Washington Post,* August 7, 1983; Cynthia Gorney, "The Shackles of Cocaine; at California's Cokenders, Face to Face with Addiction," *Washington Post,* April 15, 1984.

62. Massing, *The Fix.*

63. Christian Parenti, *Lockdown America: Police and Prisons in the Age of Crisis* (New York: Verso, 1999).

64. Massing, *The Fix,* 169. Italics in the original.

65. Ibid., 190.

66. Tonry, *Malign Neglect.*

67. Katherine Beckett, *Making Crime Pay: Law and Order in Contemporary American Politics* (New York: Oxford University Press, 1997); Loic Wacquant, *Punishing the Poor* (Durham, N.C.: Duke University Press, 2009).

68. Adler, *Land of Opportunity;* Inciardi, *War on Drugs IV.*

69. Adler, *Land of Opportunity.*

70. Ibid.; Reinarman and Levine, "Crack in Context"; Terry Williams, *Crackhouse: Notes from the End of the Line* (Reading, Mass.: Addison-Wesley, 1992).

71. Adler, *Wheeling and Dealing,* 89.

72. Inciardi, *War on Drugs IV.*

73. United States Drug Enforcement Administration, "DEA History Book, 1980–1985" (http://www.justice.gov/dea/pubs/history/1980–1985.html); Adler, *Land of Opportunity.*

74. Inciardi, *War on Drugs IV.*

75. Craig Reinarman et al., "The Contingent Call of the Pipe: Binging and Addiction among Heavy Cocaine Users," in *Crack in America: Demon Drugs and Social Justice,* ed. Craig Reinarman and Harry G. Levine (Berkeley: University of California Press, 1997).

76. Agar, "Story of Crack."

77. Bruce D. Johnson and a team of researchers found that of the 658 committed crack users in their 1988 northern Manhattan sample, about 32 percent used it over four times a day. Bruce D. Johnson et al., "Crack Abusers and Noncrack Abusers: Profiles of Drug Use, Drug Sales and Nondrug Criminality," *Journal of Drug Issues* 24, no. 1–2 (1994).

78. Agar, "Story of Crack."

79. Several observers have pointed out shortcomings in the DAWN data, but these shortcomings would not seem to question the presence of a high demand for crack. Sociologists Craig Reinarman and Harry G. Levine argue, for example, that a "mention" or blood test revealing cocaine does not necessarily explain an emergency or death. First, other drugs, like alcohol, might have been present. Second, reasons other than drug use might have been responsible for injuries or death, like head traumas or accidents. Third, the monitoring failed to distinguish between powder cocaine and crack. Craig Reinarman and Harry G. Levine, "The Crack Attack: Politics and Media in the Crack Scare," in *Crack in America: Demon Drugs and Social Justice,* ed. Craig Reinarman and Harry G. Levine (Berkeley: University of California Press, 1997). In a similar vein, medical professor John P. Morgan and sociologist Lynn Zimmer assert that DAWN statistics only measured cocaine's presence in patients and corpses. But they also noted that rising emergencies mentioning "cocaine" were indicators that crack use might be on the rise among the urban poor. "The Social Pharmacology of Smokeable Cocaine: Not All Its Cracked up to Be," in *Crack in America: Demon Drugs and Social Justice,* ed. Craig Reinarman and Harry G. Levine (Los Angeles: University of California Press, 1997).

80. David R. Simon, *Elite Deviance* (Boston: Allyn and Bacon, 1999).

81. Adler, *Land of Opportunity.*

82. Robert Jackall, *Wild Cowboys: Urban Marauders and the Forces of Order* (Cambridge, Mass.: Harvard University Press, 1997); Michael Stone, *Gangbusters: How a Street Tough, Elite Homicide Unit Took Down New York's Most Dangerous Gang* (New York: Knopf, 2002).

83. Terry Williams, *The Cocaine Kids: The Inside Story of a Teenage Drug Ring* (New York: Addison-Wesley, 1989).

84. Jane Gross, "A New Purified Form of Cocaine Causes Alarm as Abuse Increases," *New York Times,* November 29, 1985.

85. Crystal Nix, "We're Not Going, So They Have to: The Bronx Battle Cry against Crack," *New York Times,* June 22, 1986.

CHAPTER TWO

1. Bourgois, *In Search of Respect;* Paul Willis, *Learning to Labor: How Working Class Kids Get Working Class Jobs* (New York: Columbia University Press, 1977).

2. For more on drug dealing on the street, see Jacobs, *Dealing Crack;* Bruce D. Johnson, Andrew Golub, and Jeffrey Fagan, "Careers in Crack, Drug Use, Drug Distribution, and Nondrug Criminality," *Crime and Delinquency* 41, no. 3 (1995).

3. Jeffrey Gettleman, "Camden Again Ranked Most Dangerous," *New York Times,* November 27, 2005.

4. Perhaps because of embarrassment, Pablo always said that his mother received a loan from a loan shark to purchase the store. But after speaking to her personally, I learned that she filed a suit against the city, which eventually settled on making a large payment to her. She would not disclose the amount.

5. This is a fictional last name.

6. Brooks, *Black Men Can't Shoot.*

7. For disturbing accounts NYC public schools during Pablo's high school years, see Jonathan Kozol, *Savage Inequalities: Children in America's Schools* (New York: Harper Perennial, 1991).

8. Lopez, *Hopeful Girls, Troubled Boys;* Ann A. Ferguson, *Bad Boys: Public Schools in the Making of Black Masculinity* (Ann Arbor: University of Michigan Press, 2001).

9. Patricia A. Adler and Peter Adler, *Backboards and Blackboards: College Athletes and Role Engulfment* (New York: Columbia University Press, 1990).

10. For a similar observation, see Black, *When a Heart Turns Rock Solid.*

11. For a look at transnational business ownership, see Alejandro Portes, Luis E. Guarnizo, and William J. Heller, "Transnational Entrepreneurs: An Alternative Form of Immigrant Economic Adaptation," *American Sociological Review* 67, no. 2 (2002). For a look at business ownership among Dominicans in the United States, see Luis E. Guarnizo, "Los Dominicanyorks: The Making of a Binational Society," *Annals of the American Academy of Political and Social Science* 533, no. 1 (1994).

12. Merton, "Social Structure and Anomie"; Steven F. Messner and Richard Rosenfield, *Crime and the American Dream* (Belmont, Calif.: Wadsworth, 1994).

CHAPTER THREE

1. Beckett, *Making Crime Pay.*

2. David Garland, *The Culture of Control: Crime and Social Order in Contemporary Society* (Chicago: University of Chicago Press, 2001).

3. See Jock Young, "Merton with Energy, Katz with Structure: The Sociology of Vindictiveness and the Criminology of Transgression," *Theoretical Criminology* 7, no. 3 (2003).

4. Beckett, *Making Crime Pay;* Loic Wacquant, "The Great Penal Leap Backward: Incarceration in America from Nixon to Clinton," in *The New Punitiveness: Current Trends, Theories, Perspectives,* ed. John Pratt et al. (London: Willan, 2005).

5. Garland, *Culture of Control.*

6. Massing, *The Fix;* Parenti, *Lockdown America.*

7. Beckett, *Making Crime Pay;* Tonry, *Malign Neglect.*

8. Beckett, *Making Crime Pay;* Tonry, *Malign Neglect.*

9. An egregious example was the federal Anti-Drug Abuse Act of 1986, the now infamous 100-to-1 crack-to-powder cocaine rule. Tonry, *Malign Neglect.*

10. Beckett, *Making Crime Pay.* See also Michael Tonry, *Thinking about Crime: Sense and Sensibility in American Penal Culture* (New York: Oxford University Press, 2004).

11. Parenti, *Lockdown America.*

12. Bourgois, *In Search of Respect.*

13. Karmen, *New York Murder Mystery.*

14. Michele Sviridoff et al., "The Neighborhood Effects of Street-Level Drug Enforcement: Tactical Narcotic Teams in New York" (New York: Vera Institute of Justice, 1992).

15. Celestine Bohlen, "Jail Population Reaches a Record," *New York Times,* September 25, 1998.

16. Ibid.

17. Alessandra Stanley, "Rikers Melee Leaves 87 with Injuries," *New York Times,* July 14, 1990; Sam H. Verhovek, "775 Jail Beds to Be Added in New York," *New York Times,* October 20, 1990.

18. Tim Golden, "Inside Rikers Island: A Bloody Struggle for Control," *New York Times,* September 1, 1990; Martin Gottlieb, "Behind Rikers Melee: Tensions Wrought by Strain of Change," *New York Times,* August 20, 1990.

19. Thus Pablo's estimate, quoted earlier, exaggerated the number of cots in each jail dorm.

20. Golden, "Inside Rikers Island."

21. In 2009, some Rikers Island correction officers were alleged to operate a secret society called "The Program," which allowed a group of detainees called "The Team" to extort and viciously assault other detainees. Joe Gould and Rich Schapiro, "Inside the Program: Secrets of Sadistic Rikers Island Society: Inmate Tells of Beatings and Sexual Humiliation," *Daily News,* January 25, 2009. It was also alleged that The Program was responsible for the death of Christopher Robinson, who was killed in the jail in October 18, 2008. See Wil Cruz, "Mom Still Angry over Son Slain in Jail," *Daily News,* October 18, 2009.

22. I added Manolo's account of his Rikers experience to triangulate, or to add another measurement, to support Gus and Pablo's accounts. The other study par-

ticipants, like Neno, Topi, and David, were too young to have experienced Rikers, at least when Pablo and Gus were detained there.

23. Later, Manolo described how during his second detainment, the phone system changed. Detainees now punched in their own code and were allowed to speak for only ten minutes at a time, making it harder for one detainee to control the phone.

24. Golden, "Inside Rikers Island."

25. Verhovek, "775 Jail Beds."

26. For a similar account, see Black, *When a Heart Turns Rock Solid.*

27. Collins, *Violence.*

28. Golden, "Inside Rikers Island."

29. This experience supports the finding that many New York state prisoners come from the same impoverished New York City neighborhoods. See Karmen, *New York Murder Mystery.*

30. Wacquant, "From Slavery to Mass Incarceration."

CHAPTER FOUR

1. Bruce D. Johnson, Andrew Golub, and Eloise Dunlap, "The Rise and Decline of Hard Drugs, Drug Markets, and Violence in Inner-City New York," in *The Crime Drop in America,* ed. Alfred Blumstein and Joel Wallman (New York: Cambridge University Press, 2000).

2. See Dunlap and Johnson, "The Setting for the Crack Era."

3. "A Taste of Urban Violence Sours a Quiet Town's Sense of Security," *New York Times,* July 27, 1992; Mary B. W. Tabor, "Migrants of the Drug World: From Brooklyn to Buffalo," *New York Times,* February 26, 1992. Clearly, some first-generation crack dealers had already done this. For example, the powerful NYC Jamaican posses started crack businesses in Philadelphia, Baltimore, and Washington, D.C., and then in rural states such as Kansas, Ohio, Nebraska, and Missouri. See Michael Massing, "Crack's Destructive Sprint across America," *New York Times,* October 1, 1989.

4. "The 'New York Boys' Plead Guilty to Charges of Conspiracy to Distribute Cocaine and Money Laundering," PR Newswire, November 15, 1991; David Simon and Edward Burns, *The Corner: A Year in the Life of an Inner-City Neighborhood* (New York: Broadway Books, 1997).

5. Though I hung out often with Alex as a teen, I never spoke with him during the research because he was in prison, sentenced to eighteen years for a robbery conviction.

6. Massing, "Crack's Destructive Sprint."

7. Ginetta E. B. Candelario, *Black behind the Ears: Dominican Racial Identity from Museums to Beauty Shops* (Durham, N.C.: Duke University Press, 2007).

8. Sylvio Torress-Saillant, "Introduction to Dominican Blackness," in *Dominican Studies Working Papers Series 1* (New York: CUNY Dominican Studies Institute, 1999).

9. F. James Davis, *Who Is Black? One Nation's Definition* (University Park: Pennsylvania University Press, 1991).

10. Candelario, *Black behind the Ears*.

11. Collins, *Black Feminist Thought*.

12. Clara Rodriguez, *Puerto Ricans Born in the U.S.A.* (New York: Westview Press, 1989).

13. Randol Contreras, "*Angustia Racial:* Racial and Masculine Anguish among Drug Market Participants in the South Bronx" (under review at *Du Bois Review: Social Science Research on Race*).

14. David Grazian, *Blue Chicago: The Search for Authenticity in Urban Blues Clubs* (Chicago: University of Chicago Press, 2003).

15. For the theater reference, see Erving Goffman, *Presentation of Self in Everyday Life* (Garden City, N.Y.: Anchor, 1959). For "doing gender" see Candace West and Don H. Zimmerman, "Doing Gender," *Gender and Society* 1, no. 2 (1987).

16. Collins, *Black Feminist Thought*.

CHAPTER FIVE

1. Richard Curtis, "The Improbable Transformation of Inner-City Neighborhoods: Crime, Violence, Drugs, and Youth in the 1990's," *The Journal of Criminal Law and Criminology* 88, no. 4 (1998).

2. These highly visible heroin operations, though, would diminish in the coming years.

3. Beckett, *Making Crime Pay;* Tonry, *Malign Neglect*.

4. Judith A. Greene, "Zero-Tolerance: A Case Study of Police Policies and Practices in New York City," *Crime and Delinquency* 45, no. 2 (1999).

5. Benjamin Bowling, "The Rise and Fall of New York Murder: Zero Tolerance or Crack's Decline?" *British Journal of Criminology* 39, no. 4 (1999); Wacquant, "Scholarly Myths."

6. Andrew Karmen comes across these figures as he seeks to explain the real causes of New York City's miraculous 1990s murder drop. See Karmen, *New York Murder Mystery*. For a briefer but incisive critique of "tougher policing" and its relation to the 1990s crime decline, see Wacquant, "Scholarly Myths."

7. Karmen, *New York Murder Mystery*. See also Tonry, *Thinking about Crime*.

8. Karmen, *New York Murder Mystery*. See especially chapter 5, "The Drug Crime Connection."

9. Nix, "We're Not Going."

10. Treaster, "New York State Reports a Drop in Crack Traffick."

11. Bowling, "Rise and Fall of New York Murder."

12. Curtis, "Improbable Transformation." For fascinating research regarding the shift from crack to heroin use among young St. Louis drug market participants during the 1990s, see Bruce A. Jacobs, "Crack to Heroin? Drug Markets and Transitions," *British Journal of Criminology* 39 (1999).

13. R. Terry Furst et al., "The Stigmatized Image of the Crack Head: A Sociocultural Exploration of a Barrier to Cocaine Smoking among a Cohort of Youth in New York City," *Deviant Behavior* 20, no. 2 (1999).

14. Ibid.; Lisa Maher and Richard Curtis, "Women on the Edge of Crime: Crack-Cocaine and the Changing Contexts of Street Level Sex Work in New York City," *Crime, Law, and Social Change* 18, no. 3 (1993); Williams, *Crackhouse*.

15. Brand Nubians, "Slow Down," in *One For All* (Elektra Records, 1991).

16. Andrew Golub and Bruce D. Johnson, "A Recent Decline in Cocaine Use among Youthful Arrestees in Manhattan, 1987 through 1993," *American Journal of Public Health* 84, no. 8 (1994).

17. Bourgois, *In Search of Respect*; MacLeod, *Ain't No Makin' It*.

18. I already knew Elias. Years back, when I was an early teen, I visited a girlfriend in a neighborhood several blocks away. We were spending an intimate moment in a building lobby when Elias angrily walked in on us and demanded to know why I had been "looking" at him earlier. I was baffled at his accusation and grew afraid because of his reputation and age (he was a well-known drug dealer in his mid-twenties). After calling me several nasty names—like *mama huevo*—he threatened to shoot me if I kept "eyeing" him. I remained silent, internally shrinking in fear and shame.

Seeing him repeatedly in Pablo's home over a decade later revived that humiliating episode. Now I was older, bigger, and stronger; now he showed signs of decline because of hard living and middle age. I wanted revenge. However, Pablo constantly told me to "chill" whenever I engaged Elias in conversation that would bring back that humiliating episode. *Let it go,* Pablo would tell me later, *he don't even remember that shit. That shit was years ago. I don't want you to fuck my shit [business] up over that bullshit.* Although difficult, I respected Pablo's wishes. I wanted Pablo to make money too.

19. The intensifying social and economic pressures in this environment are consistent with Merton's formulation of "strain." Merton, "Social Structure and Anomie."

20. Expanding on Merton's notion of strain, Richard Cloward and Lloyd Ohlin point out that a person blocked from pursuing legitimate endeavors needs some kind of *opportunity* to create illegal paths to success. For Pablo, opportunities were clearly shrinking. Cloward, "Illegitimate Means, Anomie, and Deviant Behavior"; Cloward and Ohlin, *Delinquency and Opportunity*.

CHAPTER SIX

1. This concept builds on the work of criminologist Jody Miller, whose research showed some female street robbers using sex to rob male victims. See Jody Miller,

"Up It Up: Gender and the Accomplishment of Street Robbery," *Criminology* 36, no. 1 (1998). For similar observations, see Christopher W. Mullins and Richard Wright, "Gender, Social Networks, and Residential Burglary," *Criminology* 41, no. 3 (2003); Wright and Decker, *Armed Robbers in Action*. For a more in-depth look at this phenomenon, see Randol Contreras, "Damn, Yo—Who's That Girl? An Ethnographic Analysis of Masculinity in Drug Robberies," *Journal of Contemporary Ethnography* 38, no. 4 (2009). For in-depth discussions of masculinity, see Robert Connell, *Masculinities* (Berkeley: University of California Press, 1995); James W. Messerschmidt, *Masculinities and Crime: Critique and Reconceptualization of Theory* (Lanham, Md.: Rowman and Littlefield, 1993). For discussions of doing gender, see Candace West and Sarah Fenstermaker, "Doing Difference," *Gender and Society* 9, no. 1 (1995); West and Zimmerman, "Doing Gender."

2. See Heath Copes and Andy Hochstetler, "Situational Construction of Masculinity among Male Street Thieves," *Journal of Contemporary Ethnography* 32, no. 3 (2003); Christopher W. Mullins, *Holding Your Square: Masculinities, Streetlife, and Violence* (Portland, Ore.: Willan, 2006).

3. Philippe Bourgois and Eloise Dunlap, "Exorcising Sex-for-Crack in Harlem: An Ethnographic Perspective from Harlem," in *Crack Pipe as Pimp: An Ethnographic Investigation of Sex-for-Crack Exchanges,* ed. Mitchell S. Ratner (New York: Lexington, 1993); Dana E. Hunt, "Drugs and Consensual Crimes: Drug Dealing and Prostitution," *Crime and Justice* 13 (1990); James A. Inciardi, Dorothy Lockwood, and Ann E. Pottieger, eds., *Women and Crack-Cocaine* (New York: Macmillan, 1993); Maher and Curtis, "Women on the Edge of Crime"; Lisa Maher and Kathleen Daly, "Women in the Street-Level Drug Economy: Continuity or Change?" *Criminology* 34, no. 4 (1996); Mitchell S. Ratner, ed. *Crack Pipe as Pimp: An Ethnographic Investigation of Sex-for-Crack Exchanges* (New York: Lexington, 1993); Williams, *Crackhouse*.

4. Adler, *Wheeling and Dealing;* Maria Blom and A.H. Ton van den Berg, "A Typology of the Life and Work Styles of Heroin Prostitutes: From a Male Career Model to a Feminized Career Model," in *Growing up Good: Policing the Behaviour of Girls in Europe,* ed. Maureen Cain (London: Sage, 1989); K.N. File, "Sex Roles and Street Roles," *Journal of Addictions* 11, no. 2 (1976); Paul J. Goldstein, *Prostitution and Drugs* (Lexington, Mass.: Lexington, 1979); Marsha Rosenbaum, *Women and Heroin* (New Brunswick, N.J.: Rutgers University Press, 1981).

5. Maher and Daly, "Women in the Street-Level Drug Economy"; Thomas Mieczkowski, "The Experiences of Women Who Sell Crack: Some Descriptive Data from the Detroit Crack Ethnography Project," *Journal of Drug Issues* 24, no. 1 (1994).

6. Mieczkowski, "Women Who Sell Crack."

7. Phillippe Bourgois, "In Search of Horatio Alger: Culture and Ideology in the Crack Economy," *Contemporary Drug Problems* 16, no. 4 (1989); Bourgois, *In Search of Respect*.

8. See Kristin L. Anderson and Debra Umberson, "Gendering Violence: Masculinity and Power in Men's Accounts of Domestic Violence," *Gender and Society* 15, no. 3 (2001); Jocelyn A. Hollander, "Vulnerability and Dangerousness: The Con-

struction of Gender through Conversation and Violence," *Gender and Society* 15, no. 1 (2001); Christopher W. Mullins, Richard Wright, and Bruce A. Jacobs, "Gender, Streetlife and Criminal Retaliation," *Criminology* 42, no. 4 (2004).

9. See Darrell J. Steffensmeier and Robert M. Terry, "Institutional Sexism in the Underwold: A View from the Inside," *Sociological Inquiry* 56, no. 3 (1986).

10. Katheryn Edin and Laura Lein, *Making Ends Meet: How Single Mothers Survive Welfare and Low-Wage Work* (New York: Russell Sage, 1997).

11. For a similar observation of strippers perceiving power over men, see Elizabeth A. Wood, "Working in the Fantasy Factory: The Attention Hypothesis and Enactment of Masculine Power in Strip Clubs," *Journal of Contemporary Ethnography* 29, no. 1 (2000).

12. Connell, *Masculinities*.

13. Michel Foucault, *Discipline and Punish: The Birth of the Prison* (New York: Random House, 1975).

14. I purposely put this shameful moment in this chapter rather than in the methodology section, where it might be lost to readers uninterested in methods. Methodologically, it warns ethnographers of how a researcher is gendered, which can affect the way a participant interprets the researcher's motives. It also shows how some types of data collection can prompt relationship violence.

15. Later, I started having long conversations with Pablo about gender violence. In those talks, we discussed its causes and his underlying reasons for doing it. Yet while he started to understand it, he still refused to give women equal status. His traditional notion of manhood was too strong (*the Bible, bro*). But I can say with certainty that I later persuaded him not to do several acts of gender violence.

CHAPTER SEVEN

1. Paul J. Goldstein, "The Drugs-Violence Nexus: A Tripartite Conceptual Framework," *Journal of Drug Issues* 15 (1985).

2. Black, *When a Heart Turns Rock Solid*.

3. Paul J. Goldstein et al., "Crack and Homicide in New York City: A Case Study in the Epidemiology of Violence," in *Crack in America: Demon Drugs and Social Justice,* ed. Craig Reinarman and Harry G. Levine (Berkeley: University of California, 1997).

4. Jacobs, *Robbing Drug Dealers*.

5. Elijah Anderson, *Code of the Street: Decency, Violence, and the Moral Life of the Inner City* (New York: W. W. Norton and Company, 1999).

6. For similar accounts, see Jacobs, *Robbing Drug Dealers*. For an early theoretical look at the stages of a robbery see David Luckenbill, "Generating Compliance: The Case of Robbery," *Urban Life* 10, no. 1 (1981).

7. For a similar observation, see Philip J. Cook, "The Role of Firearms in Violent Crime," in *Criminal Violence,* ed. Marvin E. Wolfgang and Neil A. Weiner (Beverly Hills: Sage, 1982).

8. Katz, *Seductions.*

9. Ferrell, Hayward, and Young, *Cultural Criminology.*

10. For an interesting account of criminals needing drugs to do crime, see Paul F. Cromwell, James N. Olson, and D'Aunn W. Avery, *Breaking and Entering: An Ethnographic Analysis of Burglary* (Newbury Park, Calif.: Sage, 1991).

11. Jack Katz uses this term to describe a necessary trait for successful robbers. Here, I borrow it in reverse: as a trait drug dealers need to keep their drugs and cash from robbers. Katz, *Seductions.*

12. For an overview of drug-selling systems, see Goerge F. Rengert, *The Geography of Illegal Drugs* (Boulder, Colo.: Westview Press, 1996).

13. Katz, *Seductions,* 194.

14. Erving Goffman, *Interaction Rituals: Essays on Face-to-Face Behavior* (New York: Doubleday, 1967).

15. Black, *When a Heart Turns Rock Solid.*

16. Randall Collins, personal communication.

CHAPTER EIGHT

1. Elaine Scarry, *The Body in Pain: The Making and Unmaking of the World* (New York: Oxford University Press, 1985).

2. But for a brief moral regression in the early twentieth-century American South, see David Garland, "Penal Excess and Surplus Meaning: Public Torture Lynchings in Twentieth-Century America," *Law and Society Review* 39, no. 4 (2005).

3. Ronald Crelinsten, "The World of Torture: A Constructed Reality," *Theoretical Criminology* 7, no. 3 (2003). See also Herbert C. Kelman, "The Policy Context of Torture: A Social-Psychological Analysis," *International Review of the Red Cross* 87 (2005).

4. For a brief, instructive look at how government-sponsored lawyers helped the United States justify torture practices by changing torture definitions, see David Luban, "Liberalism, Torture, and the Ticking Time Bomb," *Virginia Law Review* 91, no. 6 (2005).

5. Ibid.

6. Crelinsten, "The World of Torture."

7. Luban, "Liberalism, Torture, and the Ticking Time Bomb."

8. Oliver Stone, *Wall Street* (Twentieth Century Fox, 1987).

9. For an early and still viable statement on excessive material consumption see Thorstein Veblen, *The Theory of the Leisure Class: An Economic Study of Institutions* (New York: Funk and Wagnalls, 1967 [1899]). For a look at how conspicuous consumption is moving away from excess materials and into cosmetic surgery, dietary supplements, healthy foods, and environment-friendly ("green") products, all expensive, see Michael S. Carolan, "The Conspicuous Body: Capitalism, Consumerism, Class and Consumption," *Worldviews: Environment Culture Religion* 9, no. 1 (2005).

10. Lawrence Mishel, Jared Bernstein, and Sylvia Allegrato, *The State of Working America, 2006–2007* (Washington, D.C.: Economic Policy Institute, 2008).

11. Karl Marx, "The German Ideology," in *The Marx/Engels Reader,* ed. Robert C. Tucker (New York: W. W. Norton, 1978 [1846]).

12. See for instance, the widely acclaimed film *In Pursuit of Happyness* (Sony Pictures, 2007).

13. Michael Katz, *The Undeserving Poor* (New York: Pantheon, 1989).

14. Daniel S. Murphy and Matthew Robinson, "The Maximizer: Clarifying Merton's Theories of Anomie and Strain," *Theoretical Criminology* 12, no. 4 (2008).

15. Ibid. For a fascinating discussion on how greed and its resulting crime is structural (built in to) capitalist markets, see Laura L. Hansen and Siamak Movahedi, "Wall Street Scandals: The Myth of Individual Greed," *Sociological Forum* 25, no. 2 (2010).

16. Criminologist Steven E. Barkan estimates that, annually, white-collar crime costs 716 billion dollars versus 17.1 billion dollars for street crime; in 2003, there were 113,025 white-collar work-related deaths versus 16,503 street-crime homicides (Steven E. Barkan, *Criminology: A Sociological Understanding,* 3rd ed. (Upper Saddle River, N.J.: Pearson Prentice Hall, 2006). For an account of horrible white-collar crimes, see Karen M. Hicks, *Surviving the Dalkon Shield IUD: Women V. The Pharmaceutical Industry* (New York: Teachers College Press, 1994); Matthew Josephson, *The Robber Barons: The Great American Capitalists, 1861–1901* (New York: Harcourt, Brace, and World, 1962); Paul Brodeur, *Outrageous Misconduct: The Asbestos Industry on Trial* (New York: Pantheon Books, 1985); Francis T. Cullen, *Corporate Crime under Attack: The Ford Pinto Case and Beyond* (Cincinnati: Anderson, 1987); Stephen Labaton and Lowell Bergman, "Documents Indicate Ford Knew of Defect but Failed to Report It," *New York Times,* September 2000; Morton Mintz, "Why the Media Cover up Corporate Crime: A Reporter Looks Back in Anger," *Trial* 1992.

17. Martha K. Huggins, "Moral Universes of Brazilian Torturers," *Albany Law Review* 67, no. 2 (2003); see also Crelinsten, "The World of Torture"; Sanford Levinson, "Slavery and the Phenomenology of Torture," *Social Research* 74, no. 1 (2007); Scarry, *The Body in Pain.*

18. For a discussion of the "ticking bomb" torture rationale, see Luban, "Liberalism, Torture, and the Ticking Time Bomb."

19. Huggins, "Moral Universes of Brazilian Torturers."

20. Crelinsten and Shmid identified three basic types of torturers: the sadist (who enjoyed giving pain), the zealot (who did whatever it took to get information), and the professional (who preferred no torture, but would engage in it after careful consideration). See Ronald D. Crelinsten and Alex P. Schmid, eds., *The Politics of Pain: Torturers and Their Masters* (Boulder, Colo.: Westview, 1995). However, it was hard to categorize drug robbers similarly, since they all saw themselves as the "professional" type. Also, among the most violent, it was hard to determine which was a "sadist" or "zealot."

21. In their analysis of state torture, Françoise Sironi and Raphaëlle Branche argue that kindness after torture is a psychological tactic used to further disorient the victim. See Françoise Sironi and Raphaëlle Branche, "Torture and the Borders of Humanity," *International Social Science Journal* 54, no. 174 (2002). However, since the larger aims of drug robbery torture and state torture are different (the latter wanting a lasting impact on the victim and to terrorize the victim's group), I could not apply this analysis to Gus.

22. David Matza and Gresham Sykes, "Techniques of Neutralization: A Theory of Delinquency." *American Sociological Review* 22, no. 6 (1957).

23. Collins, *Violence*.

24. See for instance, Anderson, *Code of the Street;* Marvin Wolfgang and Franco Ferracuti, *The Subculture of Violence: Towards an Integrated Theory of Criminology* (London: Tavistock, 1967).

25. Collins, *Violence*.

26. Anderson, *Code of the Street;* Collins, *Violence;* Katz, *Seductions*.

27. Collins, *Violence*.

28. However, I would not argue that all police violence results only from emotional momentum or a forward panic. Perhaps race and class inequalities can inform a forward panic, which leads to more extraordinary violence against Black suspects versus White suspects, a Black street corner man versus a White politician or a well-known celebrity. For instance, the drawn-out police chase involving Black celebrity O. J. Simpson did not end in a Rodney King–style police beating. O.J. was famous and, for that moment, still respected. Thus, police officers checked their emotions.

29. Collins, *Violence*.

30. Ibid. See especially chapter 10, "The Violent Few."

31. For a discussion of how violent robbers progress from petty to dangerous crimes, see Katz, *Seductions*.

32. Collins, *Violence*.

33. Bourgois, "Overachievement in the Underground Economy."

34. "Sammy the Bull" (real name, Salvatore Gravano) was an underboss in the Gambino crime family who was involved in numerous murders and famous for later helping law enforcement bring down the Gambino family.

35. Lonnie Athens, *Violent Criminal Acts and Actors Revisited* (Chicago: University of Illinois Press, 1997).

36. Collins, *Violence*.

37. Athens, *Violent Criminal Acts*.

38. Katz, *Seductions*.

39. Collins, *Violence,* 4.

40. Ibid., 21. To be fair, Collins does say that this book is the first part of a two-volume series. The second book "expands the frame to what has been left out ... institutionalized violence ... meso- and macro-organizations ... geopolitics" (34).

41. Danielle L. McGuire, "It's Like All of Us Had Been Raped: Sexual Violence, Community Mobilization, and the African American Freedom Struggle,"

Journal of American History 91, no. 3 (2004). For a sobering historical account during the slavery period, see Edward E. Baptist, "'Cuffy,' 'Fancy Maids,' and 'One-Eyed Men': Rape, Commodification, and the Domestic Slave Trade in the United States," *The American Historical Review* 106, no. 5 (2001).

42. Jasbir K. Puar, *Assemblages: Homonationalism in Queer Times* (Durham, N.C.: Duke University Press, 2007).

43. See, for instance, James W. Messerschmidt, "Men Victimizing Men: The Case of Lynching, 1865–1900," in *Masculinities and Violence,* ed. Lee H. Bowker (Thousand Oaks, Calif.: Sage, 1998). For a disturbing yet illuminating account of southern lynchings, see Garland, "Penal Excess and Surplus Meaning."

44. See Jasbir K. Puar, "On Torture: Abu Ghraib," *Radical History Review,* no. 93 (2005).

45. Mark Danner, "The Logic of Torture," in *Abu Ghraib: The Politics of Torture,* ed. Mark Danner (Berkeley, Calif.: North Atlantic, 2004); Mark Danner, "Torture and Truth," in *Abu Ghraib: The Politics of Torture,* ed. Mark Danner (Berkeley, Calif.: North Atlantic, 2004); Puar, "On Torture."

46. Danner, "The Logic of Torture"; Danner, "Torture and Truth"; Seymour Hersh, "The Grey Zone," *New Yorker,* May 24, 2004; Puar, "On Torture." For a disturbing account of how the U.S. military treated female detainees, especially as to rape and sexual humiliation, see Luke Harding, "The Other Prisoners," *Guardian,* May 20, 2004.

47. At the scandal's height, top U.S. government and military officials made the affair seem like the sadistic doings of a few untrained, unstable soldiers. However, journalist Seymour Hersh uncovered the torture's source: a controversial 1973 book entitled *The Arab Mind,* written by cultural anthropologist Raphael Patai. The book captivated U.S. intelligence, especially a chapter describing homosexuality as a grave taboo in Arab culture. According to Patai, its discovery would not only cause shame in the *guilty* party, but also among close family and friends. Sexually humiliating torture, then, became *the* way to handle Arab detainees. Hersh, "The Grey Zone"; Raphael Patai, *The Arab Mind,* rev. ed. (New York: Scribner, 1983). For a concise review of the book's many critiques see Ann Marlow, "Sex, Violence, and the Arab Mind" (Salon.com. http://dir.salon.com/books/feature/2004/06 /08/arab_mind, 2004).

48. Quoted in Puar, "On Torture," 20.

49. On gender performativity, see Judith Butler, *Subjects of Desire* (New York: Columbia University Press, 1999).

50. Puar, "On Torture."

51. Ibid.

52. Similarly, Abner Louima, a Haitian immigrant, was sodomized with a toilet plunger by an angry White police officer in a Brooklyn police precinct. See Mike McAlary, "The Frightful Whisperings from a Coney Island Hospitable Bed," *Daily News,* August 13, 1997.

53. James Messerschmidt, *Masculinities and Crime: Critique and Reconceptualization of Theory* (Lanham, Md.: Rowman and Littlefield, 1993); James Messer-

schmidt, *Crime as Structured Action: Gender, Race, Class, and Crime in the Making* (Thousand Oaks, Calif.: Sage).

54. See also Copes and Hochstetler, "Situational Construction of Masculinity."

55. Dorothy E. Smith, *The Everyday World as Problematic: A Feminist Sociology* (Boston: Northeastern University Press, 1987).

CHAPTER NINE

1. GrandMaster Flash and Melle Mel, "White Lines (Don't Don't Do It)" (Sugarhill Records, 1983).

2. Anderson, *Code of the Street;* Bourgois, *In Search of Respect.*

3. Collins, *Violence.*

4. Edwin Sutherland, *The Professional Thief* (Chicago: University of Chicago Press, 1937).

5. See also Werner J. Einstadter, "The Social Organization of Armed Robbers," *Social Problems* 17, no. 1 (1969).

6. Black, *When a Heart Turns Rock Solid.*

CHAPTER TEN

1. Shover and Honaker, "Socially Bounded Decision Making"; Wright and Decker, *Burglars on the Job.* Jacobs, *Dealing Crack;* Jacobs, *Robbing Drug Dealers;* Jacobs, Topalli, and Wright, "Carjacking, Streetlife, and Offender Motivation"; Jacobs and Wright, "Stick-up, Street Culture, and Offender Motivation"; Wright and Decker, *Armed Robbers in Action.*

2. Mike Collison, "In Search of the High Life: Drugs, Crime, Masculinities and Consumption," *British Journal of Criminology* 36, no. 3 (1996).

3. Likewise Mr. Conwell, an early twentieth-century professional thief, observed that "it is very common when a [thieving] mob is cutting up (dividing the proceeds of) a day's work to suggest sending a part of it to some member of the profession, not necessarily one of the mob, who is doing a bit (prison sentence). . . . Thieves are glad to be able to send it, as it is the only way they have of expressing their friendship and continued memory of him." Sutherland, *Professional Thief,* 7–8.

4. Freddy, who used to be Gus' "brother-in-law" (Gus had a child with his sister), was well versed in street robberies, muggings, and shootings. Every now and then, he dropped by Sylvio's bar to hang out with Gus and learn of new criminal opportunities.

CHAPTER ELEVEN

1. In his study of Puerto Rican crack dealers, Bourgois faced a similar problem with an upper-level crack dealer who needed his cultural capital to navigate the legal world. See Bourgois, *In Search of Respect.*

2. Devah Pager, "The Mark of a Criminal Record," *American Journal of Sociology* 108 (2003).

3. Joan Petersilia, *When Prisoners Come Home: Parole and Prisoner Reentry* (New York: Oxford University Press, 2003).

4. Ibid. A shocking example occurred in 2000, when New York State denied one ex-offender a license to cut hair. He had learned the trade in prison and wanted to make it a legal career. See Clyde Haberman, "He Did Time, So He's Unfit to Do Hair," *New York Times* (nytimes.com), March 4, 2005.

5. Bruce Western, Jeffrey Kling, and David Weiman, "The Labor Market Consequences of Incarceration," *Crime and Delinquency* 47, no. 4 (2001). Cited in Petersilia, *When Prisoners Come Home.*

6. Pager, "The Mark of a Criminal Record."

7. Black, *When a Heart Turns Rock Solid.*

8. Howard Becker, *Outsiders: Studies in the Sociology of Deviance* (New York: Free Press, 1963).

9. Petersilia, *When Prisoners Come Home.*

10. I changed the exact membership cost and commission because it was the same as the one found in the money-making program he ordered. However, the numbers I listed are not too far off.

11. Mishel et al., "The State of Working America, 2008/2009."

12. Mills, *Sociological Imagination.*

13. Clearly, fallen stars can be found across social strata and occupational fields. However, since my fieldwork involved criminality, I can only speak to the phenomenon in this sphere.

14. Emile Durkheim, *Suicide: A Study in Sociology* (New York: Free Press, 1997 [1897]).

15. Ibid.

16. In his classic study, Emile Durkheim identified three other forms of suicide: egoistic suicide, which is associated with inadequate social bonds to the group; altruistic suicide, which is associated with a powerful social bond or a strong commitment to the group; and fatalistic suicide, which is associated with oppressive regulation (e.g., slavery). Ibid.

17. Ibid.

18. Ibid.

19. Ibid.

20. Merton, "Social Structure and Anomie."

21. Bourgois, *In Search of Respect.*

22. Emile Durkheim, *Rules of the Sociological Method* (New York: Free Press, 1982 [1895]).

23. Katz, *Seductions*.

24. Timothy Black also reported a study participant who mentioned that prison life was more predictable and structured, and thus easier, than life outside. Black, *When a Heart Turns Rock Solid*.

25. Emile Durkheim, *The Elementary Forms of Religious Life* (New York: Free Press, 1995 [1912]).

CONCLUSION

1. Mills, *Sociological Imagination*.

2. David A. Shirk, "Drug Violence in Mexico: Data and Analysis from 2001–2009" (San Diego: Trans-Border Institute, 2009).

3. Ibid.

4. Ibid.

5. Traci Carl, "Progress in Mexico Drug War Is Drenched in Blood," *Associated Press*, November 11, 2009.

6. Shirk, "Drug Violence in Mexico."

7. Carl, "Mexico Drug War."

8. Ibid.

9. For a look into how Mexican Norteño musicians are sometimes killed for the once accepted practice of glorifying traffickers through folk songs, see *Dangerous Music* (Borderland Pictures Production, 2009).

10. Shover and Honaker, "Socially Bounded Decision Making"; Wright and Decker, *Burglars on the Job;* Jacobs, *Dealing Crack;* Jacobs, *Robbing Drug Dealers;* Jacobs, Topalli, and Wright, "Carjacking, Streetlife, and Offender Motivation"; Jacobs and Wright, "Stick-up, Street Culture, and Offender Motivation"; Wright and Decker, *Armed Robbers in Action*.

11. Jacobs, *Robbing Drug Dealers,* 144.

12. Ibid., 145.

13. Ibid.

14. Wacquant, *Punishing the Poor;* Loic Wacquant, "Class, Race, and Hyperincarceration in Revanchist America," *Daedalus* 140, no. 3 (2010); Loic Wacquant, "The Wedding of Workfare and Prisonfare Revisited," *Social Justice* 38 (2011).

15. Steven D. Levitt and Stephen J. Dubner, *Freakonomics: A Rogue Economist Explores the Hidden Side of Everything* (New York: HarperCollins, 2005).

16. William Bennett, *Morning in America* (Radio Broadcast, 2005).

17. Mishel, Bernstein, and Allegrato, "The State of Working America, 2006–2007."

18. Don Peck, "How a New Jobless Era Will Transform America," *The Atlantic*, March 2010.

19. Craig Reinarman and Harry G. Levine, "Crack in the Rearview Mirror: Deconstructing Drug War Mythology," *Social Justice* 31, no. 1–2 (2004).

20. Massing, *The Fix.*

21. Tonry, *Malign Neglect.*

22. Stephen R. Fox, *Blood and Power: Organized Crime in Twentieth Century America* (New York: William Morrow, 1989); Harvey A. Siegel and James A. Inciardi, "A Brief History of Alcohol," in *The American Drug Scene: An Anthology,* ed. James A. Inciardi and Karen McElrath (2004).

23. Massing, *The Fix.*

24. Ibid.

25. Ibid.

26. See, for instance, Stacy Burling, "Candidates Seek Area Tea Party's Support at Rally," *The Philadelphia Inquirer,* April 18, 2010; Tonry, *Thinking about Crime;* Katie Zernike, "Doing Fine, but Angry Nonetheless," *New York Times,* April 18, 2010.

INDEX

masculinity: drug culture, 124–125; drug dealing, 58, 101–103; panoptic, 132; partying, 99–102, 196–197; reproduction in robberies, 125–127; sexism/misogyny, 103; torture/violence, 169–175. *See also* masculinity trap

masculinity trap, 124–125

Massing, Michael, 48–50

Matza, David, 159

Merton, Robert, 5, 24, 26, 71, 224, 244n10, 255n19, 255n20

Messerschmidt, James, 173

Messner, Steven, 71

methadone, 240

Mexican Drug Wars, 236–237

Mexico, 46, 236–237

middleman, 192–193

Miller, Jody, 255n1

Mills, C. Wright, 4–5, 33, 217, 235

Mona Lisa, 26

Monroe College, 128

Morgan, John P., 250n79

Moses, Robert, 38, 55

mothers: attitudes toward dealing, 69; of study participants, 56–57, 63–66, 68–70, 118, 120, 134, 198–199

Mullay, John (Public Park), 8, 62

Murphy, Daniel, 153

New Bedford, Massachusetts, 112–113, 229

New York Boys, 87–99, 104

New York City: drug organizations, 53–54; employment, 39; politics, 39, 75, 107; zero-tolerance, 107–109

Nixon, Richard M., 240–241

Notorious B.I.G., 203

Ohlin, Lloyd, 5, 255n20

Operation Take Back Our Community, 108, 110

Pager, Devah, 209

Pan American Highway, 46–47

Parenti, Christian, 49

Partido Revolucionario Institucional, 236

partying. *See* high lifer

Patai, Raphael, 261n47

Pinochet, Augusto, 47

Policia Nacional de Colombia (CNP), 51

police: tactical narcotics team, 75. *See also* zero-tolerance

positionality. *See* insider research

prison (jail): breeding criminal self-concept, 209; conservative policies, 73–75; experiences, 84–86; study participant perception of, 86, 231–232

profit sharing. *See* drug robbers

Prohibition, 240

Providence, Rhode Island, 229–231

Pryor, Richard, 50

public health model, 49

Puerto Ricans: blaming of, 39; in the Bronx, 38–39, 44; racial makeup, 98; women, 98–99

racism: crime, 168–169; Dominican, 93, 96–97; gendered, 96–98; of study participants, 92–99; prison/jail, 81–82

rape, 170–175

Reagan Administration, 45, 49, 52

Reagan, Ronald, 74, 238

real estate elite, 39

Reinarman, Craig, 239, 250n79

religion, 232–233

Rikers Island: breeding racial hatred, 81–82; correction officers, 83–84; drug arrests of study participants, 63, 70; homophobia, 81–82; neighborhood stories, 72; overcrowding, 72–73, 75; status competitions, 76–81; survival strategies, 78–79; violence, 76–84

robbery: anomie, 224; critique of crime policies, 237–242; critique of robbery research, 2–4, 36; drug use, 142–143; homicide, 137; street culture, 3–4; street robberies, 63, 128–129, 168–169; thrills, 2–4, 128–129, 142. *See also* drug robbers

robber elite, 164–168

Robinson, Christopher, 252n21

Robinson, Matthew, 153

Rockefeller, Nelson, 240–241

Roxanne (crack), 51. *See also* crack

Rosenfeld, Richard, 71

Safe Streets, Safe City Act, 110

Sammy the Bull, 166, 260n34

DESIGNER
Lia Tjandra

TEXT

DISPLAY

COMPOSITOR
Westchester

PRINTER AND BINDER
Maple Press

COVER PRINTER
Brady Palmer